The Shadow King

THE SHADOW KING

Rex Inutilis in Medieval Law and Literature, 751–1327

by Edward Peters

New Haven and London, Yale University Press

1970

Library of Congress catalog card number: 73–118736
International standard book number: 0–300–01217–9
Designed by John O. C. McCrillis,
set in Garamond type,
and printed in the United States of America by The Carl Purington Rollins Printing-Office of the Yale University Press, New Haven, Connecticut.
Distributed in Great Britain, Europe, and Africa by Yale University Press, Ltd., London; in Canada by McGill-Queen's University Press, Montreal; in Mexico by Centro Interamericano de Libros Académicos, Mexico City; in Australasia by Australia and New Zealand Book Co., Pty., Ltd., Artarmon, New South Wales; in India by UBS Publishers' Distributors Pvt., Ltd., Delhi; in Japan by John Weatherhill, Inc., Tokyo.

TO MY WIFE

PATRICIA PETERS

AND

TO MY TEACHER

ROBERT S. LOPEZ

Contents

Preface

"But what are kings when regiment is gone,
But perfect shadows on a sunshine day?"
Christopher Marlowe, *Edward II*

"Umbra fuit, non rex . . . Rex quasi funesta."
Godfrey of Viterbo, *Pantheon*

The same metaphor served both twelfth-century chronicler and sixteenth-century playwright to express the dramatic plight of the king without power. In its various forms the figure of the shadow-king has always appealed to poets and historians, perhaps because it suggests not only a convenient allegory of mortality but also the paradox inherent in the contrast between the limits of human nature and the frequently inhuman demands of political life. The dramatic opportunities which failed royalty offered to Renaissance and later playwrights, however, and the historian's understandable affection for such general labels as *roi fainéant* to describe pusillanimous or otherwise incompetent rulers hardly serve to define with any accuracy either the historical character of early medieval kingship or the nature of political typology. The medieval ruler, although strongly supported by ecclesiastical and temporal authority, had nevertheless to control power as well—Marlowe's "regiment." The king without power or the king who used power unwisely was both a public danger and a philosophical anomaly. "Rex a recte agendo" ("the [name] king comes from right acting") —so said St. Isidore of Seville in the sixth century, and so echoed many later writers on kingship. But *recte* is an elusive term. Although many writers considered chiefly its moral implications, it had practical ones as well, and the history of what men from the eighth to the fourteenth centuries considered one aspect of "right" royal action may well illuminate one chapter in the story of medieval kingship.

The figure of the *rex inutilis,* the useless king, became a topic of political thought between the eighth and the fourteenth centuries —that is, during the period in which kingship became the characteristic political institution in Christendom. Because of the nature of the historical circumstances in which that institution emerged, most political theory was primarily concerned with the use and misuse of excessive power—in both the moral and political sense—rather than with the deficiency of power. To a considerable extent, subsequent studies of medieval kingship have followed this concern. This study proposes to trace other concerns. The problems raised by the king who lost power or became unable to wield it because of physical or mental incapacity or political misjudgment were the object of the occasionally intense, if not continuous, interest of chroniclers, poets, publicists, and jurists. The history of the type—and the history of the ways in which medieval men conceived political power to be distributed in society—must be traced in literary as well as documentary sources and must necessarily cross the boundaries of a number of scholarly disciplines, in only a few of which one man can claim any degree of competence. The history of political types and their functions in society, however, is too complex for the historian not to attempt to trace it. The relation between individual and political office—fundamental to all societies, medieval or modern—is, after all, a legal fiction. Modern political man, like his medieval predecessors, lives still by such fictions, and it may be in his interest to trace the means by which some of them were shaped and altered by six centuries of history. The Twenty-fifth Amendment to the Constitution of the United States, which deals with some of the contemporary aspects of the problem of the *rex inutilis,* is, after all, only three years old. Even now, political incapacity presents some of the most intricate constitutional difficulties which politics and law have to treat. Modern notions of *recte,* as the nature and history of that Amendment show, are in this sense as elusive as were those of St. Isidore and his successors.

Since this study touches upon numerous distinct fields which are treated as related but separate units, I have included notices of my direct sources in the footnotes. Because these fields are not treated exhaustively, I have not felt the need to add a lengthy bibliography at this point (for manuscripts cited and sources of medieval canon law, see Bibliographical Note, below, p. 247). Most of the texts upon which my arguments depend have been cited in the body of this book or in its footnotes, and I have provided translations into English where they seemed necessary. Thus any reader desiring further information on points raised in this study will find ample documentation and bibliographical references in the footnotes to the part of the text which concerns his interests.

A first book, or any book, owes far more than it can ever successfully acknowledge, let alone repay. In expressing my gratitude to friends and teachers, I can indicate only their generosity and the extent of their help, not my ability to use both as much, or as well, as I should. Professor Joseph T. Curtiss introduced me to medieval studies at Yale while I was an undergraduate, and Professor and Mrs. Thomas M. Greene of Yale have consistently provided encouragement and advice, always when I needed it most. Professor W. H. Dunham, Jr., in whose seminar the idea behind this book began, has been very generous with advice, questions, and time to read and reread this manuscript in its early stages. Professor Stephan Kuttner, both in and out of seminars, has extended to me, as to many others, his boundless kindness, interest, and advice, not the least example of which was his allowing me the hospitality of the Institute for Medieval Canon Law during two critical years of research and writing. Professor Harold Johnson introduced me to and assisted me with many of the Portuguese sources. Professors Gaines Post, Karl Morrison, Joseph Strayer, and Gerard Caspary have been generous with suggestions and advice, Professor Caspary in particular having suggested areas of research and raised questions and, most important, allowed me to use several ideas from his own important study, "The Deposition of Richard II and the Canon Law" (see chap. 5, n. 3), a work which came to me at a welcome moment. Professor Robert Benson and the Reverend John F. Kenney have given me advice and encouragement at many points, and the generosity of Professor Peter Riesenberg, who made available to me his collection of materials on some of the canonical legislation of Innocent IV, cannot be repaid ever. Professor Jeremy duQ. Adams of Yale has consistently helped me to clarify difficult points, as have the long (and to them doubtless interminable) discussions with my friends and fellow graduate students, many now professors, Diane Owen Hughes, Susan Jarvis, Lee Patterson, Stephen Kaplan, Robert Somerville, Richard Hoffmann, Noel Swerdlow, and William D. Paden. I am grateful to Mrs. Genoveva Palmieri, Miss Sandy Baker, Mrs. Eunice Konold, and Mrs. Patricia Haynes, who helped me to produce a readable and orderly manuscript.

I must express my thanks also to the Woodrow Wilson National Fellowship Foundation for fellowships in 1963 and 1967, to Yale University, which awarded me a Sterling Fellowship in 1967, and to the Graduate School of the University of Pennsylvania, which granted me a Faculty Research Fellowship for the summer of 1968. I thank the Committee of the Yale Graduate School which awarded to my doctoral dissertation, of which this book is a revision, the John Addison Porter Prize in 1967. The libraries of Yale University, the University of California, San Diego, and the University of Pennsylvania have been unfailingly cooperative throughout my research.

Early versions of some of the material in this book have appeared in *Studia Gratiana, Bibliothèque d'Humanisme et Renaissance,* and *Rivista Storica Italiana.* I am grateful to the editors of these journals for permission to reprint.

My debt in this, as in all other work, to those to whom this book is dedicated, is greatest of all. My wife, Patricia Peters, and my teacher, Robert Lopez, have given me help which is beyond acknowledgment. What I can offer in return is my love and gratitude —and the book itself.

E. P.

Abbreviations

ALMA	R. S. Loomis, ed., *Arthurian Literature in the Middle Ages* (Oxford, 1959)
Auvray	L. Auvray, ed., *Les Registres de Grégoire IX,* 4 vols. (Paris, 1890–1955), cit. by doc. no.
BEHE	Bibliothèque de l'Ecole des Hautes Etudes
Berger	E. Berger, *Les Registres d'Innocent IV,* 4 vols. (Paris, 1884–1921), cit. by doc. no.
Bezzola	R. R. Bezzola, *Les Origines et la formation de la littérature courtoise en occident (500–1200),* vol. 1, BEHE, fasc. 286 (Paris, 1944); vol. 2, BEHE, fasc. 313 (Paris, 1960); vol. 3, BEHE, fasc. 319 (Paris, 1963)
BJRL	*Bulletin of the John Rylands Library*
Carlyle	A. J. and R. W. Carlyle, *A History of Medieval Political Theory in the West,* 6 vols. (rep. New York, 1949)
CHR	*Catholic Historical Review*
CSEL	Corpus Christianorum ecclesiasticorum latinorum
DA	*Deutsches Archiv für Erforschung des Mittelalters*
Das Königtum	Theodor Mayer, ed., *Das Königtum. Seine geistigen und rechtlichen Grundlagen,* Vorträge und Forschungen, vol. 3 (Lindau-Konstanz, 1956)
EETS	Early English Text Society
EHR	*English Historical Review*
Etudes . . . LeBras	*Etudes d'histoire du droit canonique dédiées à Gabriel Le Bras,* 2 vols. (Paris, 1965)

Herculano — A. Herculano, *Historia de Portugal,* 8 vols. (9th ed., Lisbon, 1916–17)

HJ — *Historisches Jahrbuch*

HZ — *Historische Zeitschrift*

JWCI — *Journal of the Warburg and Courtauld Institutes*

MGH — Monumenta Germaniae Historica: Series

Const. *Constitutiones et acta publica imperatorum et regum*

Epp. *Epistolae*

Epp. kar. aev. *Epp. aevi karolini*

Epp. sel. *Epp. selectae*

Legum Cap. reg. Franc. *Leges II, Capitularia Regum Francorum*

Ldl *Libelli de lite imperatorum et pontificum saec. XI et XII conscripti*

Poetae *Poetae latini aevi karolini*

SS *Scriptores*

SS rer. germ. *SS rerum germanicarum*

SS rer. lang. *SS rerum langobardorum*

SS rer. mer. *SS rerum merowingicarum*

SS in us. schol. *SS in usum scholarum*

SS vern. lingua *SS qui in vernacula lingua usi sunt*

MIöG — *Mitteilungen des Instituts fur österreichische Geschichtsforschung*

PL — *Patrologiae cursus completus . . . Series secunda in qua prodeunt patres . . . ecclesiae latinae (= Patrologia Latina),* ed. J. P. Migne, 221 vols. (Paris, 1844–55, 1862–64)

PMLA — *Publications of the Modern Language Association*

Potthast — *Regesta pontificum Romanorum unde ab A. post Chr. n. MCXCVIII ad A. MCCCIV,* 2 vols. (Rome, 1875), cit. by doc. no.

Pressutti — P. Pressutti, ed., *Regesta Honorii papae III,* 2 vols. (Rome, 1858–95), cit. by doc. no.

QE — *Quadro Elementar das relaçōes politicas e diplomaticas de Portugal com as diversas potencias do mondo,* ed. Visconde da Santarem, cont. by Rebello da Silva (Lisbon, 1842ff.), vol. 9

RDF	*(Nouvelle) Revue de l'Histoire du Droit Français et Etranger*
RH	*Revue Historique*
RIS	*Rerum italicarum scriptores*
RS	Rolls Series
Rot. Parl.	*Rotuli Parliamentorum*
SATF	Société des anciens textes français
Sommer	H. O. Sommer, ed., *The Vulgate Version of the Arthurian Romances, 8 vols.* (Washington, 1909–16)
ZfRG	*Zeitschrift der Savigny-Stiftung für Rechtsgeschichte* G.A. Germanistische Abteilung K.A. Kanonistische Abteilung
ZfRPh	*Zeitschrift fur romanische Philologie*

The standard abbreviations for the *Corpus iuris civilis* and the *Corpus iuris canonici* have been used. For the serial publications of learned societies not listed above, standard national or local abbreviations have been followed: e.g. Br. = British; Wien. = Vienna; Acad. (Akad.) = Academy (Académie, Akademie); S.B., Proc., Trans., Soc. = Sitzungsberichte, Proceedings, Transactions, Society (Société); *Reg.* = *Registrum.*

Introduction

"From the monarch, as from a never-failing spring, flows a stream of all that is good or evil over the whole nation." Thomas More's observation on the role of kingship, from the first part of *Utopia,* reflects a widely held medieval and Renaissance attitude toward the nature of politics and social change.[1] From St. Augustine to Hobbes, most writers of history or political theory would have agreed that, whatever forces or institutions effect profound changes in society, it is ultimately the character of the ruler which establishes or subverts the good State. Like their medieval predecessors, political theorists and historians of the sixteenth and seventeenth centuries were most frequently concerned with the ideals of justice and morality which they assumed to be prerequisites for all good governance. In their approach to the institution of kingship, therefore, they paid most attention to the "good or evil" for which, like More, they held the monarch responsible, and they treated individual rulers accordingly as either just kings or tyrants.[2]

1. St. Thomas More, *Utopia,* ed. E. J. Surtz, S. J. (New Haven, 1964), p. 17. Cf. William Baldwin's first preface to *A Mirror for Magistrates,* ed. L. B. Campbell (rep. New York, 1960), p. 64: "The goodness or badness of any realm lieth in the goodness or badness of its rulers . . . for indeed the wealth and quiet of every common weal, the disorders and miseries of the same, come especially through them."

2. Although the term *roi fainéant* developed in the work of historians rather than in that of political theorists, contemporary political ideas played an important role in its genesis. General discussions of kingship during the sixteenth and early seventeenth centuries may be found in the following works: A. J. and R. W. Carlyle, *A History of Medieval Political Theory in the West* (rep. New York, 1949), 6:219–90, 329–462; J. W. Allen,

Book II, chapter 4, of Jean Bodin's *Les Six Livres de la République* contains one of the most elaborate analyses of the differences between the just king and the tyrant that the sixteenth century produced.[3] After describing the effects of beneficent, then of tyrannical rule, Bodin sets out in a long series of symmetrical pairs the opposing characteristics of each type and contrasts in a conventional manner the misery of the tyrant's life, death, and subsequent reputation with the corresponding felicity of those of the just king. Thus far, excepting the extensive scope and detail of his historical references and his careful attention to rhetorical structure, Bodin does not differ significantly from earlier writers on the same topic, most of whom regarded "civil," or political, history chiefly in terms of royal governance. Their overriding interest in the abstract concepts of justice, salvation, public welfare, or the precepts of natural law inclined them to treat individual rulers in terms of idealized royal types—personifications of justice and morality, on the one hand or of sovereignty and public law, on the other.

After describing these extreme types, however, Bodin goes on to note that such contrasts between idealized figures are easily seen, but that it is much more difficult to judge a prince who has in him something of both the *roy tres-juste* and the *tyran tres-meschant.*

A History of Political Thought in the Sixteenth Century (rep. New York, 1960); P. Mesnard, *L'Essor de la philosophie politique au XVIe siècle* (2d. ed., Paris, 1952); J. N. Figgis, *Political Thought from Gerson to Grotius: 1414–1625* (rep. New York, 1960); G. Weill, *Les Théories sur le pouvoir royal en France pendant les guerres de religion* (Paris, 1891); J. H. M. Salmon, *The French Religious Wars in English Political Thought* (Oxford, 1959); R. H. Murray, *The Political Consequences of the Reformation* (Boston, 1926); Guenter Lewy, "Some Theology about Tyranny," in *The Renaissance Reconsidered: A Symposium,* Smith College Studies in History, vol. 44 (Northhampton, Mass., 1964), pp. 79–90; W. A. Armstrong, "The Elizabethan Conception of the Tyrant," *Review of English Studies* 22 (1946): 161–81.

3. *Les Six Livres de la République* (Paris, 1583; photo-rep. Aalen, 1961), pp. 289–97. Cf. Bk. VI, chap. 4, p. 961. Besides the works cited in the preceding note, see also Beatrice Reynolds, *Proponents of Limited Monarchy in Sixteenth-Century France: François Hotman and Jean Bodin* (New York, 1931).

Circumstances sometimes cause a ruler to do things which seem tyrannical to some and praiseworthy to others. Since governments differ one from another according to the natures of different peoples and places, it is necessary to consider the acts of the prince with care and to avoid hastily labeling him a tyrant. "Il est bien vray que le moyen de vertu environné de plusieurs vices, comme la ligne droite entre un million de courbes, est difficile à trouver."[4]

To illustrate his point further, Bodin discusses the problem of necessary severity on the part of the just ruler and, for emphasis, contrasts some of the characteristics of the tyrant with those of the weak, overly generous king who ruins his realm by allowing governance to pass into the hands of unworthy favorites, thus setting up, in fact, ten thousand tyrannies instead of one. For Bodin excessive severity is required more often than not, and the ruler who is excessively weak, pusillanimous, incompetent, or generous may well be a greater disaster to the kingdom than one who appears to be a tyrant.[5]

The question of royal severity had, of course, been a concern of earlier political theorists and historians. In the sixteenth century alone, both Machiavelli and More had argued for its necessity, Machiavelli's remarks on the "good and evil cruelty" of *The Prince* being quite similar to Bodin's own observations.[6] William Tyndale

4. *République,* p. 297.

5. Ibid., p. 295: "Car telle simplicité sans prudence, est tresdangereuse & pernicieuse en un Roy & beaucoup plus à craindre que la cruauté d'un Prince severe, chagrin, revesche, avare & inaccessible. Et semble que nos peres anciens n'ont pas dit ce proverbe sans cause, De meschant homme, bon Roy. . . . Par la souffrance & niaise simplicité d'un Prince trop bon, il advient que les flatteurs, les corratiers, & les plus meschans emportent les offices, les charges, les benefices, les dons, espuisans les finances d'un etat: & par ce moyen le povre peuple est rongé jusqu'aux os, & cruellement asservi aux plus grands; de sorte que pour un tyran il y en a dix mil. . . ." For aspects of specific fiscal incompetence in Bodin, see now Martin Wolfe, "Jean Bodin on Taxes: The Sovereignty-Taxes Paradox," *Political Science Quarterly* 83 (1968): 268–84.

6. *The Prince,* chap. 8. The problem appears in the contrast between the rulers Basilius and Euarchus in Sidney's *Arcadia.* Cf. W. R. Briggs, "The Political Ideas of Sidney's *Arcadia,*" *Studies in Philology* 28 (1931): 137–61; E. W. Talbert, *The Problem of Order* (Chapel Hill, 1962), pp.

had given the distinction between the tyrant and the weak king dramatic expression in *The Obedience of a Christian Man:*

> Yea, and it is better to have a tyrant unto thy king: than a shadow; a passive king who does nought himself, but suffereth others to do with him what they will, and to lead him whither they list. For a tyrant, though he do wrong unto the good, yet he punisheth the evil, and maketh all men obey, neither suffering any man to poll but himself only. A king that is soft as silk and effeminate, that is to say turned into the nature of a woman—what with his own lusts, which are the longing of a woman with child, so that he cannot resist them, and with the wily tyranny of them that ever rule him—shall be much more grievous unto his realm than a right tyrant.[7]

Yet the distinction between the weak king and the tyrant usually remained on the periphery of early modern political thought. Like their predecessors, the Reformation political theorists generally upheld the doctrine of obedience to all rulers, but their attention was focused on the extreme ends of the political spectrum and not on the more frequent but less dramatic human mean. The figure of the weak king remained, as it had in Bodin and Tyndale, rather an exemplary abstraction than a political problem. Although another side of the sixteenth-century political consciousness—the progressive awareness of the contrast between the individual humanity of

---

89–120; Irving Ribner, "Sidney's *Arcadia* and the Structure of *King Lear,*" *Studia Neophilologica* 24 (1951/52): 63–88. At a slightly later period Fulke Greville discussed the figure of the weak ruler in his "Treatise on Monarchy," particularly in sections III and IV. See Fulke Greville, Lord Brooke, *The Remains: Being Poems of Monarchy and Religion,* ed. G. A. Wilkes (Oxford, 1965), pp. 55–70, and Hugh N. MacLean, "Fulke Greville: Kingship and Sovereignty," *Huntington Library Quarterly* 16 (1951/52): 237–71.

7. Cited in Irving Ribner, *The English History Play in the Age of Shakespeare* (2d. ed., New York, 1965), p. 158. Cf. the *Vindiciae contra tyrannos,* ed. and trans. H. J. Laski (rep. Gloucester, Mass., 1963), pp. 133–36, 183–213; Francis Oakley, *The Political Thought of Pierre d'Ailly: The Voluntarist Tradition* (New Haven, 1964), pp. 211–30.

the ruler and his function as the personification of the abstract ideals of justice, law, and sovereignty—is reflected in some political literature, it was to have its most profound treatment in the political and historical drama of Marlowe and Shakespeare rather than in "politick discourses" or "civil histories."[8]

Neither Bodin's observations of the complexity of political experience nor Shakespeare's portraits of tortured, all-too-human rulers appear to have had much influence on the concept of royal inadequacy, particularly as it came to be expressed by the term *roi fainéant* in the political and historiographical vocabularies of the seventeenth and eighteenth centuries. The term was to serve as a commonplace for the sort of royal inadequacy described in Bodin and Tyndale and as an approximate equivalent to another term which some medieval writers had coined to designate a similar phenomenon, the *rex inutilis.* A brief outline of the origins and early development of the term *roi fainéant* may serve to introduce the earlier history of the *rex inutilis,* since it is the one still most frequently used to label the medieval and later rulers who seem to conform most closely to Bodin's portrait of the incompetent prince.

Claude Fauchet, *Président à la cour des monnaies* and historiographer of France under Henry IV, appears to have been the first modern historian to have considered the origins of the term *roi fainéant.* The term itself made its first appearance in the fourteenth century in the *Grandes Chroniques de France* as an attempt to translate the Latin *rex nihil faciens* of some eleventh-century chroniclers.[9] These writers had used it to describe the brief rule of a fictitious Louis, son of Carloman and grandson of Louis the Stammerer: "Loys-Fai-noient . . . Sy fu ansi surnommé ou pour ce qu'il fit nule chose que l'on doive mettre en memoire ou pour ce que il

8. For Shakespeare and Marlowe, see Ribner, *English History Play.* See also E. Kantorowicz, *The King's Two Bodies* (Princeton, 1957), pp. 24–41; M. M. Reese, *The Cease of Majesty* (London, 1961); G. W. Keeton, *Shakespeare's Legal and Political Background* (London, 1967).

9. See F. Godefroy, *Dictionnaire de l'ancienne langue française,* vol. 9, *Complément* (Paris, 1938), p. 393. For the date of 1321, see Oscar Bloch, *Dictionnaire étymologique de la langue française* (Paris, 1932), 2:88.

traist une nonnain de l'abbaye de Chiele et l'epousa en mariage."[10] They had also used it to designate Louis V, the last Carolingian ruler of France. The term does not appear to have been of wide currency in the later fourteenth and fifteenth centuries, but it became somewhat more popular in the vernacular histories of medieval France produced in the sixteenth century.[11] When Fauchet came to write his *Antiquitez et histoires gauloises et françoises* in 1599, in fact, it is evident that the term had come to mean not the brevity of these kings' reigns but the dissoluteness of their characters. Fauchet set himself two tasks: he provided good grounds for disproving the existence of the fictitious *Loys-Fainoient,* and he attempted to give an accurate historical definition to the chroniclers' *rex nihil faciens, roi fainéant.*[12]

Noting that no Louis, son of Carloman, had appeared in the chronicles of Regino and others, Fauchet conjectured, rightly, that the ruler had been in fact only "supposé":

10. P. Paris, ed., *Les Grandes Chroniques de France* (Paris, 1837), 3:96–98. Cf. F. Lot, *Les Derniers Carolingiens* (Paris, 1891), p. 97, n.1.

11. A brief account of some of the most important of these may be found in A. Thierry, "Notes sur quatorze historiens antérieurs à Mézeray," in his *Lettres sur l'histoire de France, Dix Ans d'études historiques* (Paris, 1866), pp. 539–82. See also Nathan Edelman, *Attitudes of Seventeenth-Century France toward the Middle Ages* (New York, 1946), pp. 44–84; W. H. Evans, *L'Historien Mézeray et son temps* (Paris, 1930); Donald Kelley, "Fides historiae: Charles Dumoulin and the Gallican View of History," *Traditio* 22 (1966): 347–402.

12. *Antiquitez* (Paris, 1610). See Janet G. Espiner-Scott, *Claude Fauchet, sa vie son œuvre* (Paris, 1938); idem, *Documents concernant la vie et les œuvres de Claude Fauchet* (Paris, 1938); idem, "Les Théories de Claude Fauchet sur le pouvoir royal," *Humanisme et Renaissance* 7 (1949): 233–38, esp. 234. For Fauchet's place in another historiographical controversy, see Donald Kelley, "De origine feudorum: The Beginnings of an Historical Problem," *Speculum* 39 (1964): 207–28. Recent bibliographical studies of Fauchet and others of the period may be found in G. Grente, ed., *Dictionnaire des lettres françaises: Le Seizième Siècle* (Paris, 1951), and A. Cioranescu, ed., *Bibliographie de la littérature française du seizième siècle* (Paris, 1959), as well as their corresponding volumes for the seventeenth century.

> Et pour ce ie croy que ce mot de fainéant doit estre approprié à Louis le Begue, duquel quelque Chroniqueur Latin avoit dit, *Ludovicus nihil fecit;* comme fait ledit de Saint Aubin: pour *brevi et inglorio regno perfunctus est,* c'est à dire il regna peu de temps, et ne fit rien de remarque, que depuis un translateur ancien a tourné *fainéant,* au lieu qu'il devoit dire, *qui ne fait rien de memorable.* Et ceux qui depuis sont venus ont prit ce mot de fainéant en mauvais part: comme se les Latins eussent entendu *Nihili.* Car Odoran parlant de Louys quatriesme fils de Lothaire roy de France a dit: *Ludovicus nihil fecit* . . . c'est à dire, Louis qui ne fit rien, à cause de peu de temps qu'il vesquit: que ceux qui n'entendoient pas bien le Latin ont tourné fainéant.[13]

Although Fauchet's remarks on the subject are indicated by several seventeenth- and eighteenth-century dictionaries as authoritative,[14] his subtle distinction between the two meanings of *fainéant* does not seem to have influenced the subsequent history of the term during the next two centuries.

One reason for this must be sought in the very practice which inspired Fauchet to discuss the several meanings of *fainéant* in the first place. Sixteenth-century France had produced not only a revival of scholarly and antiquarian interest in her medieval past but also a number of popular histories, particularly of early rulers, complete with portraits, elaborate genealogies, coins, medallions, coats of arms, and other—usually quite spurious—iconographic material.[15] General interest in the early history of France led both students and popularizers to note in common certain features of

13. Fauchet, *Antiquitez,* fols. 396ʳ and 470ᵛ. Cf. Fauchet's "Lettre de Claude Fauchet sur les successeurs de Charlemagne," in Espiner-Scott, *Documents,* p. 198.

14. E.g. Gilles Ménage, *Les Origines de la langue française* (Paris, 1650), p. 308. For the *Dictionnaire des Théroux,* see below, n. 35.

15. See Edelman, *Attitudes of Seventeenth-Century France.* For illustrations of the popular histories, see Jeanne Duportal, *Etude sur les livres à figure édités en France de 1601 à 1660* (Paris, 1914); Robert Brun, *Le Livre illustré en France au XVIe siècle* (Paris, 1930).

medieval royalty. No less a scholar than Estienne Pasquier, for example, devoted a chapter of his *Les Recherches de la France* to popular royal surnames, remarking that such titles were given for faults as well as virtues and citing Charles *le Simple* and Louis *le Fainéant* as examples.[16] A few years later, in his polemical *Franco-Gallia,* François Hotman attacked the laxity and incompetence of later Merovingian and later Carolingian rulers chiefly to strengthen his own thesis of the powers of the popular assemblies of this early period.[17]

Some historians, to be sure, regarded the meaning of the term in much the same manner as Fauchet. Nicholas Vignier, in his *Sommaire de l'histoire des françoys,* published in 1579, sounds very much like Fauchet: ". . . Loys, qui le surnom Fait-neant a esté donné (ou pource qu'il dura peu, ou qu'en son regne il ne fait chose digne de memoire)."[18] Jean du Tillet, whose *Recueil des Roys de France* appeared shortly after Fauchet's *Antiquitez,* echoes these remarks almost verbatim.[19] None of these works, however, achieved the popularity of Bernard de Girard, Seigneur du Haillan's *Histoire générale des Roys de France,* a work which was to remain the best-known history of medieval France until the appearance of that of Scipion Dupleix between 1621 and 1648.[20] Du Haillan's work appears to have been the first major history to link the terms *fainéant* and *néantise* to both the later Carolingians and the later

16. Paris, 1611, Bk. IV chap. 21, p. 481. Cf. Bodin, *République,* p. 296, for Charles, "Fait-Neant."

17. The relevant parts of *Franco-Gallia* are chaps. 12–13. The work exists in numerous editions. See R. E. Giesey, "When and Why Hotman Wrote the Francogallia," *Bibliotheque d'Humanisme et Renaissance* 29 (1967): 581–611.

18. N. Vignier, *Sommaire de l'histoire des Françoys* (Paris, 1579), p. 166; cf. p. 213: "Odoramnus l'a [Louis V] surnommé Faitnéant: pour ce qu'il n'eut loisir de faire aucune chose memorable pour briefeté de son regne."

19. J. du Tillet, *Receuil des Roys de France, leur couronne et maison* (Paris, 1602), pp. 51–52, 191 For du Tillet, see Donald R. Kelley, "Jean du Tillet, Archivist and Antiquary," *Journal of Modern History* 38 (1966): 337–54.

20. For du Haillan, see Evans, *L'Historien Mézeray.* The edition here cited is that of Paris, 1616, vol. 1.

Merovingians and to impart to it the pejorative tone to which Fauchet was to take such learned offense.[21] Although du Haillan barely avoided the attribution of the epithet *rois fainéants* to the most famous of its subsequent bearers, the Merovingian successors of Clovis II, his attacks on their persons and on their political incapacity linked them with his scorn for Louis V, "Louis Faineant . . . pource qu'il fut homme de peu de valeur, adonné à la pailliardise, oisiveté et vices . . .,"[22] and for Charles *le Simple,* "prince idiot."[23] Du Haillan also noted the other definition of *fainéant,* that of little achievement because of a short reign, but his heaviest emphasis always falls upon the personal degeneracy of these rulers, in this respect in a manner not very different from that of Hotman.[24]

One of the first instances of the application of the term *fainéant* to the later Merovingians was the series of *Les Vrais Portraicts des Rois de France* published in 1634 by Jacques de Bie.[25] The second edition of this work, with the text expanded by short biographies of the rulers discussed, further emphasizes the *fainéantise* of the later Merovingians. De Bie's portraits might have acquired little historical significance, however, since the practice of illustrating histories of earlier rulers had become popular as early as 1522 and was to continue long after,[26] had not François de Mézeray

21. Ibid., pp. 81, 88–89, 96–97, 110–12, 118–19.

22. Ibid., p. 251; cf. p. 283f.

23. Ibid., pp. 260–63.

24. Ibid., p. 284: "Quelques uns l'ont appellé Fainéant pource qu'il n'eust aucun loisir de faire aucune chose memorable, pour la brieveté de son regne."

25. For de Bie, see Duportal, *Etude sur les livres à figure,* pp. 275–79; Evans, *L'Historien Mézeray,* pp. 47–51. The brief biographies were added by H. de Coste, the epigrams beneath the portraits by Jean Baudoin.

26. Between 1522 and 1688 there were at least eighteen popular histories printed with illustrations of individual rulers. Because many of these have not been available to me, I have not been able to check one interesting aspect of the origins of the *roi fainéant:* a popular pictorial tradition reflecting the low esteem in which such rulers came to be held. A brief note is given by Edelman, *Attitudes of Seventeenth-Century France,* p. 88. De Bie's portraits do not appear to reflect such a tradition, although others certainly may.

used them and their inscriptions to illustrate his massive *Histoire de France,* which appeared in 1643 and 1646 and was to supplant the work of Dupleix in popularity until displaced in its turn by the history of Gabriel Daniel in 1715. Mézeray, like Fauchet and others before him, used the most advanced historical techniques of his day, but his contempt for royal weakness far outweighed his sensitivity to semantics, and his comments on the last Merovingians ring with scorn:

> Nous avons assez donné à la mémoire de Clovis [II] d'avoir souffert une dizaine de ses successeurs, tous fainéants, hébetez, et plongés dans les ordures du vice.[27]

> . . . et la fainéantise, desormais hereditaire a cette premiere race, [est] cause qu'il ne se lit rien de memorable de son regne.[28]

The success of Mézeray's history and its portraits inspired Jacques Boulanger to reissue Jean de Serres's *Inventaire de l'histoire de France* in 1648 with a new series of portraits, this one including a "promenade des Rois fainéants."[29] In 1668 Mézeray published his *Abrégé chronologique ou extrait de l'histoire de France* and again gave the Merovingians short shrift: "D'ailleurs il sembloit juste que la France après tant d'idoles et de fainéans se donnast un roi effectif."[30] Thus, in spite of Fauchet's careful etymological distinctions, the figure of the *roi fainéant* had begun to take shape in the historiography of seventeenth-century France.

Other usages of the word *fainéant* hastened the process. From Malherbe to Voltaire and after, the term appears in literary satire in much the same sense as it had in Mézeray.[31] In Cotgrave's

27. François de Mézeray, *Histoire de France* (Paris, 1643), 1:142. Cf. pp. 96–115 (Clovis II to Childeric III).

28. Ibid., p. 101.

29. Duportal, *Etude sur les livres à figures,* p. 277. I have not seen the work.

30. François de Mézeray, *Abregé chronologique ou extrait de l'histoire de France* (Paris, 1668), p. 138. Cf. pp. 295–97.

31. Godefroy's earliest references to the term *fainéant* after the fourteenth century are to the satires of Malherbe, Boileau, and Voltaire. Cf. E. Littré, *Dictionnaire de la langue francaise* (Paris, 1885), 2:1597.

French-English *Dictionary* it is highly pejorative: "An idle, drowsie, lither, slothful luske; a heartlesse loytrer, a lazy fellow; one that's without wit, without vertue, without spirit; a droane, a dullard, a housedove; also a lewd companion, a loose fellow."[32] In 1683 John Bulkeel's translation of Mézeray appeared. Although Bulkeel translated *fainéans* (in the last citation from Mézeray above) as "shadows," he found it necessary when discussing Louis V to provide a gloss on Mézeray's epithet, *"Louis le fainéant"*: "Louis the lazy or Sloathful . . . [in margin, as gloss to Lazy:] Fainéant, Lazy, Idle, Do-Nothing."[33] Toward the end of the century Furetière's *Dictionnaire universel* defined *fainéant* as:

> Paresseux, oisif qui ne fait rien, ou fait peu de chose en comparaison de ce qu'il devroit faire, qui aime à ne pas travailler, ou qui ne veut rien faire. En un République bien policée on doit punir les *fainéans* Il y a des Ordonnances contre les *fainéans* et vagabonds. Ce Conseiller a vendu sa charge, il veut vivre *fainéant*. Un *fainéant*, est proprement un homme ou sans vertu, ou sans cœur, ou sans esprit, ou sans adresse . . . L'inutilité fait regarder un homme comme un *fainéant* méprisable . . . Ce mot de *fainéant* s'est dit de certains Rois de France de la première Race, parce qu'ils ne se meloient de rien, les maires du palais gouvernant les affaires de l'Etat selon leur caprice et selon leurs intérêts. On en compte XI dont le premier est Clovis II et le dernier Childeric, qui fut mis dans un couvent.[34]

Early in the eighteenth century the *Dictionnaire des Théroux* elaborated Furetière's definition and finally established the meaning of the term in French, although ironically citing Fauchet as its authority:

> Paresseux, qui ne fait rien, ou qui ne veut rien faire. *Piger, deses, desidiosus* . . . Il y a eu des Rois de la première Race

32. Randle Cotgrave, *A French-English Dictionary, with Supplements* by James Howell (London, 1650), s.v. *fainéant.*

33. François de Mézeray, *A General Chronological History of France*, trans. John Bulkeel (London, 1683), p. 198. Cf. pp. 87, 153, 199.

34. La Haye, 1727, vol. 2, s.v. *fainéant.*

> qu'on a appellés *Fainéans*. . . . On trouve dans les anciens titres et dans les chroniques, *Ludovicus nihil faciens,* Louis le fainéant; on ecrivoit meme autrefois *Fûtnéant.* Aimoin moine de Fleury dans le second livre des miracles de Saint Benoit, *Augusto Karolo rebus humanis exempto, filius eius Ludovicus successit, qui nihil fecisse praenomen sortitus est, sive quod vix duobus annis regno potius nil strenue gessit, sive quod sanctimonialem quandam, sicuti a majoribus accepimus, Kale monasterio puellarum abstractum, conjugio copulans suo, peccatum quod nihil esse noscitur, perpetravit.*[35]

Thus *fainéant* evolved in the vocabularies of scholars, popularizers of history, and literary satirists.

Fauchet may have suspected that he was fighting a losing battle, and surely the depictions of the later Merovingians and later Carolingians in many medieval chronicles and legal texts indicated something of their future at the hands of Mézeray and his successors (see discussion of some of these sources below, chap. 4). Even Mézeray, however, like Bodin and others, used the term not as an accurate means of historical description but as a commonplace of contemporary social opprobrium. Mézeray's history, like those of many of his predecessors, appealed to a wide public that was interested chiefly in the depiction of royal vices and virtues set against seventeenth-century standards of political and moral conduct. It appears to have been used in this sense, for example, to inculcate cautionary lessons into the young Louis XIV. The seventeenth century was willing to tolerate, with certain limits, depictions of royal inadequacy. These limits, however, were narrow. In his *Histoire de France,* published in 1715, Gabriel Daniel was to reduce Mézeray's invective against the last Merovingians to a few pages devoted to "quatre ou cinq de ces Rois qu'on appelle Fainéants,"[36] and to use them chiefly as illustrations of the basic political truths that:

35. *Dictionnaire universel françois et latin . . . vulgairement appellé Dictionnaire des Théroux* (Paris, 1743), vol. 3, col. 29, s.v. *fainéant.* I am grateful for this reference to Mr. Stephen Kaplan.

36. Gabriel Daniel, *Histoire de France* (Paris, 1729), 1:xlv–vii.

> Outre la leçon si commune de l'inconstance et de la décadence des choses humaines qu'on peut apprendre par tout, on en trouve ici une importante qui regarde en particulier les Princes: c'est que l'oisiveté, l'inapplication, la lâcheté, l'amour du plaisir, et du repos, ne furent jamais les fruits et les avantages légitimes d'une Couronne; qu'ils en ternissent toujours l'éclat, et que si les vertus opposées ne la soutiennent, elle n'est jamais hors du danger d'être ebranlée et de tomber.[37]

Daniel's history continued his earlier attacks on Mézeray's language and style. He did not object, however, to Mézeray's usage of *fainéant,* and he even used *rois fainéants* in a manner which suggests that it had become by his day a common term. Even Pierre Bayle's *Dictionnaire,* although it did not use the term *fainéant,* observed, in the article on David, that the worst things which could be said against a ruler were that he was a tyrant or that he gave himself up to wicked counsel, one of the stock traits of the *roi fainéant* and a topic in political literature from the Middle Ages to the present.[38] By 1700 the figure of the *roi fainéant,* given up to vices or wicked counsel or both, dominated by unworthy favorites or a wicked queen, stripped of all power of governance, and defenseless against a righteous national church, an outraged aristocracy, or a heroic popular assembly—in short, already a stock character out of the historian's repertory company—had entered the commonplace vocabulary of historians, poets, and social critics, where he has since remained.

Historical judgments often tell us more about the men who make them than about the things which are judged. The stylized, oversimplified, and essentially moral terms in which many such evaluations of rulers are couched pose a further danger for the later historian, since their comfortable vagueness lends them to other presuppositions about morals and politics than those in

37. Ibid., p. 514.

38. *Dictionnaire historique et critique* (La Haye-Utrecht, 1740), 2:254. See also Walter Rex, "Bayle's Article on David," in his *Essays on Pierre Bayle and Religious Controversy* (The Hague, 1965), pp. 197–255. On Renaissance ideas of counsel, see J. H. Hexter, *More's Utopia: The Biography of an Idea* (Princeton, 1952), pp. 99–157.

whose midst they were created. Historians, in fact, often reject the moral or political bias of their predecessors only to retain, in much of the casual terminology which that bias had helped to shape, many of the postulates of earlier historical thought. In a study of "Good Kings and Bad Kings in Medieval English History," V. H. Galbraith examined some of this bias as exemplified in medieval and Victorian attitudes toward several English rulers, particularly John and Edward I.[39] The reduction of medieval kings to the categories of "hero, saint, failure, and villain," understandable in terms of the monastic chronicler's willingness to disregard those elements of political experience which did not seem to contribute to the history of salvation—of which the abstract concept of the morality of the ruler was a constitutive element—became especially misleading in view of the peculiarly moral cast of Victorian historical thought which echoed it. The history of the term *roi fainéant,* long since extended beyond the figures of the hapless Merovingians, reflects a similar problem. The term is in fact no more valid an instrument of historical description than is the distinction between "good" and "bad" kings which Galbraith criticized.

The *roi fainéant,* far from being identical with the medieval *rex inutilis,* is a figment of seventeenth-century historical taste. In scholarship it has become an easy substitute for exactness, in popular history a vague commonplace used to label any ruler whose reign appears to have been characterized chiefly by indolence, incompetence, pusillanimity, or subjection to the wills of others. It has been used to describe, besides the last Merovingians and last Carolingians, Philip I, Louis VI, Charles VI, and Henry III of France, Stephen, John, Henry III, and Henry VI of England, and even the figure of Arthur in some courtly romances. Whatever traits—if any—these rulers shared are hardly clarified by calling them, one and all, *rois fainéants.* When a single category of kingship, itself originally a product of a far later period than that to which historians usually aply it, becomes so comprehensive as to include all these rulers, its accuracy and applicability necessarily

39. *History* 30 (1945): 119–32. Expanded version in Galbraith's *An Introduction to the Study of History* (London, 1964), pp. 3–21.

diminish. The commonplace vocabulary is convenient, even tempting, to use, but it is not very informative. The frequency with which it appears, however, should recall Bodin's observation that extremely simplified political types are easily identified, but they do not cover all—particularly the most complex—cases.

While the term *roi fainéant* may have been the brainchild of French historians and poets from the sixteenth century on, the phenomenon was not new to men of that century, nor were historians the first to note it. Neither Tyndale nor Bodin was a historian, nor were their fifteenth-century predecessors, Fortescue and Seyssel, who also expressed particular concern for royal weakness. P. S. Lewis, in his recent study *Later Medieval France,* has suggested at least one convincing reason why such concern emerged in the fifteenth century:

> The true bridles of the king of France lay in his entourage, in his agents, and in the power of those who effectively resisted them . . . In the interplay of the forces of this political society true power was to be found and the true position of the king to be ascertained. And it is upon this complex that the effect of the crisis of confidence should be assessed. The tyranny which men like Jean Juvenal des Ursins saw in France in the fifteenth century was the tyranny of royal ineffectiveness within that complex.[40]

The problem of royal ineffectiveness had grown great because the consequences of royal ineffectiveness had grown great. In the fourteenth and fifteenth centuries kings and their agents had increased the sphere of royal activity in the fiscal, judicial, and religious structures of the realm to a far greater extent than had their predecessors. Fifteenth-century rulers were acquiring extensive, explicit powers concerning and touching wider and wider areas of the life of their kingdoms. Just as the beneficent use of this new power created a greater semblance of order than most men of the

40. New York, 1968, p. 378. For this and the following pages, see also J. H. Hexter, "Claude de Seyssel and Normal Politics in the Age of Machiavelli," in C. Singleton, ed., *Art, Science, and History in the Renaissance* (Baltimore, 1967), pp. 389–415.

fifteenth century had known, so did royal ineffectiveness in governing its distribution threaten to dissolve order into chaos. The full extent of the penetration of agencies of royal power into the daily affairs of more and more men contributed to the changing attitudes concerning its misuse and helped to shape the rhetoric men devised to represent royal failure.

Men in the Middle Ages had also experienced the governance of inept or otherwise inadequate rulers, and they had worked out in some respects solutions to the legal, political, and ecclesiastical problems inherent in dealing with them. In their early forms, of course, these problems were different from those which troubled men in the fifteenth and sixteenth centuries, chiefly because the character of kingship itself was different. From late Iron Age tribal structures and Roman imperial institutions to fifteenth-century Christendom, the institution of kingship was the chief instrument by means of which increasingly articulated judicial, religious, and political structures emerged in European society.[41] This study attempts to trace the changing terms in which men formulated these problems and the solutions they devised between the eighth and the fourteenth centuries. In the early part of this period ideas of kingship were derived from Old Testament political structures, traces of Roman legal and ethical thought, and Celtic and Germanic custom. Kings and political writers from the eighth century on often appeared to weld these diverse elements into a homogeneous structure of political ideas, strengthened by the creation of a vocabulary of ecclesiastically inspired and maintained political categories based chiefly upon patristic and later interpretations of Scripture and surviving ideas of Roman law. Yet the homogeneity and accuracy of these ideas was at best artificial. They could not take fully into account the changing social organizations to which they ostensibly applied. They remained too far from the practice of rulership as men of the eighth, ninth, and tenth centuries experienced it. They centered upon the categories of the *rex iustus*, the just king, and the *tyrannus*, the tyrant. The

41. Particular studies of kingship will be cited in footnotes only. See preface, p. xi.

just king followed the precepts laid down in patristic writings on the moral end of governance. The tyrant opposed his own will to that of the divine source of his authority.[42] No matter how exalted a rationale might be constructed by those ecclesiastics who sought to spiritualize the institution of kingship within the framework of law and a theological vision of human society, their first concern had to be the legitimation of the private, personal power held by individual rulers. The Christianization of Germanic kingship thus became one of the primary objects of early medieval political thought, and this necessity contributed to the concentration upon the excessive goodness or evil which characterizes that thought.[43]

Such political conceptions offered little specific guidance to the legal and administrative problems of early medieval rulers. The clear moral dividing line between good governance and tyranny could not often serve to distinguish clearly between good and bad political judgment or between the exalted position of the Carolingian ruler in the world order and the historical circumstances in which the Carolingians wielded royal power (see discussion below, chap. 2). In practice, that power was more often than not the personal inheritance of individual men, perhaps given to them by God in theory, but sustained by force and personal loyalties in practice. Thus the high rhetoric of St. Isidore of Seville's distinc-

42. The following works offer a good introduction to the subject: W. Parsons, "The Medieval Theory of the Tyrant," *Review of Politics* 4 (1942): 129–43; J. Spörl, "Gedanken um Widerstandsrecht und Tyrannenmord im Mittelalter," in B. Pfister and G. Hildmann, eds., *Widerstandsrecht und Grenzen der Staatsgewalt* (Berlin, 1956), pp. 11–32; F. Kern, *Gottesgnadentum und Widerstandsrecht,* ed. R. Buchner (2d. ed., Darmstadt, 1962), pp. 334–38; Carlyle, *A History of Medieval Political Theory,* 1:172–73, 221–22, 229–34, 250–52; 3:38, 52–73, 112–46. Richard H. and Mary A. Rouse, "John of Salisbury and the Doctrine of Tyrannicide," *Speculum* 42 (1967): 693–709.

43. The best recent study is that of J. M. Wallace-Hadrill, "The *Via Regia* of the Carolingian Age," in B. Smalley, ed., *Trends in Medieval Political Thought* (New York, 1965), pp. 22–41. Now, see also Walter Ullmann, *The Carolingian Renaissance and the Idea of Kingship* (London, 1969).

tion between the *disciplina terroris* (the righteous use of coercive force) of the king and the *doctrina sermonis* (the establishment of orthodoxy by teaching) of the clergy was stoutly maintained by later Carolingian rulers and their ecclesiastical advisors. As late as the twelfth century, Gratian's *Decretum,* the starting point for the later highly developed study of canon law and ecclesiastical political theory, depicted the ruler chiefly in terms of his power to coerce and kill within the law. Gratian included Isidore's distinction, cited above, as well as St. Jerome's injunction to rulers to protect the powerless and Pope John VIII's threats to princes who refuse to supply force when necessary. One of the two most frequently cited passages on kingship in the *Decretum*—one to which we will later return—dealt with the dangers of a powerless king (see discussion below, chaps. 3 and 4).

The separation of theory from circumstances in early medieval political thought constitutes only one point of orientation. There existed other powers in Christian society besides those of the king. The liberties of the priestly order and of individual magnates could not always smoothly accommodate themselves to the exalted claims of kingship. The labels "custom," "tradition," and "ancient liberties," when applied to those aspects of the distribution of power in early medieval society in which such powers conflicted, served to absorb tensions and mitigate the extreme claims put forward at various times by kings, bishops, popes, or magnates. Although the theoretical claims of the king might be very extensive indeed, his governance was in fact hedged about by the actual resources of power outside his control. These resources too were elevated by appeals to God, to the legal status of ecclesiastical institutions, and to the family rights and immunities of the magnates. Thus the circumstantial restriction of royal power in the early period constitutes a second point of orientation for this study.

Early medieval political society maintained itself in a state of uneasy balance between two sets of powers, describing itself as one thing in theory while it was quite another in fact. Between the twelfth and the fifteenth centuries, however, power in political society was redistributed through new structures. Impersonal royal agents—judges, administrators, tax collectors—carried the king's authority to wider areas of the kingdom. By encroaching upon powers outside their own, kings reminded men that they were first *royal* subjects and thus diminished the claims of the barons and bishops of the feudal realms. As the king came to wield direct power less frequently, his institutional power increased. As kings came to lead their armies in person less and less, distributed their judicial authority among judges, and began to surround themselves with new definitions of law, advice, and representation, the older distinctions between the just king and the tyrant became less meaningful. During the twelfth century, as Wieruszowski has pointed out, "under the impact of new ideas infiltrating the area of political thought from more realistic quarters, the dividing line between the *rex iustus* and the tyrannus begins to fade away."[44] The earlier notion of kingship as an office, a *ministerium,* within the church—which Ladner has called the "functional" theory of kingship—gradually gave way before the idea of kingship as an office which functioned primarily for the public welfare, the *publica utilitas,* of the kingdom.[45] The king became less the *minister Dei* than the *minister utilitatis publicae.*[46] To be sure, the king often continued to reserve to himself the right to determine precisely what the public welfare was, and he never freed himself, nor ever wished to, from a role, however vaguely or contentiously defined, within the church.

The long process by which the personal, theologically conceived power of the ruler became impersonal and public led to new terms in discussions of political authority. The growth of new symbols of public power—"crown," "community of the realm," "estate of king," and the suprahuman character of the anointed ruler—all

44. Helene Wieruszowski, "Roger II of Sicily, *Rex-Tyrannus,* in Medieval Political Thought," *Speculum* 38 (1963): 46–78.

45. G. B. Ladner, "Aspects of Medieval Thought on Church and State," *Review of Politics* 9 (1947): 403–22; idem, "The Concepts of Ecclesia and Christianitas and their Relation to the Idea of Papal Plenitudo Potestatis from Gregory VII to Boniface VIII," *Miscellanea Historiae Pontificii* 18 (Rome, 1954): 49–78.

46. See Erna Buschmann, "*Ministerium Dei—idoneitas.* Um ihre Deutung au den mittelalterlichen Fürstenspiegeln," *Historisches Jahrbuch* 82 (1962): 70–102.

reflected attempts to reconcile the older private view of kingship with the newer and more legally articulate public view. During the twelfth and thirteenth centuries this process of reconciliation led to the discussion of new political types. In the reign of Roger II of Sicily, as Wieruszowski has shown, a new political abstraction appeared—the *tyrannus utilis,* the tyrant who appeared to govern lawlessly but also appeared paradoxically to benefit his realm (see above, n. 46). In 1245, at the instance of the magnates and higher clergy of Portugal, Innocent IV formalized in canon law another political type, the *rex inutilis,* the legitimate ruler whose weakness and incompetence cause disaster in his realm. Innocent's action reflected some of the tension between older and more recent views of kingship and rightful resistance and drew not only upon conventional political theory but also upon the juridical status of certain types of incompetent prelates as these had been defined in the writings of late twelfth-century canon lawyers.[47]

Between Innocent's action against Sancho II of Portugal in 1245 and the early fourteenth century, men increasingly began to consider all forms of public power as subject to description, if not containment, by law, and hence as more similar to each other than disparate. Thus imperial, papal, and royal power in the period between 1245 and 1327 were subjected to similar kinds of analysis, and men who concerned themselves with the description of, or resistance to, that power tended to describe all public powers, whether spiritual or temporal, in the same conceptual terms. Theories of resistance, deposition, and control of those holding royal power shared the same juridical framework, and it is possible after the mid-thirteenth century to consider the object of political thought and political action as the abstract figure of the *princeps*—the prince, in the Roman lawyers' sense—rather than as the distinct traditional figures of pope, emperor, or king, each with its own unique history, its own defined powers and liberties, its own particular concerns in the sphere of public authority. This study will close with an introduction to this process, but it will

47. Discussed below, chaps. 4 and 5. See also my "Rex inutilis: Sancho II of Portugal and Thirteenth-Century Deposition Theory," *Studia Gratiana* 14, Collectanea Stephan Kuttner, IV (1968): 253–305.

not pursue its implications beyond the early years of the fourteenth century. "History," Maitland once remarked, "does not proceed from the simple to the complex, but from the vague to the definite." This study will concentrate upon the "vague" period of the history of Christian kingship in which the institution served as a focal point for considerations about the legitimate nature and use of power and authority within society rather than as a means of reconciling and aligning political forces within a framework of public law which contained, or purported to contain, legitimate conceptual terms for juridical resistance.

When Innocent IV acted against Sancho II and Frederick II, he had recourse to the most dynamic tradition of political thought that the West had known since the later period of the Roman Empire, the juristic consideration of public authority in the work of twelfth-century political theorists, canon and Roman lawyers, and politically minded popes, including his great predecessor, Innocent III. By drawing upon that tradition he was instrumental in shaping and directing the chief political concerns of Europeans for several centuries, although his ideas were soon to dress themselves in secular clothing and purport to be of great antiquity in the power structures of the territorial monarchies in which men applied them. In fact, the precision of thirteenth-century papal political theory concealed the vagueness of earlier political thought and the rich variety of its sources. Innocent's notion of the *rex inutilis* was in effect the juridical definition of a political type which had long existed in the writings of chroniclers, poets, and political theorists at least as early as the eighth century. The type may be said to have emerged in part from the Carolingian rationale for the replacement of the Merovingian royal dynasty of the Franks in the mid-eighth century and in part from the practical experience of ninth-, tenth-, and eleventh-century men of individual rulers who were for various reasons unable to sustain the forceful personal governance which had of necessity come to characterize Christian kingship. The full importance of the type *rex inutilis,* however, did not lie exclusively in theories of resistance to an incompetent ruler. It was rooted not exclusively in "political theory" but more deeply in what an astute recent scholar has described as the "modes of perception" of men between the eighth and the fourteenth centuries.[48] "Political theory" in this period was rarely separated—or separable—from general ideas about the limits of human nature and the purposes of human social structures. In this respect, ideas about kingship may be said to reflect men's efforts to conceptualize and describe the changing circumstances of social organization from the tentative political structures of the post-invasion period to the emergence of the articulated kingdoms and city-republics of the fourteenth and fifteenth centuries. It is that tentative character of early political literature which justifies this attempt to include literary as well as documentary sources and to describe, in the third chapter, changing ideas of human nature as well as the particular views of kingship represented by clearly defined social groups such as the aristocratic audience of the twelfth-century epic poems dealing with a remote but relevant past.

The history of the *rex inutilis* illustrates the breadth as well as the narrowness of early medieval ideas about power. In the formulaic vocabulary of eighth- and ninth-century chroniclers, for example, the useless ruler was one who had "falsely" retained the title *(nomen)* of king while having lost its necessary adjunct, the *potestas*—the wealth, military power, and political control required of a "true" king. The historical failure of the last Merovingian kings of the Franks to conform (after the fact, to be sure) to this pattern of "true" kingship constituted at least one of the bases for the later rationale of Carolingian kingship, with emphasis upon the ecclesiastical sanction of the new dynasty overcoming its illegitimacy and concern for the forceful maintenance of political power heightened by the official view of Merovingian incompetence and indolence (see below, chaps. 1 and 2).

In the politically troubled world of the ninth and tenth centuries the very practical inability of some of the later Carolingians to defend people and *patria* was rationalized by chroniclers and poets into their loss of *virtus*. *Virtus,* an ambivalent term meaning charisma, divine favor, and actual power, thus acquired a highly

48. William J. Brandt, *The Shape of Medieval History: Studies in Modes of Perception* (New Haven, 1966), p. 69.

pragmatic sense and provided both a philosophical and historical rationale for the early stages of the Capetian and Saxon rise to power.[49] However tenuous it might ostensibly seem, the relation between the facts of early medieval political experience and the rationale which men provided for those facts is an essential element in understanding the extent of change in political theory as well as the course of change in political institutions.

Certain recurring problems in early medieval society also contributed to the formation of the type. The disparity between the theoretical power of the ruler and his often severely limited political control often could be made to account for a wide variety of political events. In the complex process of substituting new dynasties for old, whatever the reasons for the substitution, the traditional sense of dynastic legitimacy could only be overcome by the authority of powerful ecclesiastical structures and by the attribution to the old dynasty of a quality of powerlessness or incompetence which rendered its individual members unfit to rule. The myth of Merovingian degeneracy, plied by Paul the Deacon and others, parallels the myth of Carolingian degeneracy cited by the tenth-century chroniclers and that of the degeneracy of the Britons in early English historiography.

The political circumstances which necessitated the giving of royal favors to ecclesiastical or lay magnates, the history of the king's thaumaturgical powers, and the rationalization of the existence of groups of men bound by personal oaths either to maintain the Truce of God or their common liberties, all might provide occasions for raising the accusation of royal weakness. The ubiquitous feudal horror of royal officials often suggested a psychological pattern in which strong-willed (and usually low-born) men perversely controlled the weak king.[50] As the political vision of

49. The best discussion of these aspects of *virtus* is that of H. Beumann, *Widukind von Korvei. Untersuchungen zu Geschichtsschreibung und Ideengeschichte des 10. Jahrhundert* (Weimar, 1950), pp. 205–65. See also below, chap. 3.

50. On the problems of royal thaumaturgy, see Marc Bloch, *Les Rois thaumaturges* (rep, Paris, 1961), pp. 31, 146–57, 245–60. See also, for other aspects, J.-F. Lemarignier, "Structures monastiques et structures

chroniclers and satirists moved beyond the rudimentary typology of the eighth and ninth centuries, the type *rex inutilis* often came to be linked to the role of Fortune in the falls of princes and to the role of the vices, particularly *acedia,* in the psychological make-up of individuals. Even the question of the comparative "usefulness" of the crusading king and the ruler who refused to leave his kingdom raised the question, especially when the criteria for "usefulness" to the native *patria* conflicted with those for "usefulness" to the common cause of Christendom. Thus a number of political occasions lent themselves to the question of the ruler's competence without necessitating the development of a legal category of uselessness.

The literary representation of kingship also contributed characteristics to the type not always related directly to theories of rightful resistance. The *chansons de geste* often pointedly attributed to the king precisely those qualities which the audience of nobles and "knightly youth" found most dangerous in any lord—treachery, unjust favoritism, or cowardice. In many of these works kings are most powerful when they violate the rights of their vassals, least powerful when their efforts to maintain justice are most needed. In the later Arthurian romances, on the other hand, the kings were essentially rulers of *aventure* who necessarily had to be inactive at times of public crisis in order to afford the knightly hero his triumphant or disastrous quest. In monastic chronicles and hagiography the king functioned more often as the benefactor or persecutor of the institution or saint, thundering or groveling, than as a recognizable political figure. In the highly polarized rhetoric of panegyric and invective the king might appear to be almost a god himself—as in, for example, the writings of the Norman Anonymous—or, to a writer like Gregory VII, he could literally be the living instrument of Satan.

---

politiques dans la France de la fin du Xe et des débuts du XIe siecle," *Il Monachesimo nell'alto medioevo,* Settimane di studio del Centro italiano di studi sull'alto medioevo, vol. 4 (Spoleto, 1957), pp. 357–400. Eng. trans. now in F. Cheyette, ed., *Lordship and Community in Medieval Europe* (New York, 1968), pp. 100–27.

Thus opportunities for criticizing royal actions or powerlessness without accusing the ruler of tyranny, and literary motifs depicting royal incapacity for other than strictly political reasons, could combine with contemporary views of human weakness generally and contribute to the shaping of a political type. Even the later, pragmatically inclined legal and political theorists might work from such a series of general assumptions. The sharply dialectical character of the ecclesiastical concepts of *sacerdotium* (priesthood and spiritual lordship) and *imperium* or *regnum* (temporal lordship) after the pontificate of Gregory VII was to influence a more specifically juridical concept of royal inadequacy, but it too was to build upon earlier postulates concerning the *rex inutilis*.

The later twelfth and thirteenth centuries witnessed the formation of an increasingly juridical view, first of Christian society as a whole in the work of the canonists, and later of a number of separate political societies in the work of kings, lawyers, and publicists. Many canonists, building a theory of temporal power on the discussions of temporal lordship contained in Gratian's *Decretum*, cited Gregory VII's remarks concerning the powerlessness of the last Merovingian king of the Franks as a basis for considering temporal rulers as parallel to the hierarchy of prelates under papal juridical authority. After the pontificates of Alexander III and Innocent III the relations between spiritual and temporal powers were placed upon an even more precisely juridical foundation and generated the theories of the necessity of papal approval of candidates for rule, of the obedience all rulers owed the pope, and of the actionability of complaints against any temporal ruler, in certain circumstances, in the court of the pope. The ideal pope of some canonists, therefore, ruling a precisely graded, juristically organized hierarchy of spiritual and temporal powers, might draw extremely broad criteria for "usefulness" and "uselessness" in terms of the interests of Christian society as a whole. Any ruler, in such a system, might become "useless" not only for incompetence but for tyranny, crime, grave sin, or criminal negligence.[51]

51. This aspect of royal "uselessness" has been developed by Walter Ullmann in a number of studies. See esp. his *The Growth of Papal Government in the Middle Ages* (rep. New York, 1960), pp. 286–88; *Princi-*

Such a view, however, was neither universal nor permanent. The threats to the unity of Christendom represented by the growth of heresy in the later twelfth century, the disputed imperial election of 1198, and the series of crises between Philip Augustus and his vassals and rivals necessarily drew a number of strong political pronouncements from Innocent III and other popes. Innocent's own "Mirror for Princes," fragmented though it might be in a series of letters to different rulers inspired by different political circumstances and widely dispersed through the canonical *Compilatio III* and the *Liber extra* of Gregory IX, maintained a view of temporal lordship which not all rulers, nor even all canonists, were prepared to accept in its totality. Innocent's most significant contribution to the history of the *rex inutilis,* in fact, was his revision of the earlier concept of the tyrant into a juridical category which included malfeasance, incorrigibility, and criminal negligence. Later popes and canonists, notably Innocent IV, Guilelmus Durantis, and Johannes Andreae were to complement Innocent's distinction by further distinguishing the incompetent prince from the criminally negligent or otherwise criminal ruler.

As the territorial monarchies and the Empire began to articulate their own claims to juridical autonomy, their own *status, necessitas,* and *utilitas,* not simply obedience to or approval of the papacy, became the essential criteria for royal usefulness. The papal prerogative of deposing unsuitable rulers passed to other hands, but the legal character which canonists and Romanists had given to older deposition theory remained. In the fourteenth century kings could no longer simply be deserted, "chased away," tonsured, or made into penitents incapable of ruling. The growth of public law and the consequent theories of juridical resistance which accompanied it changed deposition from "an ecclesiastical to a constitutional procedure." It was no longer the world order or the welfare of Christendom that determined and shaped temporal deposition theory and practice, but the law. Men experimented (often

---

ples of Government and Politics in the Middle Ages (New York, 1966), pp. 57–86; "Law and the Medieval Historian," *XIe Congrès international des sciences historiques, Rapports* (Uppsala, 1960), 3:34–74, at 44.

very awkwardly) with theories and processes of resistance that were, so they would claim, not repugnant to the law and were therefore capable of bearing legal examination and judgment, or so it seemed to the English barons of 1308, 1327, and 1399, to the magnates of the Empire in 1298 and 1400, and even to those canonists and publicists who disputed about the removal of popes in 1294, 1378, and 1417. As the church itself came to be discussed as a political society, the qualifications of even the pope bacame subject to considerations similar to those of temporal rulers, as the series of ecclesiological crises from the abdication of Celestine V to the Council of Constance were to make painfully clear.

Throughout the period covered in this study the *rex inutilis* was always a legitimate ruler who enjoyed all—or as much as he was able to control—of the dignity and power of kingship until such time as his inadequacy rendered him unfit to rule. Thus the term was not applied to a minor who was unsuitable for—or incapable of—rule because of his nonage.[52] Neither was it used of those women who were, according to some interpretations of the alleged Salic Law, unsuitable for rule in France.[53] Although there were a number of standards of suitability which often strongly influenced succession to the throne, these did not strictly apply once rule had actually begun.

52. On the question of royal minorities in France, see F. Olivier-Martin, *Les Régences et la majorité des rois sous les Capétiens et les premiers Valois* (Paris, 1931). For England, see Joan Kennedy, *The King's Nonage* (Ph.D. Diss., Yale University, 1956). The minority of an emperor presented, of course, far fewer difficulties. Perhaps the classic pronouncement is that of Innocent III, in his *Deliberatio . . . super facto imperii de tribus electis* of 1200, trans. Brian Pullan, *Sources for the History of Medieval Europe* (New York, 1966), pp. 194–200: "It is obvious to all that it is not seemly for the boy to rule. For how could he rule others, being in need of others to rule him? How could he guard the Christian people, being himself committed to the guardianship of another person?"

53. On this characteristic, see J. de Pange, *Le Roi très chrétien* (Paris, 1949), pp. 395–98; H. de la Perrière, *Le Roi légitime* (Paris, 1910), pp. 37–66; P. E. Schramm, *Der König von Frankreich* (2d ed., Darmstadt, 1960), 1:325; R. E. Giesey, "The Juristic Basis of Dynastic Right to the French Throne," *Transactions of the American Philosophical Society*, n.s. 51 (1961): pt. 5.

Between the eighth and the fourteenth centuries no force of political revision contributed more to the changes in the institution of kingship than did the influence of theories and institutions of ecclesiastical polity on temporal political structures. Yet older scriptural views of Christian kingship remained influential throughout the period as well. In 1298 Archbishop Gerhard of Mainz opened his proclamation of the deposition of the Emperor Adolf of Nassau with the observation:

> Ut prodeat de vultu Dei iudicium et oculi nostri videant equitatem, via regia debemus incidere, nec ad sinistram, nec ad dextram declinare, ita magnum iudicantes ut parvum, quia non est personarum accepcio apud Deum.[54]

These remarks, a patchwork of scriptural quotations long familiar to clerical and lay writers on kingship, introduce the conclusion of a political process, the details of which hardly seem relevant to the high ideals of justice and equity which they proclaim. The *via regia* of the thirteenth-century imperial electors was surely different from that of the Carolingian ecclesiastics who first applied the scriptural reference to medieval kingship. Yet to the magnates who, however loosely, used them and to those who responded to them, such scriptural commonplaces often were as meaningful as the new principles of public law to which they were often so uncomfortably joined. If the history of the *rex inutilis* is essentially a study of changing ideas of political failure, it also affords a point of orientation toward changes in political thought and practice that sharpened the ideas by which men conceived the institution of kingship and formed as a result new ideas about the nature of the commonwealth.

During this period the consideration of royal inadequacy centered first upon the private person of the king and later upon his public person and the object of his governance, political society. In the sixteenth century such new fictions as that of the body

54. MGH, *Const.* 3, no. 589, p. 549: "Promulgatio depositionis per Archiepiscopum Moguntinum facta." The references are to Psalms, 16:2; Numbers 21–22; Paralipommenon I, 17, 7. See below, chap. 6.

politic, the mystical body of the realm, and the king's two bodies were to encourage the official belief that the king could do no wrong because the suprapersonal perfection of the body politic wiped away the human imperfections of the individual ruler. In the same period strong kings who learned to manipulate their new resources strengthened the institution as well. In general, the political metaphysics of the sixteenth century reflect the difficulty which men faced in separating the abstract repository of public authority from the person of the individual who momentarily embodied it. Between the eighth and the fourteenth centuries, however, the king could indeed do wrong, act foolishly, and dilapidate his kingdom. Within the vague framework of early political thought men turned to political expediency and rationalized their actions as best they could, by appeals to God, to their rights, or to the demands of the *via regia.* The traces of this tension may be found in literature as well as law and in the continually changing figures of the "good king" and the "tyrant" as well as in that of the *rex inutilis.* The role of these three types in early political thought reflects the character of the *via regia* as the *via politica* of medieval Christendom.

1

Gregory VII's Concept of the *Rex Inutilis* and Its Antecedents in Law and Historiography, 751–1100

Pope Gregory VII's use of historical materials reflects a view of the past according to which history is the record of a struggle between the forces of Christ and antichrist for the establishment of the right order of the world. This view was to constitute in large measure the perspective from which later ecclesiological and political theorists would consider history and evaluate events both in their own time and in times past. Gregory's own correspondence and the work of the Gregorian publicists thus constitutes a convenient starting point for a discussion of early medieval ideas of royal inadequacy. Gregory's own brief remarks on the subject acquired greater currency in the eleventh and twelfth centuries than did any others, and they became the basis for subsequent ecclesiastical speculation concerning the papal authority to act against temporal rulers generally and to act in the cases of *reges inutiles* in particular. The twelfth-century canonists who were to shape most ecclesiastical policy toward temporal rulers turned first to the extracts from Gregory's register incorporated in Gratian's *Decretum* and only later began to consider other alternatives than those which he had suggested.[1]

The last quarter of the eleventh century and the first few decades of the twelfth constituted not only what Fournier has called "a turning point in the history of law" but also a "turning point in the history of society."[2] The term "Investiture Contest," as most

1. Gregory VII's observations on the *rex inutilis* may be found in his register, ed. E. Caspar, MGH *Epp. sel. II* (Berlin, 1920). The most recent study of the register is that of Alexander Murray, "Pope Gregory VII and His Letters," *Traditio* 22 (1966): 149–202.

2. P. Fournier, "Un Tournant de l'histoire du droit," *RDF* (1917), pp. 129–80. The other citation is that of R. L. Poole, *Illustrations of the*

historians have long labeled the conflict which characterizes most significant political disputes of the period, hardly does justice to the wide range of issues that papal and imperial writers dealt with in the first major propaganda campaign of modern history.[3] The volume and intensity of publicistic literature, from papal and imperial correspondence to the numerous political and ecclesiological pamphlets, turned the dispute between Gregory VII and Henry IV into a comprehensive effort on the part of many contemporaries to redefine for themselves the constituent political elements of the intellectual world in which they lived.

In the course of that effort many writers came to deal in particular with the most important social concepts of the *societas christiana*. Such terms as *sacerdotium, imperium, christianitas, ecclesia,* and *iustitia* underwent a change in meaning because they had become especially important parts of the ecclesiological and political vocabularies of the early Middle Ages upon which many arguments of the conflict hinged.[4] These were the terms which, in Scripture,

---

History of Medieval Thought and Learning (rep. New York, 1960), p. 198. Surveys of recent scholarship on the period may be found in Norman Cantor, *Church, Kingship, and Lay Investiture in England, 1089–1135* (Princeton, 1958), and in the numbers of *Studi Gregoriani,* ed. G. B. Borino (Rome, 1947ff).

3. The most recent survey of the publicistic literature of the conflict is that of K. J. Leyser, "The Polemics of the Papal Revolution," in Smalley, ed., *Trends in Medieval Political Thought,* pp. 42–64. The most comprehensive survey is still that of Carl Mirbt, *Die Publizistik im Zeitalter Gregors VII* (Leipzig, 1894). The term "Investiture Struggle" has been criticized by Z. N. Brooke in "Lay Investiture and Its Relation to the Conflict of Empire and Papacy," *Proc. Br. Acad.* 25 (1939). Most of the tracts are printed in the MGH *Ldl,* 3 vols. (1891–1907).

4. For *christianitas,* see F. Kempf, "Das Problem der Christianitas im 12. und 13. Jahrhundert," *Historisches Jahrbuch* 79 (1959): 104–23; P. Zerbi, *Papato, Impero, e respublica christiana dal 1187–1198* (Milan, 1955); J. Rupp, *L'Idée de chrétienté dans la pensée pontificale des origines à Innocent III* (Paris, 1939). For *ecclesia,* see J. T. Gilchrist, "Humbert of Silva Candida and the Political Concept of *Ecclesia* in the Eleventh-Century Reform Movement," *Journal of Religious History* 2 (1962): 13–28; A. Rota in *Ephemerides Iuris Canonici* 4 (1948): 257–74; F. Merzbacher in *ZfRG,* K.A. 39 (1963): 274–361.

in the works of the patristic writers, in the canons of councils, and in diplomatic and historiographical literature designated the essential bonds of Christian society. The practice of redefining these terms resulted in part in what Maritain, discussing a different period, called, "a lifting into consciousness of the ethos of the time." That ethos was not, in the eleventh and twelfth centuries, what it had been in the eighth and ninth when these terms had come into general use. If Gregory VII was to base his own views of the papal place in Christian society upon the traditional concepts of his predecessors, he was, by redefining the vocabulary in which those concepts were expressed, to impose his own view of the ordering of Christian society upon many of his most influential successors.

Gregory's attitude toward the past was, then, ambivalent. He saw his own actions not as revolutionary but as consistent with the principles of ecclesiology that had been established in Scripture and in the works of the fathers. If he could denounce imperial claims which were based upon custom, he as frequently grounded his own claims upon the *dicta, regulae,* and *canones* of his predecessors.[5] Indeed, it is the appeal to history—or, as it often turned out, the reshaping of history—which characterizes many of the publicistic works of the period. Writers on both sides of the conflict attempted to justify their own positions by attempting to redefine a past with which their own claims would be perfectly consistent, to posit a version of the right order of the world, of which their own position would be one logical extension. By considering Gregory's concept of the *rex inutilis,* the extant evidence from earlier legal and historiographical sources, and the reaction to the Gregorian view between 1076 and 1140, I shall attempt to describe the entrance of the problem of the useless king into the legal literature of the later Middle Ages.

5. See Ullmann, *The Growth of Papal Government,* pp. 356–62, 472n. Gregory had answered imperialists' claims for the authority of custom with the observation, "Dominus non dixit, 'Ego sum consuetudo,' sed dixit 'Ego sum veritas et vita.' " See also G. B. Ladner, "Two Gregorian Letters on the Sources and Nature of Gregory VII' Reform Ideology," *Studi Gregoriani* 5 (1956): 221–42; G. Tellenbach, *Church, State and Christian Society at the Time of the Investiture Contest,* trans, R. F. Bennett (Oxford, 1948).

In 1076 and 1081 Gregory VII wrote two letters to Hermann of Metz in which he took occasion to clarify his actions against Henry IV and his supporters, "to reassure disturbed Christian consciences . . . and to summarize and codify the reasons which had determined his attitude."[6] Although subsequent interpretations of these motives often differ considerably, most of Gregory's contemporaries and most later scholars agree that the two letters contain the essence of Gregory's thought in regard to the relations between *sacerdotium* and *imperium*.[7] The occasions which brought forth these letters and the role of Hermann of Metz in the conflict between pope and emperor account in large measure for their contemporary influence. The scope within which they deal with the very elements of the Gregorian positions gives the letters an ideological importance possessed by a few other documents of the period.

The two letters are quite similar, since the letter of 1081, the longer and more important of the two, is largely an expansion of that of 1076. Both consist chiefly of citations of scriptural and historical precedent, and their character in this respect bears out the contention of some recent scholars that Gregory's political thought developed gradually throughout the course of his pontificate and

6. A. Fliche, "Les Théories germaniques de la souveraineté à la fin du XIe siècle," *RH* 125 (1917): 2; see pp. 1–67. The letter of 1076 is *Reg.* IV,2; that of 1081 is *Reg.* VIII,21.

7. The letters have been widely discussed. Besides the works previously cited, see also A. Fliche, *La Réforme grégorienne,* 3 vols. (Louvain, 1924–37); idem, *La Réforme grégorienne et la reconquête chrétienne* (vol. 8 of A. Fliche and V. Martin, eds., *Histoire de l'église* [Paris, 1940]); idem, *La Querelle des investitures* (Paris, 1946); E. Voosen, *Papauté et pouvoir civil à l'époque de Gregoire VII* (Gembloux, 1927); J. P. Whitney, *Hildebrandine Essays* (Cambridge, 1932); K. F. Morrison, Introduction to K. F. Morrison and T. E. Mommsen, *Imperial Lives and Letters of the Eleventh Century* (New York and London, 1962); idem, "Canossa: A Revision," *Traditio* 18 (1962): 121–48; Ullmann, *The Growth of Papal Government;* H.-X. Arquillière, *Saint Grégoire VII* (Paris, 1934); idem, *L'Augustinisme politique* (Paris, 1934); E. Caspar, "Gregor VII in seinem Briefen," *HZ* 130 (1924), 1–30; A. Nitschke, "Die Wirksamkeit Gottes in der Welt Gregors VII," *Studi Gregoriani* 5 (1956): 115–29. A useful collection of studies is that of H. Kempf, ed., *Canossa als Wende,* Wege der Forschung, vol. 21 (Darmstadt, 1973). Other studies cited in C. N. L. Brooke, *The Investiture Disputes,* Historical Association Aids for Teachers, no. 4 (1958).

culminated in the letter of 1081. More important for this study, both letters contain Gregory's only known references to the question of royal inadequacy, and the degree to which their texts differ on this point is perhaps a measure of Gregory's increased interest in the problem.

Within each letter most of Gregory's statements concerning the relations between *papatum* and *imperium* are buttressed by citations from a wide variety of sources. Although Gregory appears to have depended far more upon Scripture than upon patristic literature, as Arquillière has shown, his debt to earlier papal documents and to chronicle evidence should not be overlooked.[8] In fact, to the last of these Gregory turned for what is perhaps his best-known exemplum, the deposition of Childeric III, the last Merovingian King of the Franks, by Pepin and Pope Zacharias in 751. Gregory's use of this episode attracted considerable contemporary attention, constituted a particularly vulnerable point upon which his enemies could direct some of their most effective opposition, and became the starting point for later canonist and civilian speculation on the problem of the useless king.

Gregory's letter of 1076 contains his first citation of the deposition of Childeric III. Although the letter neither names the king nor remarks the cause of the deposition, an examination of the passage in which the reference occurs will serve as an introduction to Gregorian political thought and will constitute a basis of comparison with the version given in the letter of 1081. The passage is as follows:

> Now to those who say: "A king may not be excommunicated," we are not bound to reply, since theirs is such a fatuous notion. Yet, lest we seem to pass over their foolishness impatiently, we will recall them to sound doctrine by directing their attention to the words and acts of the holy fathers. Let them read what instructions St. Peter gave to the Christian community in his ordination of St. Clement regarding one who had not the approval of the pontiff. Let them learn why the Apostle said, "Be prompt to punish every disobedience"; and of whom he said, "Do not so much as take food with such peo-

8. *Saint Grégoire VII*, pp. 222–79.

> ple." Let them consider why Pope Zachary deposed a king of the Franks and released all his subjects from their oath of allegiance. Let them read in the records of St. Gregory how in his grants to certain churches he not merely excommunicated kings and dukes who opposed him but declared them deprived of their royal dignity. And let them not forget that St. Ambrose not only excommunicated the emperor Theodosius but forbade him to stand in the place reserved for priests within the church.[9]

This passage is characteristic of the entire letter, for the brevity of which Gregory had apologized at the outset. The claims that were to be carefully documented and expanded in the letter of 1081 stand out here as terse and hurried, and, because of this, they appear more obviously directed toward the immediate question of excommunicated rulers rather than toward the outlining of a systematic theory of papal-imperial relations.[10]

9. The translation is that of E. Emerton, *The Correspondence of Pope Gregory VII,* Columbia University Records of Civilization: Sources and Studies, vol. 14 (New York, 1932), p. 103, with some revisions of my own. The Latin text may be found in *Reg.* IV,2, 294 "Eis autem, qui dicunt, 'Regem non opportet excommunicari,' licet pro magna fatuitate nec etiam eis respondere debeamus, tamen, ne impatienter illorum insipientiam perterire videamur, ad sanctorum patrum dicta vel facta illos mittimus, ut eos ad sanam doctrinam revocemus. Legant itaque, quid beatus Petrus in ordinatione Sancti Clementis populo christiano preceperit de eo, quem scirent non habere gratiam pontificis. Addiscant, cur apostolus dicat: 'Habentes in promptu ulcisci omnem inoboedientiam,' et de quibus dicit: 'Cum huiusmodi nec cibum sumere.' Considerent, cur Zacharias papa regem Francorum deposuerit et omnes Francigenas a vinculo iuramenti, quod sibi fecerant, absolverit. In registro beati Gregorii addiscant, quia in privilegiis, que quibusdam ecclesii fecit, reges et duces contra sua dicta venientes non solum excommunicavit, sed etiam, ut dignitate careant, iudicavit. Nec pretermittant, quod beatus Ambrosius non solum regem, sed etiam revera imperatorem Theodosium moribus et potestate non tantum excommunicavit, sed etiam, ne presumeret in loco sacerdotum in ecclesia manera, interdixit."

10. An anonymous twelfth-century commentator left a marginal rubric on this point in the manuscript: *Reg.,* p. 546: "Contra illos qui stulte dicunt imperatorem excommunicari non posse a Romano pontifice." The letters of 1076 and 1081 are directed to a bishop and concern bishops. Their constitutional bearing is subordinate.

In this passage Gregory rhetorically directs his remarks at those bishops who continue to associate with the excommunicated emperor. He then proceeds to group together a number of examples culled from Pseudo-Isidor, St. Paul, an unspecified Frankish chronicle, and the letters of St. Ambrose. The result is a tightly knit paragraph consisting of syntactically parallel sentences, each of which is introduced by an exhortative verb in the subjunctive: *Legant . . ., Addiscant . . ., Considerent . . ., Addiscant . . ., Nec preteremittant.* Further, the verbs in each subordinate clause contribute by their force to the tone of the letter *deposuerit, absolverit, excommunicavit, iudicavit, excommunicavit, interdixit.*

Although Gregory's literary style has not been widely praised, it is here effective enough to allow the syntax of each sentence and the structure of the whole passage to reinforce the ideas expressed with some of the dramatic power which is characteristic of Gregory's strongest pronouncements.[11] Indeed, Gregory's sense of the dialectical opposition between the forces of good and evil, exemplified by his conception of his role "as Pope . . . the leader of the faithful in active battle against the Devil," accurately reflects "the moral context of his political thought" and determines his literary style.[12] That style reflects Gregory's vivid awareness of the contrast between *sapientia* and *insipientia, membra christi* and *membra antichristi, rex iustus* and *tyrannus,* and other sets of dialectical concepts, in terms of which he constantly conceived his own position as well as that of his opponents.[13]

11. For Gregory as a writer, see V. Ussani, "Gregorio VII scritore nella sua correspondenza e nei suoi dettati," *Studi Gregoriani* 2 (1947): 341–59. Cf. Erich Auerbach, "Latin Prose and Its Public in the Early Middle Ages," in his *Literary Language and Its Public in Late Antiquity and the Middle Ages,* trans. R. Manheim (New York, 1965), pp. 83–180.

12. Morrison, "Canossa," p. 130. See also Ullmann, *Papal Government,* pp. 262–309; G. Soranzo, "Aspetti del pensiero e dell' opera di Gregorio VII e lo spirito dei tempi," *Aevum* 22 (1948): 309–32.

13. Besides the studies cited above, n. 4, see Ullmann, *Papal Government,* pp. 272–310; Arquillière, *L'Augustinisme politique,* pp. 9–27; P. Zerbi, "Il Termine fidelitas nelle lettere di Gregorio VII," *Studi Gregoriani* 3 (1948): 139–48. For *Libertas,* see Tellenbach, *Church, State, and Christian Society, passim.*

Not only does Gregory's concern for the power of God in history appear in the passage under consideration, but something of his dramatic personal view of the ideological dispute as well. Intellectual and moral error exist, he implies, not only on the abstract plane of dogma but also in the daily actions of men, through their *fatuitas,* their *insipientia,* their *vanitas,* and above all their *fragilitas.*[14] One infrequently noted aspect of Gregory's letters is the strong presence of the pope's own personality and his awareness of the individuality of others. His solicitude for the soul, if not for the dignity, of Henry IV, even during the most violent stages of their quarrel, emphasizes this concern and accounts in part for the style of some of the documents which he issued.

For Gregory all of the ecclesiological disputes which his pontificate witnessed centered on the question of the proper ordering, the *norma recte vivendi,* of a single entity, Christendom, seen as a moral-legal *communitas.*[15] Within this entity there existed, to be sure, different orders and different powers. But the only successful outcome of the struggle between pope and emperor would have been one that determined who was to be superior in Christendom, the head of the *ecclesia Romana* or that of the *imperium Romanum.* Indeed, few writers during this period directed their efforts at purely ecclesiological problems. Most of the polemical tracts touched upon the question of the relationship between the spiritual and temporal powers, and some pronounced strongly on the man-

14. Cf. *Reg.,* V, 10; III, 10a. See also Arquillière, *Saint Grégoire VII,* p. 252; Ullmann, *Papal Government,* p. 24, n. 3, and p. 463; K. F. Morrison, *The Two Kingdoms: Ecclesiology in Carolingian Political Thought* (Princeton, 1964), p. 44 (citing the Synod of Meaux/Paris, 845–46, from MGH *Cap.* II, no. 293, prologue). On the Gregorian distinction between the "inner" and "outer" man, see Ladner, "Two Gregorian Letters," pp. 222–24.

15. See W. Ullmann, "Romanus Pontifex indubitanter efficitur sanctus: Dictatus Papae 23 in Retrospect and Prospect," *Studi Gregoriani* 6 (1959/61): 229–64. See also the studies of G. B. Ladner cited above and those of H. de Lubac, *Corpus Mysticum* (2d ed., Paris, 1949); Kantorowicz, *The King's Two Bodies,* pp. 302–14; A. H. Chroust, "The Corporate Ideal and the Body Politic in the Middle Ages," *Review of Politics* 9 (1947): 423–52.

ner in which the world was to be ordered. As Ullmann and others have shown, the repetition of these questions helped generate new intellectual disciplines as well as new political theories, the chief of which was to form the groundwork of classical canon law studies during the next century.[16] One of the products of these polemics and propaganda was to be a new juristic structure for Christendom. As Southern remarks:

> The great contribution of this age in the sphere of practical life was the development of a system, or, rather, a number of interlocking systems, of law of a hitherto unknown complexity. . . . By a kind of natural necessity these changes took place in every department of life, but nowhere with greater swiftness or with more general agreement than in the government of the Church.[17]

The Investiture Contest was a turning point in the constitutional history of Christendom. The thought and writings of Gregory VII contributed greatly to the subsequent direction which the *sacerdotium* was to take at other turning points.

Not the least important of these contributions was the terminology which Gregory employed to describe his vision of the proper order of Christendom. The Gregorian vocabulary, detached from its earlier connotations and transformed, went a long way toward establishing many of the categories of later political thought. That vocabulary was in turn largely shaped by critical events of Gregory's pontificate. By 1076 Gregory had deposed and excommunicated Henry IV. By 1077 the German magnates had elected Rudolph of Rheinfelden in Henry's place. By 1081 Gregory had again excommunicated and deposed Henry and had recognized Rudolph's title. By 1084 Henry's imperial army had invaded Rome, driven

16. G. Le Bras, "Le Droit romain au service de la domination pontificale," *RDF* 27 (1949), 377–98; idem, with P. Fournier, *Histoire des collections canoniques en occident depuis les fausses décrétales jusqu'au Décret de Gratien* (Paris, 1932), 2:7–150; Ullmann, *The Growth of Papal Government,* pp. 359–81.

17. R. W. Southern, *The Making of the Middle Ages* (rep. New Haven, 1961), p. 151.

Gregory from the city, and retired, leaving Rome in the hands of Gregory's Norman supporters, who sacked and burned it. This dramatic breaking of the order of the Christian world called forth increasingly detailed attempts to explain the causes of all that had taken place. In this effort Gregory's political views took on a strength and a determination that rendered them the center of the polemical literature of the period. Again Gregory turned to the past for evidence to support papal claims. He, with his followers, "challenged custom, tradition, and established practices with their own vision of the past and the argument of lasting truth."[18] And that argument was in essence ahistorical.

The full result of this development in Gregory's thought is to be found in the letter of 1081. This letter is, of course, a redaction of the earlier letter of 1076, but Gregory's changes are considerable, and the direction of his thought is clearly evident. The relevant section, parallel to the one cited above, is as follows:

> In reliance upon such declarations and such authorities, many prelates have excommunicated kings or emperors. If you ask for illustrations: Pope Innocent excommunicated the emperor Arcadius because he consented to the expulsion of St. John Chrysostom from his office. *Another Roman pontiff deposed a king of the Franks not so much on account of his evil deeds as because he was not equal to so great an office, and set in his place Pepin, father of the emperor Charles the Great, releasing all the Franks from the oath of fidelity which they had sworn to him.* And this is often done by Holy Church when it absolves fighting men from their oaths to bishops who have been deposed by apostolic authority. So St. Ambrose, a holy man, but not a bishop of the whole Church, excommunicated the emperor Theodosius the Great for a fault which did not seem to other prelates very grave and excluded him from the church. He shows in his writings that the priestly office is as much superior to the royal power as gold is more precious than lead. He says: "The honor and dignity of bishops

18. Leyser, "The Polemics of the Papal Revolution," p. 58.

admit of no comparison. If you liken them to the splendor of kings and the diadem of princes, these are as lead compared to the glitter of gold. You see the necks of kings and princes bowed to the knees of priests, and by the kissing of hands they believe that they share the benefit of their prayers." And again: "Know that we have said all this in order to show that there is nothing in this world more excellent than a priest or more lofty than a bishop."[19]

19. Emerton, *Correspondence*, p. 170. *Reg.* VIII,21 553–555: "Talibus ergo institutis talibusque fulti auctoritatibus plerique pontificum alii reges alii imperatores excommunicaverunt. Nam si speciale aliquod de personis principum requiratur exemplum, beatus Innocentius papa Archadium imperatorem, quia consensit, ut sanctus Johannes Chrisostomus a sede sua pelleretur, excommunicavit. *Alius item Romanus pontifex regem Francorum non tam pro suis iniquitatibus quam pro eo, quod tantae protestate non erat utilis, a regno deposuit et Pippinum Caroli Magni imperatoris patrem in eius loco substituit omnesque Francigenas a iuramento fidelitatis, quam illi fecerant, absolvit.* Quod etiam ex frequenti auctoritate saepe agit sancta ecclesia, cum milites absolvit a vinculo iuramenti, quod factum est his episcopis, qui apostolica auctoritate a pontificali gradu deponuntur. Et beatus Ambrosius licet sanctus tamen non universalis ecclesiae episcopus, pro culpa quae ab aliis sacerdotibus non adeo gravis videbatur, Theodosium magnum imperatorem excommunicans ab ecclesia exclusit. Qui etiam in suis scriptis ostendit, quam aurum non tam pretiosus sit plumbo, quam regia potestate sit altior dignitas sacerdotalis, hoc modo circa principium sui pastoralis scribens: Honor, fratres, et sublimitas episcopalis nullis poterit comparationibus adaequari. Si regum fulgori compares et principum diademati, longe erit inferius, quam si plumbi metallum ad auri fulgorem compares; quippe cum videas regum colla et principum submitti genibus sacerdotum et exosculata eorum dextera orationibus eorum credant se communiri; et ex post pauca: Haec cuncta, fratres, ideo nos praemissa debetis cognoscere, ut ostenderimus nichil esse in hoc seculo excellentius sacerdotibus, nichil sublimius episcopus repereri." The italicized passage in this text became *Causa* XV *quaestio* 6, *capitulum* 3, *Alius item* (for fuller discussion, see below, chap. 4). Gregory's exact source of information has not been identified. On the general importance of the passage, besides the works cited above, the following should also be consulted: Gaines Post, *Studies n Medieval Legal Thought* (Princeton, 1964); J. Watt, "The Theory of Papal Monarchy in the Thirteenth Century," *Traditio* 20 (1964): 186–211 (separately printed, New York and London, 1965); K. G. Hugelmann, *Die deutsche Königswahl im Corpus Iuris Canonici*

This text contains some noteworthy changes in the citation of the deposition of Childeric III. The name of the pope is now omitted, the reason for the deposition is now spelled out clearly, and the papal substitution of the Carolingian dynasty now occupies a prominent place in the text. The structure of the whole passage, in fact, has been altered. Instead of consisting of a few passages to indicate the papal power to excommunicate contumacious emperors, the text now reads as a paean to the superiority of the priestly order over the temporal power.

A comparison of the two texts leads to several suppositions concerning Gregory's use of historical material and perhaps the direction of his thought as well. The first is that he may have acquired more information between 1076 and 1081; this is especially likely, since there is evidence that he had libraries and archives searched during this period.[20] The second is that this information may have been particularly relevant in 1081, since Gregory had recognized *(substituit?)* Rudolph of Rheinfelden as King of Germany in 1080. Although the case of Henry IV did not resemble that of Childeric III any more closely in 1081 than it had in 1076, the events of the intervening five years evidently made the pope wish to clarify and expand certain details of his earlier reference. The new version implies more strongly the point that if Childeric had been deposed simply because of his inadequacy, how much more did Henry, who had committed unheard-of *iniquitates,* deserve the same fate? The syntactical opposition in the letter of 1081 between *iniquitates* and

(Breslau, 1909), pp. 30–41, 105–09; O. Hageneder, "Das päpstliche Recht der Fürstenabsetzung," *Archivium Historiae Pontificiae* 1 (1963): 53–95. For the passage which Gregory erroneously attributed to St. Ambrose, see G. H. Williams, "The Golden Priesthood and the Leaden State," *Harvard Theological Review* 50 (1957): 37–64.

20. Gregory himself remarked that he had had archives searched during the period: *Reg.* IV, 23. See also Poole, *Illustrations of Medieval Thought and Learning*, p. 200. Peter Damian once remarked that Gregory (then Hildebrand) had asked him in 1059 to make a search of old *decreta gesta: Opusculum Quintum, PL* 145. 89. See J. J. Ryan, *Saint Peter Damiani and His Canonical Sources: A Preliminary Study in the Antecedents of Gregorian Reform* (Toronto, 1956), p. 10, n. 4.

inutilis (esse) emphasizes the difference between the two cases. Childeric had not been deposed for his crimes. He had committed no grievous sins. He had disobeyed no commands from Rome. He had not, so far as Gregory and his most likely sources reveal, ever troubled the liberties of either the clergy or the magnates. Henry, on the other hand, was guilty in Gregory's view of all these. It is dangerous to conclude too much in the way of political theory from a rudimentary *explication de texte,* but it is at least equally dangerous to ignore the text and its implications in trying to determine the reasons for the changes which Gregory made.

Of what, then, did Childeric's uselessness, *tantae potestati,* consist? The scriptural and patristic distinction between the *tyrannus* and the *rex iustus* dominated early medieval discussions of kingship and reappears distinctly in Gregory's own thought.[21] The just ruler is *idoneus,* or suitable; the tyrant is *indignus,* unworthy.[22] The principle of suitability created a more comprehensive category which included the elementary moral distinction between the two kinds of ruler. As Kern has shown, this principle determined for Gregory the category to which any ruler belonged. However, in citing the case of Childeric, chiefly in order to indicate rhetorically the magnitude of Henry's crimes, Gregory called attention to another cause of royal unsuitability, that of political ineptitude. According to Gregory, *iniquitates* and *delicta* sufficed to turn a *rex iustus* into a *tyrannus.* However, within the *societas christiana* the suitable ruler also needed some degree of spiritual strength, good counsel, and sufficient political power to follow the demands of *iustitia.*[23] A ruler who lacked these qualities might be *inutilis* and yet not be a tyrant, nor would he automatically become a *membrum antichristi.* The suitable ruler had to avoid two extremes: he must

21. See G. Herzfeld, *Papst Gregors VII Begriff der bosen Obrigkeit (Tyrannus, rex iniustus, iniquus)* (Greifswald, 1914), esp. pp. 63–68; Morrison, "Canossa," passim.

22. Kern, *Gottesgnadentum und Widerstandsrecht,* pp. 175–212; Ullmann, *The Growth of Papal Government,* pp. 232n., 244–51, 288f. The concept of *idoneitas* did not have, in the late eleventh century, the specifically legal connotations it would possess in the letters, say, of Innocent III.

23. See *Reg.* IX, 3 and VIII, 26.

not, through iniquity, become a tyrant; nor should he, through ineptitude, lethargy, ignorance, evil counsel, negligence, physical incapacity, indifference, or greed render himself *inutilis* for the *ministerium (tantae potestati)* which he held.[24] Although, Gregory said, a ruler ought to be deposed for both kinds of unsuitability, the fault of the *tyrannus* was far greater, since it represented an active participation in the forces of the antichrist.

Gregory's view of Childeric's uselessness appears to be somewhat broader than some recent scholars, notably Ullmann, imply:

> The Christian king who acts on the basis of unqualified obedience to the Roman Church, is the king who deserves the epithet "useful"; he who does not, is "useless" . . . Usefullness to the *societas christiana* is the hallmark of the Christian king, and he proves himself useful by accepting the principles of *iustitia*.[25]

If my own suggestions are correct, Gregory suggests strongly that Childeric was, on the contrary, simply not equal to the demands of his office. Kern, on the other hand, seems much closer to the mark: "Gregory VII, with complete lucidity, emphasized in 1081 that the setting aside of Childeric III occurred not so much because of his lack of moral qualities, as because a powerless ruler was politically useless."[26] We may first note briefly that the term *potestas* occurs in all of the extant sources for the deposition of Childeric and signifies political power, not obedience. The contrast between the *potestas* of Pepin and the empty or false *nomen* of Childeric is a frequent theme of the annalists and chroniclers of the episode between the eighth and the eleventh centuries. For Gregory the opposition between Childeric's *inutilitas* and Pepin's *potestas* remains largely what it had been for Pope Zacharias, the

24. As professor Morrison has kindly reminded me, Gregory himself had expressed the hope that he would not be found *inutilis* or *insufficiens*. The expression, in spite of its long history as a papal rhetorical commonplace, takes on a more substantial sense in a man like Gregory. Cf *Reg.* I, 6; I, 8; II, 32.

25. *The Growth of Papal Government*, p. 287.

26. *Gottesgnadentum und Widerstandsrecht*, p. 50, n. 103.

Frankish annalists, and Einhard: political weakness which disrupted the temporal and spiritual order of the *regnum Francorum* and outweighed Childeric's dynastic legitimacy.

Gregory's concept of kingship as a *ministerium* differed, however, from that of the Carolingians. He envisioned temporal rulers as functioning outside the structure of the *ecclesia,* although very much under papal and ecclesiastical scrutiny. In this regard, Ullmann's remarks on the subject of *inutilitas* may be considered in another light. Gregory's thought anticipates to some extent the later development of such Romano-canonical concepts as *publica utilitas.* For Gregory the usefulness of Rudolph of Rheinfelden may well have pertained to his cooperation with the church, especially in his role as *rector et defensor ecclesiae.* In an important letter describing the ideal qualities of a new emperor, Gregory notes that he should be a *rex idoneus* and clarifies this category a few lines further. The king should be "oboediens et sanctae ecclesiae humiliter devotus ac utilis, quemadmodum christianum regem opportet."[27] In this passage *oboediens* and *utilis* are not quite synonymous. The opposite of the *rex idoneus* in Gregory's letter is "aliquis indignus." A kind of usefulness, then, might very well be linked, in contemporary cases such as that of Rudolph, to obedience to the papacy and the *Romana ecclesia.* In the case of Childeric, however, it is hardly necessary to seek as complicated an idea in operation. The structure of the passage in question, the relation of Childeric's deposition to that of Henry, and the clarity of the source material most likely available to Gregory militate against such a reading of the text.

Two further considerations should be noted. First, the sections of the two letters in which Gregory mentions the Childeric episode deal primarily not with the papal power to depose temporal rulers but with the prelatal authority of excommunication. In this respect, the citations of the cases of kings and emperors add rhetorical force to an argument dealing essentially with a commonplace of Christian doctrine in the eleventh century. Second, Gregory's modification of the term *ecclesia,* in which he restricted its earlier

27. *Reg. VIII,* 26.

sense of all Christianity to that of the clergy, particularly the clergy of Rome, tended to put temporal rulers, as we have noted, outside of the ecclesiastical structure in which they had once occupied a prominent place.[28] The place of the Childeric episode in these letters, then, indicates no novel concept of royal inadequacy at variance with all of the existing sources, but a rhetorical reinforcement of Gregory's argument for the power of prelates to excommunicate sinful Christians, however powerful they might be. Gregory may well have modified the concept of the *rex inutilis* in the course of his negotiations with the supporters of Rudolph and his own political experience. But he did not change the meaning of the term when he applied it to the last Merovingian king of the Franks. The antithesis between *iniquitates* and *inutilis* in the letter of 1081 is sufficient to show this; for a king to be *inutilis* in Ullmann's sense, he would have to be disobedient to Rome and guilty, *ipso facto,* of *iniquitates,* stemming from his *superbia* and his consequent willful rejection of the guiding principles of *dilectio, libertas,* and *iustitia.*

The first effective result of Gregory's brief discussion of the case of Childeric was to restrict action in similar cases to the pope alone. Some ninth-century sources, including Einhard, had flatly stated that the pope's authority had been the sole instrument in the change of dynasty. Other sources, to be sure, presented substantially different points of view. Whether inadvertently or not, Gregory failed to cite any version but that of the pro-papalists. Nor did he, for that matter, use the much more relevant material surrounding the deposition of Louis the Pious in 833 or any other actions taken against useless or evil rulers during the ninth and tenth centuries. By failing to consider the question of royal inadequacy except as a

28. The juridical (Ladner uses the term "feudal") bond between temporal rulers and the papacy replaced the ecclesiological bond of Carolingian political thought. This change parallelled the Gregorian attempt to discourage the sacramental character of the royal anointing. See, e.g., K. Jordan, "Das Eindringen des Lehnwesens in das Rechtsleben der römischen Kurie," *Archiv für Urkundenforschung* 12 (1931/32): 13–110; G. Soranzo, "Gregorio VII e gli stati vassali della Chiesa," *Aevum* 23 (1949): 131–58; Carlyle, 4:298–306.

rhetorical aside and by reserving constitutive action to the pope alone, Gregory removed from the hands of local powers a useful defensive instrument of action in cases of dangerously inadequate rule. As Fliche has observed, after Gregory VII papal intervention became a necessary element in all deposition action taken against temporal rulers.[29] It is the political, or the procedural, aspect of Gregory's treatment of the case of Childeric and not its constitutional novelty that is important.

Gregory added great vitality and precision to the expression of political ideas by vitrue of his sharply dialectical conception of the forces at work within the *societas christiana.* Yet his notion of the *rex inutilis* remained, on the political plane, far closer to that of Pope Zacharias than to that, say, of Pope Innocent IV. His contribution to later legal treatment of the problem was chiefly procedural: he restricted action against an inept ruler to the pope, thus in effect denying a practical right of resistance to local powers. The consequences of his views would be worked out in the publicistic battles of the late eleventh century and in the legal developments of the twelfth. His letters of 1076 and 1081 did, however, serve to lift the problem of the *rex inutilis* "into consciousness" and provided a starting point for subsequent speculation. Yet he neglected to use much material which should have been readily available to him. To discover the earliest medieval treatments of

29. This general rule held till the deposition of the Emperor Adolf of Nassau in 1298. The Merovingian ruler is not said to have been excommunicated. The sources, in fact, make it clear that he was tonsured and placed in a monastery, a fate not uncommon among rulers before the tenth century. Moreover, Gregory's noting the substitution of the Carolingian for the Merovingian dynastry suggests that this version was dictated with Henry and Rudolph in mind. By the early twelfth century the purely legal aspects of Zacharias's deposition of Childeric III had begun to appear in later citations of the case; e.g. the *Liber canonum contra Henricum Quartum,* MGH *Ldl* I, 471–516: "Franci miserunt Roman Burchardum Wirzeburgensem episcopum ad Zachariam papam XCII, ob disponendam ex eius consilio sui rem publicam; plenus Deo papa remandavit, ut Hildericus in administrando rem publicam tepidus, quandoquidem matri aecclesiae non esset proficuus, regia potestate privaretur, et Pippinum pater Magni Caroli . . . in regem ungueretur . . . Hilderico ad consulendum animae in monasterium apostolica auctoritate traditio" (p. 496). This work appeared about 1103.

royal ineptitude, the eighth-, ninth-, and tenth-century sources must be examined.

For the Carolingian chroniclers, as for the publicists of the Gregorian period, history was a work of edification. The chronicler was not only the witness to or recorder of events, but one who attempted to describe events "in a light which could explain them. [He] elaborated a truthful historical construction which rests upon a specific vision of the world, upon a specific concept of time."[30] The Carolingian-ecclesiastical vision of world order constituted the background for all of Carolingian historiography. That vision was invented not by Pepin and Charlemagne but by the ecclesiastical groups to whom they had given both power and a position from which they might reshape the intellectual life of the *regnum Francorum.*

Like Gregory VII, the Carolingian chroniclers tended to see history in terms of their understanding of their own time. The deposition of Childeric III, as it appears in ninth-century sources, reflects the political limitations of these writers as well as the limits of their knowledge of Merovingian kingship and their ability—or concern—to be historically accurate. Childeric possessed the *nomen,* or title, of king. Pepin possessed the *potestas,* or power, of governance. According to all of the extant sources, the inadvertent separation of *potestas* from royal *nomen* was the sole criterion for the transfer of the crown. Because of his lack of *potestas,* Childeric was, according to one source, "nec sibi nec aliis utilis," useful neither to himself nor to others. The possession of *potestas,* then, determined usefulness, and the quality of usefulness determined in its turn the validity of the royal *nomen.* Some chroniclers, to be sure, attempted to bridge the obvious gap between *nomen* and *potestas* by interposing a third atribute of kingship, the royal

30. P. Rousset, "La Conception de l'histoire à l'époque féodale," in *Mélanges Louis Halphen* (Paris, 1950), pp. 623–34; see pp. 623–24. See also H. Beumann, "Die Historiographie des Mittelalters als Quelle fur die Ideengeschichte des Konigtums," *HZ* 180 (1955), 449–88; D. Bianchi, "Da Gregorio di Tours a Paolo Diacono," *Aevum* 35 (1961): 150–66; Wolfram von den Steinen, *Der Kosmos des Mittelalters* (Bern, 1959), pp. 61–89.

dignitas, which gave stature to both the naked title and the raw power of governance. Such simplified elements projected back upon the events of 751 give the Carolingian representation of Childeric's deposition, as Wallace-Hadrill has noted, much more the air of propaganda than of history.

The description of the deposition of Childeric III found in Carolingian historiography was the result, however, not of consciously ordered propaganda but of a specific attitude toward kingship. This view became particularly strong in the late eighth century and grew apace until the late ninth, and its role in the chroniclers' description of the deposition of Childeric was the only one they could have given it. Childeric III became the first conspicuous *rex inutilis,* not because his own inadequacy was especially greater than that of some of his predecessors, but because the distinction between *utilitas* and *inutilitas* in the person of the king had become a part of the historical background of the Carolingian world order. Not the intrinsic character of the events of 751 but the chroniclers' coloring of those events provided Gregory VII with his useful and influential exemplum.

Einhard tells the story of the events of 751 in the first chapter of his *Vita Karoli Magni:* " The race of Merovingians, from among which the Franks were accustomed to crown their kings, is said to have lasted until Childeric, who, at the order of Stephen, the Roman pontiff, was deposed and tonsured and placed in a monastery."[31] Einhard goes on to note that the Merovingians had for a long time held no power but only the "empty name" of king, be-

31. Ed. L. Halphen (Paris, 1947), pp. 6–8. The background is described in J. M. Wallace-Hadrill, *The Long-Haired Kings and Other Studies in Frankish History* (New York, 1962); E. Caspar, *Pippin und die römische Kirche* (Berlin, 1914); idem, "Das Papsttum unter fränkischen Herrschaft," *Zeitschrift fur Kirchengeschichte* 54 (1935): 132–266; E. Perels, "Pippins Erhebung zum Königtum," *Zeitschrift fur Kirchengeschichte* 53 (1934): 400–16; W. Levison, *England and the Continent in the Eight Century* (Oxford, 1946); L. Halphen, *Charlemagne et l'empire carolingienne* (Paris, 1937); H. Buttner, "Aus dem Anfangen des abendländischen Staatsgedankens: Die Königserhebung Pippins," *HJ* 71 (1951): 77–90; R. Buchner, "Das merowingische Königtum," W. Schlesinger, "Uber germanisches Heerkönigtum," and E. Ewig, "Zum christlichen Königsgedanken im

cause the wealth and power of the kingdom had long since slipped into the hands of the mayors of the palace. The king retained only "the name, the long hair and beard. . . . With the exception of the useless name of king and a meager livelihood, he had nothing of his own other than one villa and a small number of servants." Einhard completes the portrait with a description of the journey of the king in an oxcart, drawn by a herdsman *rustico more agente,* to the ceremonies at the March field.

Other Carolingian writers, including Paul the Deacon, had commented upon the weakness and even the degeneracy of the later Merovingians. Among the chronicles the *Annales laurissenses minores* give a typical account:

> In the year 750 Pepin sent ambassadors to Pope Zacharias at Rome in order to inquire about the kings of the Franks, who were of the royal dynasty and were called kings but had no power in the kingdom, save that of signing charters in their own name. They had no real royal power, for they did only what the Frankish mayor of the palace wished: they went to the March field according to the ancient custom, where they received the gifts given by the people to the kings. . . . Pope Zacharias therefore, according to the apostolic authority, answered them that it seemed better and more useful to him, that he who had power in the kingdom should be called king and should be king, rather than him who was falsely called king. The pope therefore sent to the king and people of the Franks that Pepin, who held the royal power, should be called king and should be thus placed upon the royal throne. This was done through the unction of St. Boniface, Archbishop of Soissons. Pepin was called king, and Childeric, who had been falsely called king, was tonsured and placed in a monastery.[32]

Frühmittelalter," all in Theodor Mayer, ed., *Das Königtum,* vol. 3 of *Vorträge und Forschungen* (Lindau and Konstanz, 1954).

32. MGH *SS* I, 116. The standard survey of bibliography for the period is that of Wattenbach-Levison-Löwe-Buchner, *Deutschlands Geschichtsquellen im Mittelalter. Vorzeit und Karolinger,* 4 vols. with Beiheft, *Die Rechtsquellen* (Weimar, 1952–63).

The anointing of Pepin was later repeated by Pope Stephen II.[33] With some exceptions, these are the accounts of the events of 751 of which Gregory VII was later to take notice.

The deposition of Childeric and the elevation of Pepin to the Frankish throne occurred at a critical moment in Frankish history. Not only was the *stirps regia* of the Merovingians displaced, but a new element was introduced into the political makeup of Frankish kingship, that of Rome. A new flow of Christian political ideas began to work upon Frankish political institutions, the idea of the *rex iustus,* whose spiritual prefiguration had been David and whose duties were to constitute the chief topic of discussion in later political literature.[34] A dynastic change which probably owed more to simple power politics than its chroniclers cared—or were able—to indicate gave patristic and scriptural political ideals a prominent place in the structure of Frankish government. Tellenbach says: "It

33. *Liber pontificalis,* ed. L. Duchesne (Paris, 1886), 1: 447–48. The contemporary *Vita Zachariae* makes no mention of the pope's role. On the significance of the anointing, see L. Levillain, "L'Avènement de la dynastie carolingienne et les origines de l'Etat pontifical (749–751)," *Bibliothèque de l'Ecole des Chartes* 94 (1933): 225–95; R. Holtzmann, "Die Italienpolitik der Merowinger und des Königs Pippin," in *Das Reich. Festschrift Johannes Haller* (Stuttgart, 1940), pp. 95–132; Theodor Schieffer, *Winfried = Bonifatius und die christliche Grundlegung Europas* (Freiburg i.B., 1954), pp. 256–64.

34. Caspar ("Das Papsttum unter frankischen Herrschaft," p. 132) claims that "With the papal-Carolingian alliance of the mid-eighth century, the middle ages begin . . . [citing Ficker]. The *responsum* of Zacharias to Pepin's ambassadors was the most influential act of the whole medieval period. It opened a new chapter in the theme of Church and State and a new epoch in history." The early rationale of Carolingian kingship is certainly a watershed in the history of the State. Besides the studies cited above, one may refer to Carlyle, 1:210–92; H. Fichtenau, *The Carolingian Empire,* trans. Peter Munz (rep. New York, 1964), pp. 47–73. The Carolingian conception of royal power has been the subject of a number of scholarly exchanges, many of which are conveniently described in C. E. Odegaard, "The Concept of Royal Power in the Carolingian Oaths of Fidelity," *Speculum* 20 (1945): 279–89. See also M. Lemosse, "La Lèse-majesté dans la monarchie franque," *Revue du Moyen Age Latin* 2 (1946): 5–24; Walter Schlesinger, "Herrschaft und Gefolgschaft in der germanisch-deutschen Verfassungs-geschichte," *HZ* 176 (1953): 225–75.

would be a much closer approach to the problem to see that as a result of Pepin's reign the theocratic conception of kingship as a function or office developed in the intellectual world of western monarchy."[35]

The development of new conceptions of kingship, however, or the definition of formerly imprecise postulates could and did turn out to be something of a double-edged sword. Once the right of resistance had been articulated in moral or juridical terms, all those who subsequently profited from that process had not only to profess to observe the new terms but also to guard against their more powerful and ambitious subjects' acquiring theories of resistance which might be used against the new monarch. Pepin, Charlemagne, and Louis the Pious in the early years of his reign profited from the increased ethical prestige of kingship, but Louis himself and his successors were hard put to prevent the ethical standards of kingship from becoming juridical weapons for dissident political forces within their own kingdoms.

The sources that describe the events of 751 give two distinct versions of the means by which the change of dynasty was accomplished. According to one group, Pepin deposed Childeric by virtue of the authority, and at the express command, of Pope Zacharias. According to the second group, the pope merely approved an action which had been instituted and completed by Pepin and the Frankish magnates, and the anointing of Pepin was the only constitutive part which the church had in the entire affair. The two versions were not, to be sure, competitive in a political sense: one was not pro-Merovingian and the other pro-Pepinid. The difference between the two is really in the degree of ingenuousness that each attributes to Pepin.

To read back into the eighth- and ninth-century sources the issues which were to occupy such a large part of the political consciousness of Europe between the eleventh and seventeenth centuries is tempting. The elements of the later constitutionalist-monarchical dilemma are all there: a wicked or inept, but legiti-

35. "Europa im Zeitalter der Karolinger," in *Historia Mundi* (Bern, 1956), 5: 401.

mate, ruler; a vigorous and popular, but nonroyal, claimant; a source of authority outside the king (the papacy) which claims competence to dispose of the crown; the employment of a novel ritual in order to secure widespread approval of and support for the candidate; finally, a well-publicized expression of ultimate concern for the order and welfare of the kingdom. The events of 751 mark, in fact, the beginning of later medieval deposition proceedings, and they instituted the pattern that was to be repeated frequently in the next nine centuries.

But these elements were neither as powerful nor as clearly defined in 751 as they would be later. The pattern lacked the one unifying principle that would strengthen it: a sufficiently abstract concept of public law. Such concern for the public order as was expressed in 751 was forced into a framework of ideas strongly colored by the ecclesiological character of political thought. The eighth-century idea of *utilitas communis* did not constitute a point of view that could consider the interests of the state—or, indeed, such a thing as a state at all—as directed toward a common welfare to which the church contributed only a limited direction and over which it exercised at best a limited amount of control. The Carolingian *regnum*—later *imperium*—was an attempt to unify Frankish society conceived as an *ecclesia* under a supreme governor. "The new Frankish-Christian universalism did not develop unassisted out of the Roman imperial idea but was considerably aided by the unity of the Church. The *imperium christianum* of Charlemagne did not of itself possess that unity; it derived it from the *Ecclesia,* the *regnum Christi,* which, in its own way, the *imperium* sought to typify."[36]

The sources, moreover, are remarkably silent about other important aspects of the removal of Childeric. To what extent did the elevation of Pepin depend upon the support of clerical and lay magnates? To what extent did the Frankish church, in its frequent eighth-century councils and its powerful monastic prelates, influence the form, if not the substance, of the deposition? Was there,

36. E. Ewig, "Zum christlichen Königsgedanken im Frühmittelalter," p. 69.

as Perels has suggested, a difference of opinion as to the nature of their respective roles on the parts of Pepin and Zacharias? To be sure, even later deposition proceedings do not always explicitly answer these questions; yet the extremely simplified depiction of the events of 751 must prevent a too strict adherence to such theories as that of the long-planned Carolingian climb to the Frankish throne. And Einhard's *rex rusticus*—or even *rex stultus*—must remain the state portrait of Childeric III.

Although the sources differ as to the precise nature of the roles of Pepin and Zacharias, there is no difference of opinion at all concerning the character of the king whom Pepin displaced. The tendency of the chronicle sources to concentrate upon the figure of Pepin, his embassy to Rome, Zacharias's response, and his coronation places the new dynasty squarely in the center of the process. Childeric, always a shadowy figure, stands, as it were, outside of the proceedings and bears the brunt of a uniformly unfavorable representation in all of the sources.

Childeric "had no power in the kingdom." He was the king "with whom no regal power remained." He possessed only the *nomen* of king, not the *potestas*.[37] The author of the early ninth-century *Breviarium Erchanberti* records a fictitious exchange between pope and king on the subject of Childeric's *nomen* and lack of *potestas*. Even though this work, far more even than that of Einhard, deserves to be called a piece of Carolingian propaganda, the following conversation captures the spirit of most of the other sources:

> Before Pepin was raised to the kingship a pope named Stephen came into Frankish territory from Rome to ask the said prince to aid him against Haistulf, king of the Lombards . . . [Pepin] answered, "I have a lord king, and I know not what he might wish to do." The pope then turned to the king and asked for

37. On the subject of *nomen-potestas*, see H. Fichtenau, "Karl der Grosse und das Kaisertum," *MIöG* 61 (1953): 237–334 (cf. his *The Carolingian Empire*, p. 71); H. Beumann, "Nomen Imperatoris. Studien zur Kaiseridee Karls des Grossen," *HZ* 185 (1958), 515–49; Arno Borst, "Kaisertum und Namentheorie im Jahre 800," in *Festschrift Percy Ernst Schramm* (Wiesbaden, 1964), 1:36–51.

> aid. The king replied, "Do you not see, Father, that I possess neither the power nor the dignity of king? In what manner, then, might I possibly help you?" "Truly," said the Pope, "such is indeed the case, since you are not worthy of such an honor." Turning to Pepin, the pope said, "By the authority of Saint Peter, I say to you: tonsure this one and place him in a monastery, for where else might he live? He is useful neither to himself nor to others." The king was then tonsured and placed in a monastery; then the pope said to Pepin, "The Lord and the authority of St. Peter chose you, that you should be a prince and king of the Franks."[38]

Nec sibi nec aliis utilis est: in this anecdote, as in the other sources, Childeric's uselessness derives from his lack of *potestas*. But the pope's remarks imply something more, a personal insufficiency which renders Childeric unfit for any work whatsoever. It is not that the king wills not to aid the pope; he is unable to do so. Whether his incapacity has been caused by others or not, his docile compliance suggests that he is not averse to his lack of power and dignity, or that if he is, he has accepted his situation with a distinctly unregal fatalism. The author of the *Breviarium* does not probe for causes. He is interested in the phenomenon before him, a king who paradoxically possesses the *nomen,* but not the *potestas,* of king. The concern of the pope is to rectify the anomaly, not to analyze it. The contrast between *nomen* and *potestas* thus becomes a central issue; the problems of the Merovingian monarchy remain at best peripheral.

The antithesis between *nomen* and *potestas* in these sources is somewhat misleading. The frequent use of these terms in opposition to justify the events of 751 would indicate that they had been traditional terms for the expression of political ideas. This, however, cannot be proven to have been the case. Ewig has noted that *utilis* and *efficax* were attributes not of royalty in the Merovingian

38. *Erchanberti Breviarium,* ed. G. H. Pertz, MGH *SS* II, 328. On the work, see H. Löwe in Wattenbach-Levison-Löwe-Buchner, *Deutschlands Geschichtsquellen,* 3:349–50. This curious piece of political propaganda has not yet been adequately studied. It was written around 826.

period but of the nobility.[39] Nor was the notion of kingship as a *ministerium* frequent before the reign of Louis the Pious.[40] According to some accounts, including that of Tacitus, kingship among the Teutonic peoples had depended neither upon leadership in battle nor upon efficiency in governance. Early Germanic kings, so this view goes, were royal because they belonged to a royal dynasty, a *stirps regia,* which was, in DeVries's words, also a *stirps divina.*[41] Other views differ considerably: one suggests that Merovingian kingship was the result of combining into one figure the qualities of Tacitus's *rex* and *dux* into a *Heerkönig.* Whatever the original character of Germanic kingship, by the mid-eighth century dynastic legitimacy had become a powerful deterrent to changes of royal family. Childeric's "uselessness" and deposition probably indicated the weakening of dynastic legitimacy as a result of the changing circumstances of economic and political power among the Franks during the early eighth century. The chroniclers' distinction between the king's *nomen* and *potestas* suggests only a placing of political emphasis within a more complicated sequence of events and causes, not the application of a traditional terminology to an expected change of dynasties.

39. "Zum christlichen Königsgedanken," pp. 15–63. The formal address "Utilitas vestra" was an epistolary commonplace among the Merovingians.

40. H. Liebeschutz, "Wesen und Grenzen des karolingischen Rationalismus," *Archiv fur Kulturgeschichte* 33 (1950): 37–39. For other royal terminology, see Schlesinger's study, cited above, n. 34, and D. H. Green, *The Carolingian Lord: Semantic Studies on Four Old High German Words: Balder, Fro, Truhtin, Herro* (Cambridge, 1965), esp. pp. 216–32.

41. J. de Vries, "Das Königtum bei den Germannen," *Saeculum* 7 (1956): 289–309; O. Höfler, "Der Sakralcharacter des germanischen Königtums," in *The Sacral Kingship. La Regalità sacra. Contributions to the Central Theme of the VIIIth International Congress for the History of Religions, Rome, 1955* (Leiden, 1959), pp. 664–701. A powerful critique of the theory of divine Germanic kingship is the excellent study by Philip Grierson, "Election and Inheritance in Early Germanic Kingship," *The Cambridge Historical Journal* 7 (1941): 1–22. See also Karl Bosl, "Reges ex nobilitate, Duces ex virtute sumunt," in his *Frühformen der Gesellschaft in mittelalterlichen Europa* (Munich-Vienna, 1964), pp. 62–73.

Patristic and scriptural ideals of kingship became institutionalized on a large scale for the first time in the West at the Carolingian court. In the figure of Charlemagne the Germano-Roman and the Christian-scriptural traditions of kingship met in the person of a single ruler. For a moment the West witnessed a king who was fully aware of both traditions and who used the power of one to balance the claims of authority made by contemporary representatives of the other. Charlemagne saw himself as at least the equal of the pope and the Eastern emperor, chiefly by virtue of his view of the Germanic past and his place in that tradition of kingship.[42]

The Carolingians did not assume the kingship of the Franks simply by rejoining the separated *nomen* and *potestas* of the Merovingians or by tonsuring the last Merovingian ruler.[43] *Potestas* alone, since it had at best a limited character in later patristic writings and among the Franks, could not have served as a legitimate cause of dynastic change until it became increased by *honor, virtus,* and *dignitas.* The political role of these had been formulated by ecclesiastical thinkers, not Frankish nobles. The King of the Franks had, by adopting a view of kingship derived from patristic thinkers, come to be judged according to standards similar to those by which he himself had formerly judged his ministers. Since the new structure of Frankish kingship had been erected largely by ecclesiastical thinkers, the church would henceforth play a considerably expanded role in the political life of the kingdom. The result of this role was the articulation of the old ecclesiastical idea of kingship as a *ministerium.* For a time, in the person of a strong

42. See H. Löwe, "Von Theoderich dem Grossen zu Karl dem Grossen," *Deutsches Archiv* 9 (1952): 353–401; H. Beumann, "Die Historiographie des Mittelalters," p. 479, n. 1, and p. 480; H. Fichtenau, *The Carolingian Empire,* pp. 66–73.

43. In 1954 Schramm suggested that Childeric had not been tonsured at all, but scalped *(Herrschaftszeichen und Staatssymbolik* [Stuttgart, 1954], 1:127). Recent studies, however, tend to confirm clerical tonsuring: E. Kauffmann, "Uber das Scheren abgesetzter Merowingerkönige," *ZfRG,* G. A. 72 (1955): 177–85; K. Sprigade, "Abschneiden des Königshaares und kirchliche Tonsur bei dem Merowingern," *Die Welt als Geschichte* 22 (1962): 142–61; A. Cameron, "How Did the Merovingian Kings Wear Their Hair?" *Revue Belge de Philologie et d'Histoire* 43 (1965): 1203–16.

king, the view of kingship as an office might be kept more theoretical than practical. In the case, however, of a ruler whose control over his prelates and magnates was less strong, political and moral errors might be changed to moral deficiency and hence unsuitability. When this in fact occurred in the reign of Louis the Pious, the concept of the *rex inutilis* became somewhat more complicated than the simple separation of *nomen* and *potestas* might indicate. Ecclesiastical critics of Louis were to join the idea of negligence, with its ambivalent Roman and canonical overtones, to a catalogue of personal moral shortcomings and thus to develop a deposition theory much more complicated and politically unstable than that worked out in 751.

Louis the Pious, the first Carolingian to be deposed, lost his throne eighty-two years after the last Merovingian. During that period the Frankish monarchy had undergone a series of striking changes, none of which were more important than the ecclesiastically influenced structure of government and the ecclesiastical concept of the character of royal governance. Since churchmen had worked out the role of kingship in the Carolingian Empire, the juridical nature of that Empire resembled strongly the juridical nature of the Frankish church. The aspect of the deposition of Louis the Pious to be kept most firmly in mind, then, is its character as an ecclesiastical procedure, specifically a form of penance, since its form and substance derived from ecclesiology, not directly from the precedent set by the events of 751.

The primary account of Louis's deposition is the *Relatio compendiensis,* which the assembled bishops had made in order to record and to publicize the emperor's penance.[44] The *Relatio* consists of a statement of the proceedings, a list of eight charges against Louis, and a brief conclusion. A summary of this document made for Bishop Agobard of Lyons is the only other extant source

44. MGH *Legum sect.* II, *Cap. reg. Franc.* II, no. 197, 51–55. See Karl Morrison, *The Two Kingdoms,* pp. 3–67, 178–246; Wallace-Hadrill, "The *Via Regia* of the Carolingian Age"; Ullmann, *The Growth of Papal Government,* pp. 119–228; Arquillière, *L'Augustinisme politique,* pp. 94–131.

of information for the hearing.[45] Although these texts are descriptions of an essentially ecclesiastical process, they illuminate the terms in which ninth-century men envisaged the degradation of a legitimate ruler. The *Relatio* begins with a statement that the bishops have assembled to treat of things which have led to scandal in the church, the ruin of the people, and the destruction of the kingdom. These disasters had been the result of Louis's negligence. The emperor had failed to discharge the terms under which he held his *ministerium*. He was declared to be subject to a public penance before the assembly, which would forever deprive him of the right to bear arms, and to a private penance afterward. Such is the character of the episcopal actions in 833.

The specific faults with which Louis was charged had occurred over the preceding fifteen years and, in one case, included a charge for which the emperor had already performed penance, that of having caused the death in 819 of his nephew Bernard, King of Italy. Other charges include the violation of the terms of the *Ordinatio imperii* of 817 by attempting to create a patrimonium for his fourth son, Charles. Louis had violated liturgical feasts by holding a general court, "against the Christian religion and against his vow without any public utility or evident necessity, deluded by the wicked counsel of evil men."[46] He had tried and convicted in their absence innocent laymen and clerics. He had failed to protect his own *fideles* in the courts and had permitted the delivery of unjust judgments and even tolerated perjury. He had made several military expeditions "in the kingdom committed to his care, not only uselessly, but without any counsel or purpose." He had acted

45. MGH *Legum sect.* II, *Cap. reg. Franc.* II, no. 198, 56–57. For Agobard, see A. Bressolles, *Saint Agobard: Evêque de Lyon (760–840)* (Paris, 1949); J. A. Cabaniss, *Agobard of Lyons: Churchman and Critic* (Syracuse, New York, 1953).

46. *Relatio*, p. 53. For the Process itself, see L. Halphen, "La Pénitence de Louis le Pieux à St.-Médard de Soissons," *Bibl. de la Faculté des Lettres de Paris*, fasc. 18 (Paris, 1904), pp. 177–85; idem, *Charlemagne et l'empire carolingienne* (Paris, 1947), pp. 225–303; Arquillière, *L'Augustinisme politique*, pp. 122–40; B. Simson, *Jahrbucher des fränkischen Reiches unter Ludwig dem Frommen* (Leipzig, 1876), 2:31–78; Morrison, *The Two Kingdoms*, pp. 224–25.

against his own sons as against his enemies. Finally, he caused all these evils to come about not only through his negligence and improvidence but through having used his power rather for the common destruction than for the common welfare, he, who ought to have been the *dux salutis et pacis eidem populo.* The *Relatio* concludes with the observation that the church, which had been scandalized by the sins, had now been satisfied by the public penance.

Although the charges of the Synod of 833 were to be completely refuted two years later, the very fact of their having been put forth invites their comparison with the events of 751. In neither case is there evidence of a judicial process of deposition. The cutting of Childeric's hair and his being placed in a monastery did not constitute a deposition any more than did Louis's public penance. The significance of both actions lies in another area than that of the specific deprivation of certain kinds of political power. Childeric and Louis were first made unsuitable for rule as individual men. The ritual cutting of Childeric's hair and the formal public penance of Louis gave each a different personal *status* from that required of a king. Louis's penance rendered him unable ever to bear arms or to return to his former *status* in life.[47] Although the evidence is not sufficient to suggest that Childeric, too, was made a penitent, it is clear that the action taken against him was designed to have the same effect as that taken against Louis. Both became unsuitable for rule, not through what would later become a deposition process, but through changes in their personal *status* which disqualified them in ecclesiastical rather than in political terms from keeping

47. For the ecclesiastical character of the deposition, see Kern, *Gottesgnadentum,* pp. 338–45, and the works of Halphen, Morrison, and Arquillière cited in the preceding note. On the similar deposition of the Visigothic King Wamba in 685, see A. K. Ziegler, *Church and State in Visigothic Spain* (Washington, 1930), pp. 113–17; F. X. Murphy, "Julian of Toledo and the Fall of the Visigothic Kingdom in Spain," *Speculum* 27 (1952): 1–27. For a later ecclesiological parallel, see the *Liber extra* of Gregory IX *(Corpus iuris canonici,* ed. Aem. Friedberg [rep. Graz, 1959], vol. 2, col. 112), 1.19.1, a letter from Innocent III to the Bishop of Faventino.

power. Both episodes reveal strong ecclesiastical influences. Both begin with the ruler's ineptitude or negligence and proceed to make that fact a public disqualification through an ecclesiastical ritual. In 751, however, Childeric's lack of *potestas* had violated men's idea of the order of the world. In 833 Louis's negligence is seen more sharply in terms of a moral failure on his part to execute the functions of the *rex iustus*.[48]

The deposition of Louis, moreover, indicates the increased political strength of the Frankish church. In 751 Zacharias alone had sanctioned the change of dynasty. In 833 the role of Gregory IV was distinctly subordinate to that of the Frankish bishops. The episcopal order, not the pope, arranged the deposition of Louis. In their description of the proceedings the bishops proclaimed that the king was answerable to the church for the *necessitas regni*, the *salus ac populis totius utilitas*, the *regni honor atque stabilitas*, and the *utilitas publica*. The use of these terms, some of them from Roman law, marks the beginning of a kind of political discussion which would run through the whole of the Middle Ages. The Carolingian concepts of *felicitas regni* and *ordo* became sharpened and acquired a practical, as well as an ecclesiastical, connotation by means of the revival of such legal concepts as *respublica* and *publica utilitas*. Although the ninth-century meaning of *respublica* often made the term seem synonymous with *ecclesia*, it was to have an important future in political discussions as a means of describing the *populus christianus*, the *societas christiana*, or, as the ninth-century popes would begin to call it, *Christianitas*, in its social and legal aspects. The king did not possess, but administered, a *regnum in sibi commisso*. If he flagrantly violated his *ministerium* by opposing his own *voluntas* to *the voluntas Dei*, he became a *rex iniquus*. If, on the other hand, he failed to act righteously out of ineptitude or carelessness, he became a *rex negligens*, lacking *dili-*

48. See M. David, *La Souveraineté et les limites juridiques du pouvoir monarchique du IXe au XVe siècle*, Annales de la Faculté de Droit et des Sciences Politiques de Strasbourg, 1 (Paris, 1954), pp. 112–19. The study of H. Büttner (cited above, p. 48, n. 31) places great emphasis upon Pippin's revolution seen against contemporary ecclesiastical concepts of *ordo*.

gentia. Childeric had been *inutilis* because he had lacked the *potestas* required of a Christian king (a quality which Theodulf was to associate specifically with David, the prototype of the Carolingian ideal ruler).[49] Louis had been a *rex negligens* because, although he possessed the *potestas* which Childeric had allowed to slip away from him, he failed to use it properly and on occasion allowed wicked men to use it improperly. He resembles Childeric chiefly in that both cases could not be made to follow the only clear-cut action which political writers knew against a ruler, that of considering him a tyrant. In consequence, the two depositions of 751 and 833 provided occasions for other ideas of kingship to emerge. The result shows a much less coherent view of kingship as a political institution than that sometimes attributed to the early Carolingians.

For the Frankish bishops in 833, as for Gregory VII in 1081, the standards of Christian kingship were suprahistorical because they were based upon a moral view of an ecclesiastical polity. The sanction for this view stood outside human time, and its fulfillment did not depend upon temporal circumstances. The bishops, in their own view more directly aware of the extratemporal ends of kingship, considered themselves the only ones capable of admonishing—or replacing—the king, as they said, "propter auctoritatem ministerii nostri." If the king failed in his high duty, the episcopal order was prepared to direct the fortunes of the *regnum Francorum*—or, for that matter, the *imperium Romanum*—and to use the principle of suitability, *idoneitas,* to select a new ruler. The *potestas-nomen* of 751 had become a *dignitas, ministerium,* and *honor*

49. In MGH *Poetae,* vol. 1, ed. E. Dümmler, p. 577, 13. Discussed by E. R. Curtius, *European Literature in the Latin Middle Ages,* trans, W. Trask (New York, 1953), p. 180. For David in Carolingian political thought, see P. E. Schramm, "Das Alte und das Neue Testament in der Staatslehre und Staatssymbolik des Mittelalters," in *La Bibbia nell' alto medioevo,* Centro italiano di studi sull' alto medioevo, settimane de studio X (Spoleto, 1963), pp. 229–56; H. Steger, *David Rex et Propheta. König David als vorbildliche Verkorperung des Herrschers und Dichters im Mittelalter, nach Bilddarstellungen des 8.–12. Jahrhunderts,* Erlangen Beiträge zur Sprach- und Kunstwissenschaft 6 (Nürnberg, 1961): 121–32.

which guaranteed the *felicitas regni.* Its possessor was a *defensor,* an *advocatus,* and an *adiutor* of the *ecclesia.*

The terms describing the ordering of society in the *Relatio* of 833 appeared elsewhere in ninth-century literature. Perhaps the most important of these occasions was the Council of Paris in 829, which produced a *Relatio* similar to that of 833. The Council noted the division of "the whole body of the Holy Church of God" into two powers: the *persona sacerdotali* and the *persona regali.* They based this division upon the famous letter of Pope Gelasius to the Emperor Anastasius, in which the pope had said, "There are two powers, August Emperor, by which the world is ruled, the sacred authority of the pontiffs and the regal power."[50] The bishops' *totius sanctae Dei ecclesiae corpus* became the ninth-century equivalent for Gelasius's *mundus.*[51] The duties of the king within the ecclesiastical framework of 829 consisted chiefly of caring for the church, his appointment of prelates and suitable royal advisors, the education of his own children, and his role in relieving the clergy of the burden of wordly cares, *negotia saecularia.* He fulfilled, in short, a *ministerium* which paralleled, but did not supplant, that of the priesthood.

The numerous Carolingian tracts on royal conduct, the mirrors for princes or *Fürstenspiegeln,* echoed these views. Jonas of Orleans's treatise *De institutione regia* culled much of its advice from the *Relatio* of 829, of which Jonas had probably been one of the authors.[52] Jonas's most recent editor, Reviron, sums up the author's view of kingship neatly:

50. *Episcoporum ad Hludowicum imperatorem relatio,* MGH *Legum sect.* II, *Cap. reg. Franc.* II, no. 196, 26–51. See also Ullmann, *The Growth of Papal Government,* pp. 125–34.

51. This point has been made by a number of commentators on Gelasius's text. See, e.g., Ladner, "Aspects of Medieval Thought," pp. 404–09. For later use of Gelasius's formula, see A. K. Ziegler, "Pope Gelasius I and His Teaching on the Relation of Church and State," *CHR* 27 (1941/42): 412–37; L. Knabe, *Die gelasianische Zweigewaltentheorie bis zum Ende des Investiturstreits* (Berlin, 1936); W. Ensslin, "Auctoritas und Potestas. Zur Zweigewaltenlehre des Papstes Gelasius I," *HJ* vol. 2 (1954), 661–68.

52. Jonas's treatise has been edited by J. Reviron, *Les Idées politico-religieuses d'un évêque du IXe siècle: Jonas d'Orléans et son "De institu-*

> The royal power appears to have a conditional character: if the king does not fulfill properly the function corresponding to his title, if he does not properly exercise his ministry, if he does not govern by law, the sovereign loses the name of king and merits no other name than that of tyrant. . . . The power [of the prince] does not appear as a possession, but as a charge, an office, a ministry.[53]

Jonas's chief sources (and the sources for the two *Relationes)* were the later fathers: Isidore of Seville, Gregory I, Fulgentius of Ruspe, and Pope Gelasius. He also made use of the eighth-century political tract of Pseudo-Cyprian.[54] To the eight-century idea of kingship uniting *nomen* and *potestas* was now added a moral dimension,

---

tione regia," étude et texte critique (Paris, 1930). For other studies, see Carlyle, 1:199–274; E. Delaruelle, "En Relisant le De institutione regia de Jonas d'Orléans: L'Entrée en scéne de l'épiscopat carolingien," in *Mélanges Louis Halphen*, pp. 185–92; Arquillière, *L'Augustinisme politique*, pp. 98–104; on the temper of the Carolingian episcopacy, see Morrison, *The Two Kingdoms*, and the recent excellent survey of Jacques Boussard, *The Civilization of Charlemagne* (New York, 1968), pp. 92–117. On the genre *speculum principum* in the ninth century, see A. Werminghoff, "Die Fürstenspiegel der Carolingerzeit," *HZ* 53 (1902): 193–214; L. K. Born, "The *Specula Principis* of the Carolingian Renaissance," *Revue Belge de Philologie et D'histoire* 12 (1933): 583–612; L. Wallach, *Alcuin and Charlemagne* (Ithaca, 1959), pp. 5–96, 227–54; for Irish examples, see T. O'Donoghue, "Advice to a Prince," *Eriu* 9 (1921/23): 43–54; R. M. Smith, "The *Speculum principum* in Early Irish Literature," *Speculum* 2 (1927): 411–45.

53. Reviron, *Jonas d'Orléans*, p. 81.

54. For Gregory I, see H. Hürten, "Gregor der Grosse und der mittelalterlichen Episkopat," *Zeitschrift fur Kirchengeschichte* 73 (1963): 16–41; Jean Gaudemet, "Patristique et pastorale: La Contribution de Grégoire le Grand au 'Miroir de l'évêque' dans le *Décret* de Gratien," *Études . . . LeBras*, 1:129–39. The influential *De Veritate praedestinationis* of Fulgentius of Ruspe is in *PL* 65. 647D–648A. For the text of Pseudo Cyprian, see S. Hellmann, *Pseudo-Cyprianis de XII abusivis seculi*, Texte und Untersuchungen zur Geschichte der altchristlichen Literatur, Reihe 3, Band 4 (Leipzig, 1909), pp. 1–62. Generally useful is M. L. W. Laistner, *Thought and Letters in Western Europe*, 500–900 (2d ed., London, 1957), pp. 315–21.

according to which not only political weakness, but moral shortcomings, could cause a ruler to be useless and hence *indignus.* The moral cast of ninth-century political literature caused such terms as *indignus, negligens,* and *iniquus* to supplant *inutilis,* and to place the removal of Louis the Pious in an ecclesiastical framework. The year 833 witnessed neither the first nor the last such such use of an ideal invoked to aid the demands of practical expediency.

The *Relationes* of 829 and 833, the moral-educational tracts to princes of Jonas, Sedulius Scottus, Smaragdus, Hincmar, and others, the prologues to *capitularia,* the political vocabulary of annalists and chroniclers, and the literary vocabulary of panegyrists and biographers developed these ideas of Christian kingship throughout the ninth, tenth, and eleventh centuries. In spite of the emphasis upon the moral duties of a Christian king, however, the political problems of 751 had not been entirely solved nor had other aspects of royal inadequacy. The chief of these, physical or mental incapacity, also made its appearance in the political affairs of the ninth and tenth centuries.

During the last years of Charlemagne's reign the order which he and his father had temporarily imposed upon the Frankish kingdom gradually began to crumble.[55] Many of the difficulties which beset Louis the Pious during the later years of his reign resulted from this disintegration, many occurring as late as they did only because Louis had for so long energetically kept them in check. The loss of real power at the center of the kingdom, the formation of separate *regni* within the territory of a single ruler, the increased influence of prelates and magnates, and the purely administrative difficulties of the kings remind us of the other side of Carolingian kingship—its continuity in many respects with that of the

55. The series of studies by F. L. Ganshof may be consulted: "La Fin du règne de Charlemagne: Une Décomposition," *Zeitschrift für schweizerische Geschichte* 28 (1948); "Observations sur *l'Ordinatio imperii* de 817," *Festschrift Guido Kisch* (Stuttgart, 1954); "Louis the Pious Reconsidered," *History* 42 (1957); see also T. Schieffer, "Die Krise des karolingischen Imperiums," in *Aus Mittelalter und Neuzeit. Festschrift . . . Gerhard Kallen* (Bonn, 1957).

Merovingians. Other elements of this continuity would also serve to sharpen the distinctions between theoretical and practical kingship in the ninth and tenth centuries. One of these was the respect which magnates retained for dynastic legitimacy.[56] In the ninth and tenth centuries *idoneitas* may have meant moral righteousness to the clergy, but it also meant Carolingian blood to the magnates. Another was the royal practice of patronizing ecclesiastical establishments. The purely ecclesiastical form of the proceedings against Louis the Pious was probably a result, ironically, of the reforms which the Carolingians had made in the structure of the Frankish church. Like Childeric, Louis was also forced into a monastery, "ut quid terram occupat?" The monasteries, "ces prisons politiques du siècle," remained a symbol of the ultimate authority by which Christian kings ruled, within whose walls those who had been found *indignus* might await at least the salavation of their souls, if not the restoration of their forfeited names.

The form of government which Pepin, Charlemagne, and Louis had shaped and worked to maintain gave way to forces similar to those which had caused the Franks to rid themselves of the Merovingian dynasty. The existence of magnates—some, indeed, within the family itself—who were sufficiently powerful not only to maintain their independence of the ruler but to influence him as well all but wrecked the high vision of Christian kingship formulated in the seventh and eighth centuries and virtually institutionalized by the Carolingians. One of the chief reasons for the survival of kingship as an institutional office during the later ninth and tenth centuries was in part the flexibility which the literature surrounding the depositions of Childeric and Louis had imparted to it. The crowning and anointing of Pepin and the deposition of Louis had added the dimensions of real political power and intelligent political action to more purely ecclesiastical theories of kingship. The demands of the late ninth and early tenth centuries called these dimensions into consideration time and time again. During this

56. See J. M. Wallace-Hadrill, "The Franks and the English in the Ninth Century," *History,* n.s. 35 (1950): 202–18; F. Lot, *Les Derniers Carolingiens* (Paris, 1891), pp. 378–94.

period Tacitus's old distinction regarding leadership among the Germanic peoples, "reges ex nobilitate, duces ex virtute sumunt,"[57] came to be reversed. Because of the material pressures upon kingship, such royal officials as Boso of Vienne became kings, "not *ex nobilitate,* but entirely *ex virtute.*"[58] *Virtus,* as a criterion for royal suitability, tended to supplant *nomen, potestas,* and *dignitas.* It, too, had several meanings. To Hincmar *virtus* was "not so much exterior courage which, to be sure, is necessary for secular rule, as for the courage of spirit, good morals, since often the negligence of the spirit leads to the loss of the courage of rulership."[59] In view of the dangers that faced the kingdoms, however, *virtus* also meant physical courage, bravery, efficiency, and power.

Virtus, magnanimitas, and *audacitas* became the honorific designations of kingship during the late ninth and tenth centuries.[60] The *dignitas regia* required a forceful maintenance which the later Carolingian rulers were not always able to provide. Thus the theories of royal idoneity that had been put forth by the church had to be tempered by the practical considerations that had already been evident in 751. The *rex iustus* came to be, of necessity, a powerful ruler as well. Such leaders as Boso, who were not originally kings at all, became kings because of their ability to rule in practice. Boso's career gave a sharpness to the ideas of *regimen, negocium regale, principatus, praesidium, adminiculum,* and *tuitio,* which

57. Tacitus, *Germania,* c. 7. See the relevant remarks of Walter Schlesinger in "Herrschaft und Gefolgschaft," and Karl Bosl in *"Reges ex nobilitate, Duces ex virtute sumunt."*

58. L. Boehm, "Rechtsformen und Rechtstitel der burgundischen Königserhebungen im 9. Jahrhundert. Zur Krise der karolingischen Dynastie," *HJ* 80 (1961): 39. See also H. Beumann, "Die Historiographie des Mittelalters," esp. pp. 472f, and his *Widukind von Korvei,* pp. 205–65.

59. Hincmar of Rheims, *Ad proceres regni, pro institutione Carlomanni regis et de ordine palatii,* PL 125. 993–1008, chap. 10, col. 997.

60. See, e.g., H. Löwe, "Regino von Prüm und das historische Weltbild der Karolingerzeit," in *Geschichtsdenken und Geschichtsbild im Mittelalter,* Wege der Forschung, vol. 21 (Darmstadt, 1961), pp. 91–134. Cf. *"Epitaphium Bosonis regis,"* MGH *Poetae,* IV, 1027–28: "Regis in hoc tumulo requiescunt membra Bosonis / Hic pius et largus fuit, audax, ore facundus."

came to be considered the practical counterparts of—and therefore parts of—the more morally oriented ecclesiastical theories of *idoneitas*.

Kingdoms had been created out of the *regnum Francorum* before the reign of Louis the Pious. However, no Carolingian ruler before Louis had been faced with a series of revolts as great as that which began with the rebellion of Bernard of Italy in 818 and did not end till Louis's own death in 840. This political disintegration resulted in a decline of the influence of both bishops and emperor. Not until 1076 would an emperor stand as high as Charlemagne had in 800; not until Gregory VII would the ecclesiastical powers be able to humble an emperor as the bishops had in 833.

The *reguli* of Aquitaine, Provence, Italy, Western Francia, and Lorraine brought down the Carolingian ideal of kingship into the particularized political arenas of half-formed kingdoms. The disparity between the material powers of these rulers and the high claims they made for themselves reflects at once the contention that Carolingian kingship depended more in the long run upon the strength of individual rulers and the importance of the institution of kingship in political life. The vigorous kings of the period—Boso, Charles the Bald, Arnulf—brought a high degree of *virtus* to their reigns, often without the elaborate ecclesiastical justifications that had aided their immediate predecessors. Except for Charles, their connection to the Carolingian dynasty was usually weak; their personal prowess overrode any question of their dynastic illegitimacy. Finally, Boso and Arnulf completed in the sphere of practical politics the process begun by Pepin of demanding from a king the same qualities that the king demanded of his ministers.

The question of practical efficiency is well illustrated by the deposition of Pepin of Aquitaine in 848. In 838 Pepin's father, also Pepin, died, leaving his kingdom to his son. Louis the Pious, however, chose to disinherit his grandson and to give Aquitaine to his fourth son, Charles. Charles's difficulties with his own nobles, with the Northmen, and with his brothers prevented him from acting against Pepin. However, Pepin's magnates in Aquitaine deposed him themselves. The circumstances of the deposition are by no means clear. The sources, in fact, begin to reflect another important aspect of the period, a marked lack of documentation of the kind available for the deposition of Louis the Pious or even a historiographical tradition of the kind available for the removal of Childeric III. For Pepin there only exist scattered notices in annals, none of which remotely resembles the *Relatio* of 833 or the first chapter of Einhard.

Pepin, it seems, had refused to organize his kingdom against the raids of the Northmen and had allowed it, in fact, to fall into such disrepair that the "Aquitanians, on account of Pepin's idleness and inactivity, sent to Charles and in the city of Orleans nearly all the more noble men with the bishops and abbots elected him king and consecrated him solemnly by anointing with the sacred chrism and by episcopal benediction."[61] Although the clergy appears to play a prominent role in the coronation and anointing of Charles, the magnates appear to have been the constitutive force in ridding the Aquitanians of their former king. Pepin's *desidia* and *inertia*, it may be noted, are not identical with the moral laxity of Louis the Pious, although they do belong to the vocabulary of vices and virtues and hence possess at least some moral-ecclesiastical connotations.[62] A physically inactive ruler proved to be *indignus* to the Aquitanians because they saw a threat to their very survival. Although they were to discover later, to their dismay, that they were not so easily rid of Pepin II, the magnates' action against him in 848 remains a striking example of the contemporary practical view of Carolingian kingship stripped of all ecclesiastical associations save those of terminology.

61. *Annales Bertiniani,* MGH *SS* I, 443, *ad. an.* 843. Cf. *Rodolfi Fuldensis annales,* ibid., p. 367, *ad. an.* 851.

62. For Pippin, see Morrison, *The Two Kingdoms,* p. 220, n. 15; G. Eiten, *Das Unterkönigtum im Reiche der Merowinger und Karolinger,* Heidelberger Abh. zur mittleren und neueren Geschichte, Heft. 18 (Heidelberg, 1907), pp. 155–58, 165–66, 170–71; L. Auzias, "L'Origine carolingienne des ducs féodaux d'Aquitaine et des rois capétiens," *RH* 173 (1934); idem, *L'Aquitaine carolingienne, 778–987,* Bibl. méridionale, 2e série (Toulouse-Paris, 1937), 28:124–270.

The death of Lothaire I in 855 provides another example. At his death, his kingdom was divided according to the Merovingian and Carolingian custom, and Provence fell the lot of "an epileptic cipher," Charles, who died in 863. Chroniclers of the reign note that he had been "useless and unsuitable for the royal name and honor."[63] Charles's physical incapacity became, in the annalist's terms, *inutilitas* and *inconvenientia.* Thus the attributes of the *rex inutilis* came to include physical, as well as mental and political, ability. Charles's cousin, Carloman of Italy, also physically incapacitated, appears to have been prevented only by episcopal laxity and his own death from having been deposed by Pope John VIII.[64]

The most significant deposition between 833 and 1076, however, was that of the Emperor Charles III in 887. Charles, like Charles of Provence and Carloman of Italy, had been forced by illness to neglect his governance. Arnulf of Carinthia, capitalizing on Charles's illness and the treachery of the emperor's advisors, deposed Charles and made himself emperor.[65] By the late ninth century the theological ideal of the *rex iustus* had been linked to other, more explicit, ideas of kingship. Incapacity, inefficient generalship, and a lack of political ability all colored the distinction between royal *nomen* and royal *potestas.* The moral concept of *virtus* had in its turn expanded in a similar manner. If the vocabulary of ecclesiastical political theory changed only slightly, the connotations of in-

63. *Annales Bertiniani, ad. an.* 861.

64. MGH *Epp.* VII, *Epp. Kar. Aev.* V, no. 163, pp. 133–34; *Annales Fuldenses, ad. an.* 879; *Annales Bertiniani, ad. an.* 879. For the case of Rudolph of Burgundy, see R. Poupardin, *Le Royaume de Bourgogne (888–1038). Etude sur les origines du royaume d'Arles,* BEHE, fasc. 163 (Paris, 1907), p. 114.

65. Texts and commentary in E. Dümmler, *Geschichte des Ostfrankischen Reiches,* vol. 3: *Die letzten Karolinger—Konrad I* (Leipzig, 1888), pp. 286–92; G. Tellenbach, *Königtum und Stämme in der Werdezeit des deutschen Reiches* (Weimar, 1939), pp. 31–40; P. Kehr, "Aus den letzten Tagen Karls III," *Deutsches Archiv* 1 (1938): 138–46: W. Schlesinger, "Kaiser Arnulf und die Entstehung des deutschen Reiches," *Wege der Forschung* (Darmstadt, 1963), 1:94–109; H. Keller, "Zum sturz Karls III," *DA* 22 (1966): 363–84.

dividual terms in that vocabulary acquired a breadth which they had not possessed in 751.

Although tracts for the instruction of princes tended to continue to describe kingship in language borrowed from Pseudo-Cyprian and Jonas of Orleans, there is some evidence that practical considerations forced their way into this genre as well. In the early works of Hincmar of Rheims, for example, conventional political rhetoric dominates the discussion of political theory. In Hincmar's later works, however, the practical side of the royal *ministerium* is emphasized more and more frequently. The *virtus* which justifies the *potestas dominandi* is the *virtus* of men like Boso, Louis II of Italy, and Louis III of France. It partakes of the *scientia gubernandi*, a concept which appears first in the mid-ninth century as one of the qualities of the *rex idoneus*.[66]

The political literature of the ninth century contained a sophisticated vocabulary for discussions of kingship. This vocabulary never, however, functioned to express a purely moral standard of royal qualifications. The practical demands made upon Carolingian rulers gave to such terms as *virtus, potestas,* and *dignitas* a concrete practical dimension they were never to lose. Further, the character of the sources that seem to make no clear distinction between the moral and the practical planes of royal attributes militates against a too facile acceptance of popular surnames and apochryphal character analyses in determining the contemporary judgments upon inept or incapacitated rulers.[67] In a sense Gregory VII was wiser than perhaps he knew in restricting himself to a reasonably clear version of the deposition of Childeric III, particularly in the light of the documentation of later deposition proceedings. Moreover, Gregory was not the only eleventh-century writer who neglected the ninth and tenth centuries. Instead of looking to the chronicles and annals of this period or to the letters of popes from Zacharias

66. It is used, for instance, by Nithard in describing the failure of Lothar I: *Historiarum Libri IV,* MGH *SS* II, 668, *ad. an.* 842.

67. See S. Honoré-Duvergé, "L'Origine du surnom de Charles le Mauvais," in *Mélanges Louis Halphen,* pp. 345–50; A. Eckel, *Charles le Simple,* in BEHE, fasc, 124 (Paris, 1899), p. 141.

to Sylvester II, eleventh-century writers looked to the fathers, just as twelfth- and thirteenth-century canonists would look to Gratian.

Lot has said of the tenth-century territorial monarchies that in them "the authority of the king depended essentially upon his personal qualities, upon his personal ascendancy, and, above all, upon the circumstances of his reign."[68] In such cases as those of Charles the Simple, Lothaire, and Louis V of France the chroniclers' attitude toward kingship and the failings of individual kings reinforces the accuracy of Lot's observation. Even the high Carolingian ideal could not of itself attribute to kingship a *dignitas* of sufficient political significance so as to remain above the exigencies of practical politics, on the one hand, and above the conglomeration of private jurisdictions, on the other. The moral *negligentia* of Louis the Pious had come to be less important politically than the material *negligentia* of some of his successors. Among the tenth-century rulers the ideal was perhaps best fulfilled by Eudes, who, as Regino notes, possessed the beauty, size, strength, and wisdom needed to rule the *respublica*.[69] The French had, by the tenth century, experienced enough inept or weak rule to be well aware of its attendant dangers. They added a political set of connotations to the ecclesiastical terminology of the eighth and ninth centuries. The ecclesiastical revolution under the early Carolingians had created a theoretical structure of kingship, and the history of this structure during the three subsequent centuries began to turn what originally had been public morality into something which resembled public law.

In the ninth and tenth centuries the imperial pattern of Carolingian kingship had been temporarily reconstructed by local powers and directed at local needs. When the political power of

68. *Les Derniers Carolingiens*, p. 170.

69. Regino of Prüm, *Chronicon* ed. F. Kurze, MGH *SS in us. schol.* (Hannover, 1890), pp. 129–30; cf. Richer, *Historiarum Libri IV, MGHS SS* III, p. 570. For the early Capetians generally, see C. Pfister, *Etudes sur le règne de Robert le Pieux* (Paris, 1885), pp. 141–208; W. M. Newman, *The Kings, the Court, and the Royal Power in France in the Eleventh Century* (Toulouse, 1929), pp. 10–18, 25–31, 76–101. For the last Carolingians, see the studies of Lot, Eckel, Eiten, and Auzias, cited above.

kingship expanded in the late tenth and eleventh centuries, the practical criteria that had become attached to the Carolingian ideal remained effective. The procedures used against unsuitable rulers during the ninth and tenth centuries, however, never entirely became principles of public law. Power politics may have added to the existing vocabulary of political thought, but it created few categories of its own. Gregory VII's view of papal authority over temporal rulers was to be met with by imperial theories which countered it at every turn, but nowhere more effectively than at the question of the *rex inutilis*. There, the imperial publicists turned not to Carolingian political theory but to political practice, and they found not papal hegemony over temporal rulers but the power of local magnates concerned with immediate public welfare.

In the ninth and tenth centuries, then, physical or mental incapacity, administrative ineptitude, moral negligence, or political error might singly or in combination make a ruler *inutilis*. Any of these was sufficient cause for powers within his kingdom to take action against him. Since, however, the terminology of chroniclers tended to remain uniform over this period, it is sometimes difficult to determine precisely the criteria applied in a given case. Nevertheless, the practical demands made upon the later Carolingians tended to strngthen the bond between the ideal and actual qualities of the ruler by borrowing the already established political vocabulary of the eighth and early ninth centuries.

Gregory VII, whose political views were akin to those of the early ninth-century popes and bishops, restored the question of royal suitability to the ecclesiastical sphere. In his attitude toward Henry IV and Childeric he selected from among a number of approaches to the problem of the *rex inutilis* which had been developed, but not systematized, between the seventh and eleventh centuries. Gregory's political views, however, were subordinate to his wider vision of the Christian life. Tellenbach and others have called this a vision of the right order of the world.[70] Gregory did not always

70. The best discussion is that of Tellenbach, *Church, State, and Christian Society*.

draw clear distinctions between his role as a leader of Christians within the *corpus mysticum* of the church and his role as a public power within the empire. His view of kings and emperors simultaneously as public figures and individual humans subject to excommunication and other ecclesiastical punishments reflects the ambiguity of his conception of his own role.

In Gregory's view it was sufficient for a ruler to fail as a Christian in order to render his rule illegitimate. There is some evidence, in fact, that Gregory thought that this was what Henry IV had done. Moreover, the sources for the deposition of Childeric III suggest that king's having made his own rule illegitimate. Some scholars view Zacharias's reply a *responsum,* not a constitutive declaration of deposition.[71] Henry's own public penance at Canossa implies that he, too, may have made himself unfit for rule by performing the same kind of penance as had Louis the Pious. Gregory returned the emphasis of royal suitability to the individual moral character of the ruler and viewed royal inadequacy and royal wickedness as the consequences of spiritual corruption. The eleventh- and twelfth-century changes in moral theology were to give Gregory's view a theological as well as a legal continuity with twelfth-century political thought.

The question of the *rex inutilis,* however, was not central in the dispute between Henry IV and Gregory. Nevertheless, several writers on both sides took occasion to comment on the pope's remarks in regard to Childeric. Most opinions other than those of Gregory himself did not have an effect that lasted beyond their own time. But together they constitute the first widespread consideration of the question in the Middle Ages, and they form part of the background to the work of the decretists in the twelfth century.

The most prominent and articulate opponent of Gregory's views on the deposition of Childeric was the unknown author of the *Liber de unitate ecclesiae conservanda.*[72] Much of the first part of this

71. Caspar, "Das Papsttum unter fränkischen Herrschaft," pp. 137f.

72. Ed. W. Schwenkenbecher, MGH *Ldl* II, 173–284, and separately in MGH *SS in us. schol.,* the edition used here. The work has been convincingly attributed to Walram of Naumberg. See B. Gaffrey, *Der Liber de*

treatise deals with Gregory's claim that popes might depose rulers in general and with the citation of the Childeric episode in particular. The author propounds a dualist *civitas Dei* composed of the *ecclesia Dei* and the *res publica imperii,* at whose head is Christ, *rex et sacerdos.* By attempting to rule both *ecclesia* and *res publica,* Gregory VII, in the author's view, had violated both the Catholic and the public faiths.[73] In his work the author examines several of Gregory's citations concerning past depositions of rulers by popes. The episode of Childeric is discussed at several different points in the tract, and the author brings to bear a remarkable knowledge of Merovingian history on the question of Gregory's accuracy. His chief references are as follows:

> Therefore Childeric reigned not in fact but in name, since the whole disposition of the kingdom and all of its power were with the mayors of the household, as the divine dispensation had long before ordained. For Chlodoveus, son of the great king Dagobert, opening the tomb of Saint Dionysius the martyr, broke the arm [of the body] and was immediately stricken with insanity. Not long afterwards he ended his life and his reign. Such presumption to so sin against a saint of God was expiated upon his posterity, since, as we read in the Deeds of the Franks, from that time diverse disasters befell the kingdom of the Franks. Afterwards, two of his sons, Clotarius and Childericus, perished in their youth . . . Theodoricus, the third brother, was afflicted by many adversities, both before and after he became king.
>
> . . . [Pepin], when he was head of the household in the

unitate ecclesiae conservanda im Lichte mittelalterliche Zeitanschauungen (Berlin, 1921;) Carlyle, 4:243–49; 3:109–11; Z. Zafarana, "Richerche sul *Liber de unitate ecclesiae conservanda,*" *Studi Medievali,* ser. 3, no. 7 (1966), pp. 617–700; Arquillière, *L'Augustinisme politique,* pp. 357f.; Mirbt, *Die Publizistik im Zeitalter Gregors VII,* pp. 52f.; Ullmann, *The Growth of Papal Government,* pp. 404–07; Voosen, *Papauté et pouvoir civil,* p. 193.

73. *Liber de unitate,* p. 45. The expression *publica fides* used here coordinately with *catholica fides* is a striking example of the strict dualism propounded by the author.

Frankish kingdom, that is, prefect of the palace, and all the royal power and dignity belonged to him, was the first of the prefects of the palace to be chosen king. He was consecrated with the blessing of the holy Boniface, Archbishop of Mainz, the judgement of Pope Zacharias having been obtained beforehand, since the consent and authority of the Roman pontiff seemed necessary for this matter. Burchard of Wurzburg, a bishop of holy life, with other messengers suitable for this mission, was sent to him by command of the princes to consult the oracle of his opinion and receive his response concerning the question, how might they reform the realm of the Franks and restore it to the state of its former dignity. For a long time it had lacked the prerogative of royal honor, since the one who was called king possessed nothing but the shadow of an empty name. Neither the wealth nor the power of the kingdom nor any ordering of its affairs rested with him but rather with the head of the household who controlled the palace. Therefore it seemed to them just and fitting that hereditary succession to the whole royal dignity and power be taken away from (Childeric) and that the royal title be transferred to Pepin, at that time prefect of the palace, who was worthy of it by virtue of his nobility and courage. Seeing that he vigorously carried on the government of the household and of the armies of the realm, it would be appropriate for him to receive the title of king along with the labors and duties of the office. When Pope Zacharias had considered this proposal and deemed it just and expedient, he gave his consent to it, and afterwards Pope Stephen confirmed this judgement. Pepin was made king by common consent of the princes, and Childeric the tonsured crown and habit of the monastic life in place of the empty name of king.

. . . [Childeric], who possessed nothing of either the regal power or the regal dignity, but only the name of king . . . [should] be placed in a monastery, because he appeared to be more worthy of being crowned with the monastic tonsure than with the regal diadem.

> Childeric is described as having nothing of the regal power or dignity . . . he was not a lord of others, nor a rector, because the name king derives from ruling rightly.

> Now as [Zacharias confirmed the decision of the Frankish princes] . . . it seems that the above-mentioned Pope Gregory, also called Hildebrand, unjustly imputed to Zacharias and Stephen, holy pontiffs of the Roman church, the acts of deposing Childeric from the kingship solely by their own authority and of absolving the Franks of the oaths of fidelity which they had sworn to him, when perchance the princes of the realm would have considered it unworthy to swear an oath [in the first place] to a man of the sort described above.[74]

These passages reveal several characteristics of the author of the *Liber.* His reading appears to have been extensive, since much of his material is found only in Merovingian and early Carolingian chronicles. He is familiar with political terminology, since he cites the usual relevant scriptural and patristic passages. He attempts to describe not only the immediate circumstances of the deposition but a chain of events deriving from one cause, the sacrilege committed by Chlodoveus. He thus shares the view of some Carolingian writers, including Paul the Deacon, one of his sources, concerning the progressive degeneracy of the later Merovingians, which resulted in their loss of *fortuna.*[75] He portrays Pepin and the mag-

74. Paragraphs 2 and 5 are from Brian Tierney, *The Crisis of Church and State, 1050–1300* (Englewood Cliffs, N.J.), pp. 80–82. The other translations are by the author. In Schwenkenbecher's edition (MGH *SS* in *us. schol.)* the paragraphs correspond to the following pages: par. 1, p. 36; par. 2, pp. 2–3; par. 3, p. 6; par. 4 p. 37; par. 5, p. 3.

75. The legend of Merovingian degeneracy is closely tied to that of Chlodoveus (Clovis II, 638–657) as found in the *Gesta Dagoberti Regis Francorum,* in M. Bouquet, *Recueil des historiens des Gaules et de la France* (Paris, 1739), 2:596. Also in MGH *SS rer, Mer.* II, 425. A more grisly version is that of the *Liber historiae Francorum,* MGH *SS rer, Mer.* II, c. 44, p. 316. Fredegar's continuator mentions the affliction of Clovis only in passing. An example of the Carolingian use of the legend, perhaps for propaganda purposes, may be found in Paulus Diaconus, *Historia Langobardorum,* ed. G. Waitz, MGH *SS rer. Langob.* VI (1878), p. 218.

nates as the mainstays of a kingdom that did not deserve to share the misfortunes of its ruling dynasty. He repeats, more than any other contemporary, the version of the deposition that Gregory had most conspicuously neglected, that which attributed the deposition to the Frankish magnates, not to the pope, and he omits any mention of a decisive role even for the Frankish clergy.

He objects strenuously, moreover, to the slightest comparison between Childeric and Henry IV: "But in our own time, the king and emperor, born and raised in the kingship, appears to the judgement of men worthy as much by reason of his own virtue as by that of his forefathers."[76] Gregory, to be sure, had pressed no such analogy, but his rhetorical linking of Childeric with Henry IV may have suggested a resemblance between the cases of the two to Gregory's less discriminating readers.

The author of the *Liber* represents a view of kingship which is more elaborate than that of Gregory. His frequent use of such terms as *honor, dignitas, labor,* and *officium* is a far cry from the Carolingian distinction between *nomen* and *potestas* only. The increasing frequency, from the tenth century on, of such concepts as *dignitas, honor, maiestas,* and *splendor imperii* or *regni* reflects the new theories of kingship that were to flower in the twelfth and thirteenth centuries. These attributes, when joined to the articulation of concepts of public law which worked through the person of the king, would give considerable weight to the concepts of throne, crown, and *persona regis* in the later Middle Ages.[77]

The works of the pro-Gregorian publicists and collectors of canons generally are usually restricted to citing or paraphrasing Gregory's own remarks. Since his citation of the Childeric deposition had been intended to illustrate absolution from oaths and excommunication rather than deposition per se, his remarks were not usually developed outside of their original context as they would

76. *Liber de unitate,* pp. 6–7.

77. Two recent studies are those of H. Wolfram, *Splendor imperii. Die Epiphanie von Tugend und Heil in Herrschaft und Reich,* in *MIöG,* Ergänzungsband 20, Festschrift dur Jahrtaussendfeier der Kaiserkrönung Ottos des Grossen, Heft 3 (Cologne-Graz, 1963); Kantorowicz, *The King's Two Bodies,* pp. 383–450, 42–86.

be, for instance, at the hands of the decretists and decretalists. Bernold of Constance, Bonizo of Sutri, and the author of the *Disputatio vel defensio Paschalis papae* all cited the Childeric deposition, although not always from Gregory's registers, nor always correctly.[78]

Gregory VII's contribution to history was twofold. His view of the relations between *sacerdotium* and *imperium* became one of the cornerstones of the structure of later theories of papal monarchy. His diligence in trying to restore proper practices to a corrupt church resulted in the first of the great ages of canon law. His interest in archival sources of early canonical material has already been noted. The impetus which this interest gave to the recovery of older texts was considerable. In the area of authenticating texts, collecting canons, and verifying sources the late eleventh- and early twelfth-century canonists laid the groundwork for the classical period of the canon law. In concentrating their work upon the figure of the pope these canonists also determined the future of judicial thought on the *rex inutilis*.

The major eleventh-century canonical collections were not politically inspired. The constitutional issues which had troubled Christendom in the last quarter of the eleventh century do not leave overt traces in these works. The texts which would later become the "political material" in Gratian's *Decretum* are to be found originally illustrating ecclesiological, not political, problems. Yet these texts were later to become the main points of departure for the canonists' discussions of the relations between *papatum* and *imperium* in the twelfth and thirteenth centuries.

A number of these early canonical collections reproduced Gregory's reference to Childeric and Zacharias.[79] Even the most com-

78. Bernhold's *Tractatus de solutione iuramentorum* is in *PL* 148. 1254–55. Bonizo of Sutri, *Liber ad Amicum*, in *PL* 150. 844, repeats his garbled version in his *Liber de vita Christiana*, ed. E. Perels (Berlin, 1930), p. 129. Cf. *Disputatio vel defensio Paschalis Papae*, ed. E. Sackur, MGH *Ldl* II, 644; *Liber canonum contra Henricum Quartum*, above, p. 46, n. 29.

79. See Friedberg, *Corpus iuris canonici*, vol. 1, cols. 755–56. For the early collections, see Fournier-Le Bras, *Histoire des collections canoniques*, vol. 2; Ullmann, *The Growth of Papal Government*, pp. 359–81.

plete and influential of these, however—that of Ivo of Chartres—dealt with the texts in terms of the absolution of subjects from oaths to rulers, not deposition. Normally the collectors transmitted the texts with no comment whatsoever. As the science of canon law developed, however, these texts came to be read, taught, and learned in conjunction with the scholarly commentaries that later glossators produced. Eventually the glosses and *summae* were to acquire almost as much authority as the original texts themselves. During the classical period of canonistic scholarship, from 1140 to 1340, all canonists knew the Gregorian text and were familiar with the main scholarly approaches to it. In the fourteenth century, after the official collections had ceased to appear, canon and civil lawyers found the traditions of legal scholarship preserved in such works as the *Speculum iuris* of Guillelmus Durantis, the *Rosarium* of Guido de Baysio, and the *Commentaria* of Panormitanus. In this form the texts and the scholarly traditions of the canon law became familiar to most fourteenth- and fifteenth-century jurists.

By the late fourteenth century the *Decretum* and the later decretal collections had been subjected to a complex and vast apparatus of scholarship which included not only the evolving political ideas of the canonists and popes but those of rulers, lawyers, philosophers, and classical scholars. The new institution of scientific jurisprudence on the part of the Roman and canon lawyers not only influenced the church but profoundly contributed to the changing conceptions and structures of twelfth-, thirteenth-, and fourteenth-century monarchies and to increasingly precise theories of public law.

Consequently, such a text as that of Gregory VII on Childeric had a long and complex history. In canon law its inclusion in eleventh-century collections, in Gratian's *Decretum,* and its earliest interpretation in the works of Rufinus, Stephen of Tournai, and Huguccio gave it a prominent, if anachronistic, place in twelfth- and thirteenth-century political thought. Other texts than that of Gregory might have better served as starting points for later discussions of royal inadequacy in the following two centuries, but Gregory's text did in fact exist, was widely known, and achieved a degree of prominence which other episodes, such as that of Louis the Pious, failed to achieve. Thus Gregory VII inadvertently shaped one aspect of later attitudes toward the problem of the *rex inutilis*. The conception of kingship in Carolingian and later writers, however, reflected other, less easily definable concepts of royal power. Kingship, like society itself, could not simply be arbitrarily redefined, even by such a visionary as Gregory. The roots of that institution lay not only in Carolingian *publizistik* but in the Christian concept of human nature, and its failings were embodied in the literature of vices and virtues, in criteria of individual unsuitability for high ecclesiastical and secular office, and in the tension between conflicting concepts of royal power on the part of kings and nobles, some of which find expression in the work of chroniclers and poets. It is with some of these roots that the following chapter will be concerned.

2

The Name of King: Rhetorical and Literary Representations of Royal Inadequacy to 1150

Papal and imperial correspondence, publicistic pamphlets, tracts for the instruction of princes, and monastic chronicles were not the only sources which contribute evidence for the history of the *rex inutilis* between the eighth and the twelfth centuries. In tracing the background of Gregory's letter of 1081, it has been necessary to neglect not only other ecclesiastical approaches to the problem but also a strong, if neither systematic nor precisely articulated, lay view. The vocabulary of twelfth-century political chroniclers, colored by rhetorical convention and inspired usually by a view of human nature and conduct strongly influenced by the precepts of moral theology, was to provide a framework not only for later popes and canonists but for poets as well when they had cause to deal with the affairs of kings. The attempts on the part of popes from Gregory VII to Innocent III to deflate the ecclesiastical character of royal and imperial authority coincided with the efforts of chroniclers, political theorists, and poets to formulate a secular-based theory of royal effectiveness, a task made more difficult by the rapidly changing character of kingship itself. If the twelfth century is, as Jolliffe has observed, a "protean age" of kingship, its multiformity may be accounted for in part by the variety of ideas from which its notions of kingship were derived and of their alteration in the growth of royal governance.[1]

1. J. E. A. Jolliffe, *Angevin Kingship* (New York, 1955), pp. 17f. See also E. Kantorowicz, "Kingship under the Impact of Scientific Jurisprudence," in M. Clagett et al., eds., *Twelfth-Century Europe and the Foundations of Modern Society* (Madison, Wisc., 1961), pp. 89–114.

"The medieval king," Maitland once remarked, "was every inch a king, but just for this reason he was every inch a man, and you did not talk nonsense about him. You did not attribute to him immortality or ubiquity or such powers as no mortal can wield. If you said he was Christ's vicar, you meant what you said, and you might add that he would become the servant of the devil if he declined towards tyranny."[2] Although Maitland was chiefly concerned with the Tudor jurists' fiction of the king's two bodies and the idea of the king as a corporation sole, he obviously intended his stricture to apply to the whole medieval period. Further, he categorized all such fictions as "metaphysiological nonsense" and contrasted them with what he called "the natural way in which the king was regarded in the middle ages." In his study *The King's Two Bodies* Kantorowicz traced the medieval antecedents of some of Maitland's "nonsense" and found (as Maitland himself surely must have found) that the "natural" way of considering kingship was only one of a number of ways, some of which would have seemed to Maitland quite unnatural indeed. The dual role of medieval kings—that of individual Christian men, on the one hand, and of quasi-juristic personifications of divine law, on the other—remained one of the central difficulties of political thought throughout the Middle Ages.

Both views of the king's role remained prominent, neither ever quite becoming the basis of a systematic theory of governance. Neither was sufficiently consistent, comprehensive, or realistic to exclude the other. Each view consisted rather of postulates about the nature and purpose of royal power. That which emphasized the individual humanity—and consequent frailty of judgment—of the ruler aided tentative theories of rightful resistance. The view which stoutly maintained the king's "divinity"—with all of the necessary qualifications that writers used to hedge its implications—strengthened the theoretical basis of the centralizing process of royal governance from the eleventh century on. Sometimes each influenced the other: the tyrant often remained in theory God's vice-gerent, even though his human pride prevented his ruling justly. Neither

2. "The Crown as Corporation," in *Collected Papers of Frederick William Maitland,* ed. H. A. L. Fisher (Cambridge, 1911), 3:244–70.

view, finally, could guarantee political stability. John of Salisbury and others maintained that tyrants might be destroyed, and generations of unanointed French barons continued to make war on generations of liturgically anointed French kings.[3] Both aspects of kingship and the views they represented served rather as collections of observations on the nature of political society whose value lay chiefly in the use to which they were put by individual men on specific occasions.

The strength of each of these views varied according to time and place. It also varied according to men's ability or willingness to discuss kingship in terms other than those found in the limited political vocabulary of the patristic and Carolingian periods. The vocabulary of the twelfth-century chroniclers was shaped not only by what men knew or thought of kingship as a political institution but by what they thought of men as individuals, moved in their actions by God or Satan, by the impulses of virtues and vices, by the balance or imbalance of the humors, or by the dictates of Fortune. The vocabularies of moral theology, literary convention, and heroic literature all contributed in part to the depiction of royal inadequacy in the twelfth century.

3. John of Salisbury, *Policraticus,* ed. C. C. J. Webb (Oxford, 1909). John discusses the distinctions between the *princeps* and the *tyrannus* at IV, 1; VI, 1; VIII, 17, 16. For his famous doctrine of tyrannicide, see III, 15; VIIIl, 8. H. Liebeschütz, *Medieval Humanism in the Life and Writings of John of Salisbury,* Studies of the Warburg Institute, ed. F. Saxl, vol. 17 (London, 1950); idem, "Englische und europaische Elemente der Erfahrungswelt des Johanns von Salisbury," *Die Welt als Geschichte* 11 (1951): 38–45; J. Dickinson, "The Medieval Concept of Kingship and Some of Its Limitations as Developed in the Policraticus of John of Salisbury," *Speculum* 1 (1926). Like many other theorists, John does not concern himself directly with the *rex inutilis;* cf. *Policraticus,* IV, 9 (in reference to Aeneas being chosen as leader of the Trojan exiles): "Compatriotis omnibus ducem dedit, virum armis et pietate praesignem. Alias enim dux esset inutilis cum sine viribus regna adquiri non valeant aut sine iustitia retineri." On other aspects of twelfth-century theories of kingship, see Marc Bloch, *Les Rois thaumaturges,* pp. 31, 146–57; F. Behrends, "Kingship and Feudalism according to Fulbert of Chartres," *Medieval Studies* 25 (1963): 93–99; Geoffrey Barraclough, "Medieval Kingship," in his *History in a Changing World* (Norman, Okla., 1956), pp. 64–72.

William of Malmesbury, in his *De gestis regum anglorum,* gives the following description of Ethelred II's failure to act as a king: "Rex interea strenuus et pulchre ad dormiendum factus, tanta negotia postponens, oscitabat; et si quando resipuerat ut vel cubito se attolleret, confestim, vel gravante desidia, vel adversante fortuna, in miserias recidebat."[4] The sudden change in the king's character is accounted for in terms of several possible causes, none of which appears to interest William, since he does not choose—or is not able—to single out one as the chief cause. Two of these causes reflect the attitude of chroniclers toward human behavior. The phrase *gravante desidia* comes from the vocabulary used in cataloguing the vices and virtues, and it possessed a strong connotation of moral deficiency. The other, *adversante fortuna,* was an example of the recurring use of the idea of fortune as an agent in human actions, a concept which would become stronger between the twelfth and the sixteenth centuries.[5] William was not interested here in the psychology of human behavior, probably because, like most of his contemporaries, he lacked a view of human motivation that could provide him with a vocabulary and a frame of reference for analyzing it. The king's actions, his avoiding *negotia,* are of interest; his neglect may be attributed to one or more of a number of causes, such as the consequences of a vice, the hostility of fortune, the advice of wicked counselors, the power of an evil queen, or simply impulse.

William offers the alternatives of *fortuna* and *desidia* almost in passing. For him, whatever the causes of Ethelred's failure, its consequences are of far greater interest. If Ethelred had suddenly become a tyrant, the change in him could easily be attributed to his pride, always a good source of motivation among the great. If he had, on the other hand, suddenly become strong, just, and victorious, his triumph over pride and his subordination of his own will to that of God would have been a cause for rejoicing and perhaps a

4. W. Stubbs, ed., RS (London, 1887), pp. 188–89.

5. For Fortuna, see H. R. Patch, *The Goddess Fortuna* (Cambridge, Mass. 1927), and A. Doren, *Fortuna im Mittelalter und der Renaissance,* Vorträge der Bibliothek Warburg, 1922/23, 1. Teil (Leipzig, 1924), pp. 70–144.

homiletic digression on the figure of the *rex iustus.* The king's inaction, however, could not be fitted into the conceptual polarity of pride and humility which distinguished the tyrant from the good ruler. Hence William offers other possibilities, but he does not choose to elaborate on either of them.

William of Malmesbury's borrowings from philosophy and theology were not unusual for a man of his calling. A brief survey of those aspects of moral theology, particularly the relation of the vices and virtues to patterns of human conduct, of rhetorical convention, of heroic literature, and of trends in twelfth-century historiography which helped to shape the chronicler's view of royal inadequacy, may reveal some details of the conceptual frame of language within which chroniclers and poets attempted to explain the shortcomings of royalty.

Early medieval approaches to problems raised by human behavior often concentrated on the Pauline *homo renatus,* "new man," or *homo christianus* at the expense of the *homo carnis,* or natural man.[6] Before 1200 this concentration was reflected especially in the search for a frame of reference in which to categorize and describe the theological consequences of human conduct. The most obvious examples of perfect human conduct, the lives of the saints, were not always the best to use. As early as the sixth century Gregory I had remarked that saints' lives were not necessarily models for Christian conduct, but rather aids to piety: "Sed haec [the life] infirmis veneranda sunt, non imitanda."[7] The saint's life was a mod-

6. Two recent studies are those of B. Rey, "L'Homme nouveau d'après St. Paul," *Revue des Sciences Philosophiques et théologiques* 48 (1964): 603–29; 49 (1965): 161–95; Walter Ullmann, "Some Observations on the Medieval Evaluation of the Homo Naturalis and the Christianus," in *L'Homme et son destin d'après les penseurs du moyen âge, Actes du premier congrès international de philosophie médiévale, Louvain-Bruxelles, 1958* (Louvain-Paris, 1960), pp. 145–51, elements of which are expanded upon in Ullmann, *The Individual and Society in the Middle Ages* (Baltimore, 1967), a work which should be approached with the cautionary remarks of Gaines Post, in *Speculum* 43 (1968): 387–90, in mind.

7. See the discussion by W. F. Bolton, "The Supra-Historical Sense in the Dialogues of Gregory I," *Aevum* 33 (1959): 206–13.

el of virtue, just as the career of Roland, Beowulf, or William of Orange was a model of the warrior's ethic. However, neither paradigm provided a working model for imitation. Saints and legendary warriors typified schemes of perfected characteristics. They served as illustrations of the process by which the individual and human was transcended by the ideal and abstract. Both were to be admired—the saints more so—because they personified the highest values of an ideal pattern. They could not, nor were they intended to be, exactly imitated.

When writers on moral theology wished to describe a more generally applicable frame of reference for human conduct, they turned, after the sixth century, to the moral psychology embodied in the catalogues of vices and virtues which had originally developed as monastic guides for spiritual conduct.[8] These catalogues played an important role in Christian society, not only influencing monastic conduct, but often serving as pastoral guides and as vehicles of social criticism. In the thirteenth and fourteenth centuries they began to be adapted in sermons and popular literature to serve the interests and needs of laymen as well as clerics, a process which culminated in the great scenes in *Piers Plowman* and which became the basis for much of secular satire from Skelton and Brandt to John Bunyan.

Aside from their rich career in later medieval and Renaissance literature, discussions of the vices and virtues had other uses. They constituted handy points of departure for discussions of morality and human behavior, whether in the form of penitentials or ser-

8. The most comprehensive study is that of Morton W. Bloomfield, *The Seven Deadly Sins* (East Lansing, Mich., 1952). For *acedia,* see the excellent study of Siegfried Wenzel, *The Sin of Sloth: Acedia in Medieval Thought and Literature* (Chapel Hill., N.C., 1967), from which much of my approach in the following pages derives. There is also the brief summary by Dietrich Rupert, *Tristitia. Wortschatz und Vorstellung in den althochdeutschen Sprachdenkmälern,* Palaestra, Bd. 227 (Gottingen, 1959), esp. pp. 9–16. Except when Wenzel's book is mentioned specifically, references below are to his earlier article, "Acedia 700–1200," in *Traditio* 22 (1966): 73–102. On the general popularity of the theme of vices and virtues, see A. Katzenellenbogen, *Allegories of the Vices and Virtues in Medieval Art* (rep. New York, 1964).

mons. They provided an easily comprehensible guide for Christian conduct to pastors and confessors. Finally, they developed a vocabulary which served as an approach not only to morality but to psychology as well. This vocabulary, which had been developed to describe purely spiritual states, had begun as early as the ninth century to be applied to the planes of mental and physical behavior, particularly in the cases of *acedia,* and *tristitia.* In the history of these, particularly *acedia,* lay the beginning of later speculations concerning human, if not specifically royal, sloth, negligence, and inaction.

John Cassian, one of the founders of Western monasticism, defined *acedia* as "taedium sive anxietatem cordis," whose chief symptoms were *otiositas, somnolentia,* and *instabilitas mentis et corporis,* the chief defense against which was intensive manual labor.[9] In early monastic literature *acedia* was chiefly a spiritual phenomenon, but as early as the ninth century it had begun to designate something broader than that. In Alcuin's *Liber de virtutibus et vitiis ad Widonem comitem* (799–800), one of the first works to adapt the scheme of vices and virtues to the lay state, *acedia* is a spiritual disease whose effects can be seen in a general weakening of the will:

> Acedia est pestis, quae a Deo famulantibus multum nocere probatur, dum otiosus homo torpescit in desideriis carnalibus, nec in opere gaudet spirituali, nec in desiderio animae suae laetatur, nec in adiutorio fraterni laboris hilarescit, sed tantum concupiscit et desiderat, et otiosa mens per omnia discurrit. . . . ex qua nascitur somnolentia, pigritia, operio boni, instabilitas loci . . . tepiditas laborandi, taedium cordis. . . . Nonunquam otiosus inveniatur servus Dei.[10]

Hrabanus Maurus's definition of *acedia* generally follows that of Alcuin, shifting the emphasis slightly from the debilitation of the will to the consequences of the vice in man:

9. Bloomfield, pp. 71–72; Wenzel, pp. 75–76, John Cassian, *De institutis coenobiorum,* ed. M. Petschenig, CSEL 17 (Vienna, 1888), X.1; idem, *Collationes patrum,* ed. Petschenig, CSEL 13 (Vienna, 1886), V.16.

10. Wenzel, p. 78. See also L. Wallach, "Alcuin on Vices and Virtues," in his *Alcuin and Charlemagne,* pp. 231–54; *The Sin of Sloth,* pp. 35–37.

> Acedia, quem tepor mentis et segnities noxia oritur, quae hominem *inutilem* ad omne opus bonum ac proclivem ad interitum reddit. Unde scriptum est: Otiositas inimica est animae [Prov. 20:4] . . . ita ut *inutiliter* faciat eum torpore, et minime in bonis operibus desudare. . . . Dum otiosus homo torpescit in desideriis carnalibus.[11]

In these Carolingian writers the idea of *acedia* is already linked with many of the terms which were to become equally applicable to such royal inactivity as that of Ethelred, cited above. *Inutilis, otiositas, torpor mentis, segnitia,* and *negligentia,* terms which cluster around the vice *acedia* in the work of these early writers, were also to cluster about the shadowy royal figures, the explanation of whose failures was to prove so difficult a task to their chroniclers.

In the elaborate analysis of spiritual behavior schematized by Hugh of St. Victor in the twelfth century, *acedia* appears particularly as a sin against *negotium.*[12] Since it is the result of an illicit collaboration between man and Satan, it is more than the simple proclivity to sin which is a consequence of man's fall from grace. In Hugh's work *acedia* appears to be a definite psychological state as well as a spiritual illness. Other twelfth- and thirteenth-century writers on the vices and virtues expanded Hugh's view. In the *De fructibus carnis et spiritus, tristitia* is linked to *acedia* and the two become aspects of a single state of mind and spirit: "Tristitia (seu acedia) est ex frustrato contrariis voto turbatae mentis anxietudo, et rei bonae gerendae taedium. Eius comite sunt desperatio, rancor, torpor, timor, acidia, querela, pusillanimitas."[13] At the end of the twelfth century Alanus de Insulis continued the exposition of *acedia:* "Accidia est animi torpor quo quis aut bona negligit inchoare aut fastidit perficere. Dividitur autem in has species: desidiam, pigritiam, pusillanimitatem, negligentiam, improvidentiam, incircumspectionem, tepiditatem, ignaviam."[14] At this stage of its

11. *PL* 101. 470D; also Wenzel, p. 78, for Jonas of Orléans.

12. See Roger Baron, "La Situation de l'homme d'après Hugues de Saint-Victor," in *L'Homme et son destin,* pp. 431–36; Wenzel, pp. 94–97.

13. *PL* 175. 383–84, 176. 525–26.

14. *PL* 176. 1000–01; Wenzel, p. 97.

history *acedia* is firmly linked to the neglect of *bona opera,* the demands of *negotium,* and the list of psychological-spiritual *species* which form part of it.

In his *Summa de arte praedicatoria* Alanus outlines a sermon *contra acediam.*[15] For exempla he turns to the Old Testament, and to kings and heroes in particular, contrasting particularly David at war with David neglecting his duties in the palace. Samson and Solomon provide similar examples. Old Testament figures, existing in the unanchored imagination of the medieval Christian intellect, often served to illustrate theological truths and dogmatic pronouncements which had little to do with their historical role in Jewish history. Kings served to illustrate far more than purely royal careers; hence there is no necessity to see direct political parallels in Alanus's analogies. The prince, however, was considered by many to be particularly subject to *acedia,* and Alanus's remarks on David, Samson, and Solomon certainly had more than an allegorical relevance to those who read them. These rulers' neglect of their duties was thus linked to *acedia.* As a result of their neglect, their own subjects, deprived of their forceful, just rule, gave themselves up to even worse crimes. The homilist, if not primarily a political thinker, could draw a harsh political analogy to illustrate the truths of moral theology. His readers in their turn did not neglect their own political experience in seeking the spiritual content of Alanus's treatise.

By the time of Alanus catalogues of vices and virtues had long since moved out of their monastic surroundings into the wider world of secular clergy and laymen. If *acedia* had not yet become the mysterious disease of Petrarch and the root of the fashionable sixteenth-century affliction, melancholia, it was at least well able to be applied to physical and mental aspects of human conduct.[16] Its

15. Wenzel, pp. 97–98. Alanus's text has been edited by O. Lottin in *Medieval Studies* 12 (1950), and in his *Psychologie et morale au XIIe et XIIIe siècle* (Gembloux, 1960), 6:27–92. For a somewhat dissenting view of Wenzel's analysis, see P. Michaud-Quentin, "La Classification des puissances de l'âme au XIIe siècle," *Revue du Moyen Age Latin* 5 (1949): 15–34; *PL* 210. 125–28.

16. For Petrarch, see Wenzel, *The Sin of Sloth,* pp. 155–63. For later Renaissance melancholia, see Lawrence Babb, *The Elizabethan Malady: A*

relation to the terms *pigritia, desidia, negligentia, tepiditas,* and *ignavia* connected it to the chroniclers' analysis of the characteristics of the *rex inutilis.* These relationships may account for the attribution to the last Merovingians of such characteristics as the moral degeneracy so frequently implied in many of the sources.

The transformation of *acedia* from a spiritual to a mental state reflects what Wenzel terms "the rational ordering and expression of traditional doctrines," which took place throughout the twelfth century.[17] This transformation was aided, of course, by other characteristics of theological terminology. The imagery used in discussing the vices and virtues came originally from the world of practical activity, its transition to the spiritual plane being most evident in the *Psychomachia* genre of the fourth and fifth centuries. Moreover, the life of the individual Christian was repeatedly described from early times in terms of activity, diligence, and service. The twin notions of spiritual and physical diligence were never, semantically at least, very far apart. In patristic political thought the magistrate was expected to be as diligent in ordering the life of the *respublica* as the individual Christian was in ordering his spiritual life or as the father was in ordering his family. Nowhere is the similarity of spiritual and physical imagery more closely intertwined than in the ideas of the *militans Dei* and the *Ecclesia militans,* which emerged in the fifth and sixth centuries and again in the eleventh and twelfth.[18]

Part of the background of these changes was the idea of the Christian as a *servus Dei* in both a literal and a figurative sense. The

---

Study of Melancholia in English Literature from 1580 to 1642 (East Lansing, Mich., 1951), esp. pp. 1–72; R. Klibansky, E. Panofsky, and F. Saxl, *Saturn and Melancholy: Studies in the History of Natural Philosophy, Religion, and Art* (London-Edinburgh, 1964).

17. Wenzel, p. 101.

18. See A. Harnack, *Militia Christi. Die christliche Religion und der Soldatenstand in den ersten drei Hundertjahren* (Tübingen, 1905); C. Erdmann, *Die Entstehung des Kreuzzugsgedankens,* Forschungen zur Kirchen- und Geistesgeschichte, Bd. 6 (Stuttgart, 1935); C. Thouzellier, "Ecclesia militans," in *Etudes . . . LeBras,* 2:1407–23.

figure appears frequently in the New Testament, from which it strongly influenced epistolography and literary convention from the fifth century on. Among patristic writings nowhere is the image expressed more forcefully than in a discourse of St. Augustine: "Debet enim, qui praeest populo, prius intellegere se servum esse multorum. Et hoc non dedigneteur: non, inquam, dedignetur servus esse multorum, quia servire nobis non dedignatus est dominus dominorum."[19] In political terms, as we have seen, this idea later reappeared with great force in Carolingian political thought. In ecclesiastical rhetoric also, the image of the Christian as a *servus* provided writers with a whole range of references relating to servitude and, consequently, with material for the discussion of Christian vices and virtues in terms of the vices and virtues of servitude.

Such concerns most often appeared in the devotional or humility formulas used in private correspondence and public documents. And such formulas usually express in a conventional way the incompetence or unworthiness of the writer, either to God or the person being addressed, or to some task which the writer has been set.[20] Without going too deeply into the classical antecedents of this convention or dealing at length with what Curtius called late Roman literary mannerism, we may give some attention to those aspects of Christian *formulae* which emphasize the incompetence or the inadequacy of the writer.

Much of the terminology for such expressions of personal inadequacy came from the New Testament, which contained innumerable references to man as a *servus* or *minister*. One product of this repeated usage, which derived from the authority-formula,

19. Ed. G. Morin, "Discours inédit de St. Augustin pour l'ordination d'un évêque," *Revue Bénédictine* 30 (1913): 398.

20. A study of these is that of K. Schmitz, *Ursprung und Geschichte der Devotionsformeln,* Kirchengeschichtliche Abh., Heft 81 (Stuttgart, 1918). See the critique by E. R. Curtius in *European Literature in the Latin Middle Ages,* Excursus II, "Devotional Formula and Humility," pp. 407–13. The use of such expressions of self-deprecation as *imbecillitas mea* and *infirmitas mea* does not appear to have been frequent in early epistolography. See Sister M. E. O'Brien, *Titles of Address in Christian Latin Epistolography to 543 A.D.* (Washington, D.C., 1930), pp. 74–75.

was the papal epithet *servus servorum Dei.*[21] From that aspect of the humility-formula, which expressed the inability of the writer to fulfill his calling at all without the constant support of the authority that had entrusted him with the task, came the variations of the papal formula, the references to the writer as the *minimus, infirmus,* or *inefficax servus servorum* (or *sanctorum) Dei.*[22] Since early medieval writers tended to shape their arguments around the nature of their metaphors, the topics of vices and virtues suitable to servants or slaves—faithfulness, efficacy, and devotion—abound in this literature.

In keeping with the servant-minister theme of much early correspondence was the necessity of disavowing one's own innate abilities and, more specifically, one's worthiness. Protestations of one's own inadequacy usually centered upon the polar pairs of terms *dignus-indignus* and *idoneus-inutilis,* the emphasis thereby falling upon innate unworthiness rather than upon functional inadequacy. Such formulas as *N. nomine absque merito episcopus* and *imbecillitas* or *insufficientia mea* also reflect the sharp distinction between the title and the individual's suitability for the title, although usually in a quite rhetorical way. However, the term *inutilis* is not often used by the writer in reference to himself. Although *humillimus, ultimus, minimus,* and *immeritus* are often appended to *servus* and *servulus,* few writers call themselves *inutilis.* Unlike the honorific connotations of many of these terms, the meanings of *inutilis* appear to have been such that the word was unsuitable for use even in rhetorical protestations of one's own inadequacy. One set of meanings may have derived from scriptural usage, particularly the text from Matthew (25:30): "Et inutilem servum eiicite in tenebras exteriores." Another set may have influenced later treatments of the term *inutilis* in eighth- and ninth-century glossaries, in which the term is glossed usually with terms suggesting mental and moral deficiency. Such terms as *ignavus, iners, desidius, segnis,* and *negligens* all appear in these glossaries in connection

21. Schmitz, *Devotionsformeln,* pp. 120–53; L. Levillain, "Servus Servorum Dei," *Le Moyen Age* 40 (1930): 5–7.

22. *Devotionsformeln,* pp. 120–53.

with *inutilis,* even as late as the eleventh-century dictionary of Papias.[23] When early medieval writers wished to refer to their own unworthiness in stronger terms than those conveyed by *humillimus* and *ultimus,* they generally turned to *insufficiens* and *incompetens* rather than to *inutilis, ineptus,* or *negligens.*

When ecclesiastical writers turned from the literary conventions of epistolography to those of historiography or poetry, they retained their sense of the terms discussed above. The religious zeal praised in individuals became the zeal for good governance, and such virtues as *cura, solicitudo, studium,* and *reverentia* characterize good rulers in historical as well as epistolary works.[24]

The just king was *idoneus* or *dignus.* Although these terms had earlier meant legal, then moral worth, *idoneus* later came to describe good governance in a more practical sense. The rhetorical opposite of *idoneus,* when one described oneself, was either *indignus* or *immeritus.* When, however, one wished to criticize an unfit prelate or ruler, the opposite of *idoneus* appears to have been *inutilis.* In this conjunction *inutilis* appears to have meant "unsuitable" for a broad variety of reasons. If the chief reason for the ruler's unsuitability was his tyranny, *inutilis* gave way to *tyrannus.* Although the *servus*-formula was not frequently applied to rulers, the *minister*-formula *(minister Dei,* later *minister publicae utilitatis)* remained a commonly used political concept and thus may

23. See G. Loewe, *Prodromis corporis glossariorum latinorum* (Leipzig, 1876); G. Goetz, *Corpus glossariorum latinorum,* 7 vols. (Leipzig, 1888–1923); Papias Grammaticus, *Vocabularium* (Venice, 1496); *Ignavus* (Goetz, 4:545); *Iners* (Goetz, 4:353); *Ineptus* (Goetz, 4:353); *Inefficax* (Goetz, 4:353; 5:302); *Desidia* (Goetz, 4:49, 226, 329, 505); *Segnis* (Goetz, 4:169, 284, 390); *Negligens* (Goetz, 4:376–78). The term *inutilis* was extremely pejorative not only in the sense of its citation in Matthew (quoted above) but also in general late-Roman usage. See *TLL,* vol. 7, fasc. 2, cols. 274–80, s.v. *inutilis,* esp. the citation from the *Regula* of St. Benedict: "Frater . . . non . . . intentus lectioni . . . non solum sibi inutilis est, sed etiam alios distollit."

24. A comprehensive survey of the language of political panegyric is that of A. Kühne, *Das Herrscherideal des Mittelalters und Kaiser Friedrich I,* Leipziger Studien auf der Gebiet der Geschichte, Bd. 2 (Leipzig, 1898), esp. pp. 4–44.

have been influenced by the connotations of these terms as they had been developed in patristic and later rhetoric.

The royal virtues that interested most writers were chiefly those which might be expressed in terms of piety: *pius, religiosus, sanctissimus, christianissimus.* The pious ruler cared especially for the clergy and for ecclesiastical institutions. As one writer said of Lothar: "Nam ipse juste iudicavit, pacem composuit, aecclesias defendit, iniquos dampnavit, elemosinas distribuit et quae Dei sunt, exquisivit."[25] Royal expressions of piety took the form of concern for the law and for justice, and from this concern came the ecclesiastical emphasis upon the royal protection of those who were not strong enough to enforce their own claims to justice: widows, clerics, orphans, and paupers. The king who fulfilled these duties was *misericors, clemens, mitis.* Kühne's observation that ecclesiastical writers tended to attribute the same qualities to all reasonably well-behaved rulers is consistent with a similar phenomenon evident in hagiography. The attribution to different saints of the same miracles, the uniform pattern of types of the saint's life, and the loss or acquisition of legendary elements in the lives of individual saints all reflect the de-individualization of much of medieval biography and historiography. The type, the sum total of desirable attributes, was the ideal, whether saint or king.[26]

Thus the collection of traits which characterizes the just king is not the sum total of perfectable individual traits of the individual personality but essentially a discarding of individuality in favor of a conventional set of moral characteristics or, rather, categories which substitute conventional traits for individual ones and make each just king's life resemble that of every other just king. The typical is, nevertheless, valuable—if not individually accurate—because it provides us with a "sharp insight into the collective attitudes, or frame of mind, of an earlier time." This approach to human char-

25. Kühne, p. 7.

26. See the interesting remarks of Walter Ullmann on the general subject of medieval royal biographies in his *Principles of Government and Politics in the Middle Ages* (2d ed., New York, 1966), pp. 299–300. The theme of royal biography has not yet been fully studied.

acter sheds some light on the early medieval idea of royal inadequacy. The *rex inutilis,* like the useless prelate or the negligent Christian man, is one who has failed to create for himself a moral personality, who has retained his individual human weakness instead of acquiring abstract moral traits external to himself. There grew up, in consequence, a set of conventional terms of description for such rulers. Between the eighth and the eleventh centuries there grew up the formation of a conventional terminology for describing royal inadequacy, the chief themes of which were mental incompetence, political weakness, physical incapacity, and subjection to one or more of the deadly vices.

By the twelfth century the concepts of *acedia* and other vices and the conventional terminology of political discussions had contributed to a background against which royal inadequacy might be viewed, although that background was not, in the strict sense, either legal or political. The idea of a twelfth-century renaissance has long intrigued students of medieval cultural history. Its chief aspect, that of the return to—and the revival of interest in—the Latin classics sometimes obscures an equally powerful aspect, that of the revival of interest in the more recent past. Like Charlemagne, the central figure of a still earlier "renaissance," twelfth-century society expressed an interest in its own postclassical past. Charlemagne had looked toward Theodoric; Frederick Barbarossa and the authors of the *chansons de geste* looked toward Charlemagne. The heroic national past constituted for many twelfth-century men a repository of ideal social relationships which the increasingly more complex forms of human association tended to neglect.

Not only knights, kings, chroniclers, and panegyrists turned to the less remote past. During the eleventh and early twelfth centuries even the church attempted to restore itself to what it considered its earlier, purer status. If kings and prelates found their heroic prototypes in the past, the nobility found there a world in which its counterparts occupied the center of social, economic, and political interest. Secular literature is aristocratic rather than royal, and it reflects better than many other sources the aristocratic view of kingship in the twelfth century.

The world of the heroic epic, whether specifically Christian or not, is centered on the figure of the warrior-hero. The hero's exploits against superior—and frequently nonhuman—opponents, his brief triumph, and, almost inevitably, his destruction constitute the central theme of this literature, and others aspects of life—social, political, and economic—are strictly subordinated to these major interests. Consequently, there is little resembling "political theory" to be found in these works. There is, rather, a series of postulates about society in terms of the hero and his role among men. The hero of the epic is often not royal at the time of his greatest exploits, and the picture of kingship which the epics reflect is often the result of peripheral relationships between social institutions and the theme of heroic adventure. When the hero himself happens to be or to become a king, only those aspects of his rule which reveal or pertain however remotely to his heroism receive much attention.[27]

Although kingship is thus subordinated to a concept of the heroic life which often does not center on the king, it is a necessary institution in the heroic world. The king must distribute largess, settle disputes, and give to his people a status higher than that of kingless tribes. The opening lines of *Beowulf,* for example, describe the contrast between the wretchedness of the Danes when they had no king at all and their power and well-being when Scyld Scefing became their lord.[28] At the other end of the period of heroic litera-

27. For German literature, see Hermann Schneider, "Herrscher und Reich in der deutschen Heldendichtung," in *Das Reich. Festschrift für Johannes Haller* (Stuttgart, 1940), esp. pp. 144–45: "The heroes, whose poeticized deeds were heard by a courtly audience, itself composed of lords and their retainers, dwelt in a distant, half-real world, without political cohesion and without political society. Their kings wielded mighty swords and had open hands, but they were not military leaders, not political rulers. Everything political and economic lay far from this world of courtly appearance." For the audience of French and German literature of this period, see Georges Duby, "Dans la France du Nord-Ouest. Au XIIe siècle: Les 'Jeunes' dans la société aristocratique," *Annales, Economies-Sociétés-Civilisations* 19 (1964): 835–46.

28. *Beowulf with the Finnsburg Fragment,* ed. A. J. Wyatt and R. W. Chambers (Cambridge 1914), lines 1–11. Modern English translations

ture the opening scenes of *Huon de Bordeaux* reveal an aging Charlemagne imposing his worthless son as king against the will of his assembled barons and the barons accepting the son as being better than having no king at all or having a stranger come to rule them.[29]

Within the conventionalized epic world, however, occasions do occur in which the problem of royal inadequacy becomes an issue of interest. In *Beowulf,* for example, the problems of kingship occupy an unusual place, and Beowulf's first great exploit in the poem is to defeat Grendel, a monster whom the king of the Danes, Hrothgar, is incapable of destroying. Hrothgar's inability to protect his own men within his own hall—his *inutilitas*—offers Beowulf an opportunity to display his own heroism. Hrothgar is at the end, Beowulf at the beginning, of a heroic life. Hrothgar's failure, the poet says, is a natural one, the result of old age: "This was a king blameless in all ways, till old age, which has done hurt to many, robbed him of the joys of strength."[30] Hrothgar himself is perfectly aware of his own weakness, and in one of the most striking speeches of the poem (vv. 1698–1784) he makes his own incapacity the starting point for a description of heroic behavior in political terms, comparing his own career with that of Beowulf, and contrasting both, through the medium of ideal lordship, with examples of royal inadequacy.

The speech falls into three distinct parts. In the first part Hrothgar contrasts Beowulf with Heremod, who after having acquired great power and fame, sank into joyless tyranny. "Learn from this," says Hrothgar to Beowulf, "lay hold on virtue." The second part repeats the differences between good and bad lords, this time, however, in general terms. God gives to some men land, power, and

---

from *Beowulf* below are from E. K. Gordon, *Anglo-Saxon Poetry* (rep. London, 1954), pp. 3–62. Line numbers from Wyatt-Chambers edition.

29. Ed. F. Guessard and C. Grandmaison, *Anciens Poètes de la France* (Paris, 1860).

30. Lines 1185–87. Beowulf is already renowned when he arrives in Denmark (cf. K. Sisam, *The Structure of Beowulf* [Oxford, 1965], pp. 22–23), but it may be suggested that the Grendel episode initiates the hero into kingly, rather than purely "heroic," society.

wealth: The lord "lives in plenty; nothing afflicts him, neither sickness nor old age; nor does sorrow darken his mind, nor does strife anywhere show forth sword hatred, but all the world meets his desire."[31] Then pride springs up, bringing with it greed and avarice. The lord's watchfulness has slackened:

> He bestows no golden rings in generous pride, and he neglects and forgets the destiny which God, the ruler of glory, formerly gave him, his share of honors. At the end it comes to pass that the mortal body sinks into ruin, falls doomed; another comes to power who bestows treasures gladly, old wealth of the earl; he takes joy in it.

The third part of the speech again contrasts two individuals, this time Beowulf and Hrothgar himself. Hrothgar tells the hero to keep himself from such passions:

> Now the repute of thy might endures for a space; straightway shall age, or edge of sword part thee again from thy strength, or the embrace of fire, or the surge of the flood, or the grip of the blade, or the flight of the spear, or hateful old age, or the gleam of eyes shall pass away and be darkened; on a sudden it shall come to pass that death shall vanquish thee, noble warrior.

Hrothgar then describes his own early strength, which had protected his people for so long that he thought he had no more enemies left. Then came the reverse, "sorrow after joy," and Grendel threatened the king who was no longer able to protect his people.

31. This and the next two passages from the speech on lines 1715–57. To a certain extent this speech is a "mirror for princes." Some scholars have regarded it as a Christian compendium of royal virtues as these were worked out between Augustine and Pseudo-Cyprian—e.g. L. L. Schucking, "Das Königsideal im Beowulf," *Bulletin of the Modern Humanities Research Assoc.* 3, no. 8 (1929): 143–54 (also in *Englische Studien* 67 [1932]). W. W. Lawrence, *Beowulf and the Epic Tradition* (rep. New York, 1961), pp. 48–58, contends that the patterns of royal life in the poem are those of seventh-century England. It is hard to agree with J. Leyerle ("Beowulf the Hero and King," *Medium Aevum* 34 [1965]: 89–102) that Beowulf exemplifies the rash king and Hrothgar the prudent king.

The aesthetic hero, one whose superiority to others lies in physical strength and courage, is destroyed, as Auden once pointed out, not so much by death as by the passage of time.[32] The hero, however, has some degree of control over the alternatives open to him. He may corrupt himself through pride and greed, or he may avoid these and succumb to inevitable decline or sudden death. Since time is the only force which can deprive the hero of his heroic qualities, it assumes the role of enemy. "Sorrow after joy" is the constant theme of the epic, just as it is in the later *Niebelungenlied:* "nach liebe leit." Hrothgar's speech deals not so much with heroic conduct as with the hero's difficulties in living in time.

The formal arrangement of Hrothgar's speech, the studied shift of emphasis from individuals to humanity in the abstract, and the constant concern revealed by Hrothgar for Beowulf's future conduct reinforce the rhetorical distinctions between excessive pride and degeneration, the two grim courses open to the hero.[33] Beowulf, like all other heroes, must succumb to pride, to the passage of time, or to sudden death. He has control only over the first of these. At the end of the poem, after Beowulf has shown himself to have rejected the way of Heremod through his just rule over the Geats, he is faced with a choice similar to that which had faced Hrothgar at the beginning of the poem. He may choose not to fight the dragon, just as Hrothgar had chosen not to attempt to battle Grendel, but he chooses to fight instead. Both alternatives would be honorable. There is throughout the early parts of the poem no criticism of Hrothgar because of his incapacity. Beowulf's final choice marks him out as the exceptional hero but does not detract in retrospect from the character of Hrothgar. Of the two men, Hrothgar's self-knowledge and objectivity suggest that his is the more difficult ordeal; for a lord to be unable, through no fault of his own, to defend his people, is a calamity. Yet the Danes remain loyal to him, a suggestion of the place he occupies in the scale of heroic behavior which the poem continually probes.

32. *The Enchafèd Flood, or the Romantic Iconography of the Sea* (London, 1951), pp. 83–84.

33. A good discussion of the Heremod references is that of A. Bonjour, *The Digressions in Beowulf, Medium Aevum* Monographs, vol. 5 (Oxford, 1965), pp. 46–53.

Hrothgar's incapacity is caused by his advanced age *(yldo),* the epic equivalent of the legal term *senectus,* a condition that was one of the canonically recognized causes for certain ecclesiastical exemptions. His decline is dramatized by the contrast with the line of vigorous rulers described at the poem's beginning, including the youth of Hrothgar himself. The balance between the order, music, and light within Heorot, the *felicitas regni* of the Danes, and the chaos and darkness which exist outside it is broken by the king's weakness, and Grendel becomes a symbol not only of the powers of disorder but of Hrothgar's diminished might.

During the preparations for Beowulf's fight with Grendel the poet dramatizes Hrothgar's incapacity: "The protector of the Scyldings went out of the hall; the warlike king was minded to seek Wealtheow the queen for his bedfellow." Hrothgar is still warlike (the poet is not, I think, being ironic at this point). Although he still rules the Danes, his place as protector is taken by Beowulf. But Hrothgar's failure has no political consequences. In the epic, or elegiac, world of Beowulf, kingship is chiefly one more ground upon which heroism may be tested. Hrothgar's inadequacy is honorable because it is inevitable. Since the king has avoided the moral dangers of the heroic world, his incapacity because of old age is described in terms of personal, rather than political or social, failure.

For all of its restricted political scope, however, *Beowulf,* standing at the beginning of the eighth century, is remarkable for the extent to which kingship and governance do constitute important themes in it. Turning from that work, with its repeated systematic confrontations between order and disorder, between heroic and nonheroic conduct, to the tenth-century *Waltharius,* reveals the extent to which political issues thave ceased to play integral parts in the epic. The inadequacy of Gunther in the *Waltharius* appears much more specifically in terms of battle strategy than of any wider area of political responsibility.[34] Gunther, whose conduct,

34. Ed. K. Strecker (Berlin, 1924 and 1947). See J. K. Bostock, *A Handbook on Old High German Literature* (Oxford, 1955), pp. 224–36. The author makes some interesting comments on Gunther's legal position on pp. 227–28. See also F. J. E. Raby, *A History of Secular Latin Poetry in the Middle Ages* (2d ed., Oxford, 1957), 1: 262–69.

though technically legal, is hardly respected even by his own men, occupies a key role in the poem not because he is king of the Burgundians but because he alone is in a position to provide opposition to Walter. Although he is continually accused of stubbornness, *superbia,* and *infelicitas,* he suffers no political consequences from his defeat by Walter, nor is his ineptitude sufficient to lose for him the loyalty of Hagen, the most complex and, in some respects, the most admirable figure in the poem.

Ultimately, it is not Gunther's royal inadequacy which merits the sharpest criticism, but his cowardice and ineptitude in battle: not his tyranny but his bad generalship. In a brief speech toward the end of the poem Walter directs Hildegunde to mix wine and to bind up the wounds of the three survivors, Hagen, Gunther, and himself. Hagen, says Walter, is to be tended first, Walter himself next, and Gunther last,

> utpote segnis
> Inter magnanimum qui paruit arma virorum,
> Et qui Martis opus tepide atque enerviter egit.

Gunther loses his honor because he had been lax in battle and "had done the work of Mars reluctantly and without strength." Gunther's failure, first to fight himself, and second to use his forces wisely, reflects the contemporary concern for military qualities in rulers not only in literature but in actuality. The ruler who refused or was unable to fight for the *patria* was just as unfit as one made useless by old age or other forms of incapacity.[35]

Although it may be dangerous to read the theological senses of the terms *pigritia* and *segnis* into Gunther's character, it is also impossible to ignore their connotations. The poet of the *Waltharius* describes a battle which takes place at the border of the Burgundian kingdom between two traveling strangers and a band of Burgundian warriors led by the king himself. The atmosphere is far different from that of Heorot and the courtly life of the Danes. In this re-

35. Most recently, Gaines Post, "*Pugna Pro Patria,*" in his *Studies in Medieval Legal Thought,* pp. 435–52. For Ethelred *Unraed* of England, see Margaret Ashdown, *English and Norse Documents Relating to the Reign of Ethelred the Unready* (Cambridge, 1930).

spect, the kingship of Gunther is a lesser institution than that of Hrothgar. Further, although Walter is the heir of the king of Aquitaine, he is presented alone, and his heroic qualities, like Gunther's unheroic qualities, must be proven in the limited, circumscribed, nonpolitical episode of the battle, not, as was the case with Hrothgar, in the more expanded world of Heorot, of the Danes as a people, or of the connections between heroic behavior and good rulership.

In describing a "lay" view of medieval kingship it is dangerous to draw too sharp a dividing line between "lay" and "clerical" ideals. The ecclesiastical concern for royal *strenuitas* in the pursuit of justice had secular as well as clerical implications. As is evident from the speech of Hrothgar, laymen were concerned with moral character as well as with power and heroic qualities. From the lay point of view the king should exhibit the qualities of bravery, generosity, and faithfulness to those who had sworn allegiance to him.

The heroic and ecclesiastical views of kingship had much in common, although the ecclesiastical view survived in documents much more coherently than did the heroic. Other closely related aspects of kingship are also to be found in the two views. The ecclesiastical view of the king as an anointed deputy of God paralleled, if it did not influence, the Germanic notion of sacral kingship with its attendant ritual. Although the sacral character of ancient Germanic kingship is beyond the scope of this study, traces of its influence appear to have lingered in folklore and literature, and on several occasions questions of taboo and the relation between the physical integrity of the king and that of his land exist even in comparatively recent and sophisticated sources. Such folk-tale motifs as that of the cuckold king who overlooks his wife's unfaithfulness so as not to disturb the order of the kingdom, the avaricious king who refuses to hire troops to defend his people, the maimed king who is unsuitable for rule, and the enchanted king were remarkably tenacious on the minds of medieval men. They reappear as motifs in historiography and legal literature as well.[36]

36. For the theme of the weak king in folklore, see Stith Thompson, *Motif-Index of Folk-Literature* (Helsinki, 1932–36): J221.1; W152.6;

Among these, the two most striking motifs that appear frequently in conjunction with the figure of the *rex inutilis* are those of the wicked (or supernatural) queen and the evil counselors. Without going deeply into the relation of the first of these motifs to the biographies of such historical queens as Fastrada, wife of Charlemagne, or Judith, wife of Louis the Pious, an episode from the *Heimskringla* may serve as a type of the motif. Harald Fairhair, Snorre Sturlusson tells, "made Snaefrid his wife and loved her so passionately that he forgot his kingdom and all that belonged to his high dignity." When his wife, who had been an enchantress, died, Harald refused to have her buried, but dressed her in costly garments and sat her at his side, ignoring her death and allowing the affairs of the kingdom to deteriorate more grievously than he had before. Finally a counselor found a way to break the enchantment that had preserved the queen's body and to bring the king to his senses: "now the king comes to his understanding again, threw the madness out of his mind, and after that day ruled the kingdom as before. He was strengthened and made joyful by his subjects, and his subjects by him, and the country by both." The figure of the wicked queen is a frequent topic of poets and chroniclers throughout the Middle Ages.[37]

D759.7; P10–19. See also E. Hoffmann-Krayer and H. Bächthold Stäubli, eds., *Handwörterbuch des deutschen Aberglaubens* (Berlin, 1927–42), 3:126f.; 4:504, 1361; 5:1394; 6:161–62, 963; 7:874; 8:584, 630f., 1385, 1511f.; Tom Peete Cross, *Motif-Index of Early Irish Literature,* Indiana University Publications: Folklore Series, vol. 3 (Bloomington, Ind., 1952), pp. 416–18. See also next note.

37. Snorre Sturlason, *Heimskringla: The Saga of the Norse Kings,* trans. S. Laing, rev. Peter Foote (London, 1961), chap. 25, pp. 69–70. The most thorough survey of kingship in the sagas is that of F. York Powell and G. Vigfusson, *Corpus poeticum boreale* (London, 1883), 2:477–80. Other interesting treatments of kingship in the area of folklore, myth, and religion are those of Heinrich Zimmer, *The King and the Corpse* (New York, 1948); Joseph Campbell, *The Hero with a Thousand Faces* (New York, 1949); P. Wolff-Windegg, *Die Gekronten. Sinn und Sinnbilder des Königtums* (Stuttgart, 1958). For Irish analogies, see John R. Reinhard, *The Survival of Geis in Medieval Romance* (Halle, 1933); Myles Dillon, *The Cycles of the Kings* (Oxford, 1936), pp. 68–74, 83–89; idem, *Early Irish Literature (Chicago,* 1948), pp. ii–xvi, 82, 86–93, 101–23.

The second motif, that of the evil counselors, was to have even more influence in historiography. The right of the nobility to advise the ruler was one of the most bitterly contested claims in the political history of the Middle Ages. The power of the counselor was considerable, both in theory and practice. Moreover, it was the counselor, not the king, who could do more damage to the interests of the nobility. The king was a natural part of aristocratic society. Few nobles could aim to supplant the reigning dynasty, but many could aspire to a voice in the royal council. When the king fell under the influence of evil men—usually lowborn as well—the proper center of aristocratic political interest was breached. In the Germanic poems the figures of Hugdietrich and Ermanrich are well-known examples of rulers who have fallen under the influence of evil advisors.[38] On occasion, frequently in the *chansons de geste,* the bad advisors are relatives, often children, of the king.

The views of kingship, governance, and political order set forth in early medieval literature reflect the interest of individual noblemen rather than the more comprehensive views of ecclesiastical political writers. Anglo-Saxon, Irish, Scandinavian, and Germanic literatures, moreover, generally deal with the more remote reaches of Germanic history, the period of the invasions or earlier. In the French *chansons de geste,* however, the historical period is more nearly contemporary to that of the poet and his audience, and the lay view of kingship derives less from remote folklore, legend, and oral tradition than from written sources, contemporary attitudes, and recent experience.[39]

38. See now Joel T. Rosenthal, "The King's 'Wicked Advisors' and Medieval Baronial Rebellions," *Political Science Quarterly* 82 (1967): 595–618.

39. A general survey may be found in Grace Frank, "Historical Elements in the *Chansons de geste,*" *Speculum* 14 (1939): 209–14. Of particular use for the study of kingship in these poems have been the studies of A. Euler, *Das Königtum im altfranzösischen Karlsepos,* Ausgaben und Abh. aus der Gebiet der romanischen Philologie, Heft 65 (Marburg, 1886), and F. Werner, "Königtum und Lehenswesen im franzosischen Nationalepos," *Romanische Forschungen* 25 (1908): 321–443. Other studies of particular use have been those of J. Frappier, "Réflexions sur les rapports des chansons de geste et l'histoire," *ZfRPh* 73 (1957): 1–19,

Perhaps the most striking aspect of kingship in the *chansons de geste* is what Auerbach termed the royal paralysis in the face of the nobility's defiance or demands of honors.[40] Such inability as that of Charlemagne in the *Chanson de Roland* to determine a policy of his own making is reflected in the lack of influence which the king has in disputes between vassals and may help to account for the humorous or stupid figure which the emperor cuts in other works. In Germanic and Scandinavian literature the king is usually the greatest of the heroes. In the *chansons de geste,* however, he occupies a more limited sphere of activity. If, on the historical plane, such a ruler as Charlemagne occasionally reflects the highest ideals of Christian kingship and heroic values, he occupies a less powerful place on the immediate plane of action and characterization. The *chansons de geste* emphasize the human weakness of the king not as Malory and Shakespeare would, in order to exploit the irony of the contrast between the humanity and the public esteem and dignity of the ruler, but simply to bring the ruler down to a level at which he is powerless in the clash between aristocratic forces, upon which the action of the poems usually centers. The action in the *chansons de geste* is linked to the battlefield and the isolated, fortified castle rather than to the court and to the barons who oppose the king and each other, rarely to the king himself.[41]

In the French epics kings may be deposed for any of a number of reasons, very few of which correspond to what is known of contemporary historical practice and theory. The ruler may abdicate or be deposed because of old age, helplessness, or the failure of his vassals to answer his summons for aid. The crown is generally hereditary, often to the disadvantage of the kingdom, since unworthy sons often seem to succeed worthy fathers. In contrast to later royal

---

and R. R. Bezzola, *Les Origines et la formation de la littérature courtoise en occident (500–1200),* BEHE, fascs. 286, 313, 319 (Paris, 1944–60), See also the long review article by A. Viscardi, "Le Origini della letteratura cortese," *ZfRPh* 78 (1962): 269–91.

40. *Mimesis* (New York, 1953), p. 156.

41. A brief summary of references to weak kings in the *chansons de geste* is found in Werner, "Königtum und Lenehwesen," pp. 325, 366–67.

practice, fiefs descend to the most able, not the eldest, son.[42] The principle of suitability appears to operate more successfully within the ranks of the nobility than within ruling dynasties. The power of the king, at least in theory, is considerable. Royal power usually appears at its greatest, however, when the king uses it to disinherit a worthy heir or to deprive a baron of something that is rightly his, rarely when the administration of the kingdom is in question. Even the figure of the king on Crusade was not without its darker side. The fate of the historical Louis VII and the Emperor Conrad revealed the practical problems of royal weakness which the Crusade spirit could not overcome. In the *Heimskringla* the two kings Eystein and Sigurd argue their respective greatness: Sigurd calls Eystein sluggish and cowardly, while Eystein retorts that a king who stays at home to protect his kingdom and subjects is more useful than one who abandons his duties to go on a Crusade.[43]

Kings in the *chansons de geste* appear to acquire wicked advisors more easily than do their counterparts in Germanic literature. In *Li Romans de Garin de Loherain* Pepin's wicked counselors are characterized: "N'ot si felons en soisante pais."[44] These rulers, whose names are those of the historical last Carolingian kings of the ninth and tenth centuries, seem to exist only in order to harass, or to be harassed by, their powerful subjects. Even Charlemagne sometimes becomes a fool or a senile and greedy old ruler. Those *chansons* which turn upon political themes—usually succession to the throne—generally contain some statement of ideal kingship in order to provide a contrast with the usual actions of the old king or the heir. In the *Couronnement de Louis,* for example, the opening lines express such an ideal:

> Reis qui de France porte corone d'or
> Prodom deit estre et vaillanz de son cors;

42. E.g. in *Renaut de Montauban.* See J. Flach, "Le Compagnonnage dans les chansons de geste," in *Etudes romanes dédiées à Gaston Paris* (Paris, 1891), pp. 153–54.

43. P. 300. The problem is not unusual. See the text from St. Anselm cited by Southern in *The Making of the Middle Ages,* p. 50.

44. Ed. P. Paris (Paris, 1833), line 811. Cf. lines 805–87.

Et s'il est om qui li face nul tort,
Ne deit guarir ne a plain ne a bos,
De ci qu'il l'ait o recreant o mort:
S'einsi nel fait, dont pert France son los;
Ce dist l'estoire: coronez est a tort.[45]

The barons, who prefer a weak king to a stranger, accept Louis and thank God "Qu'estranges reis n'est sur nos devalez."

Charles then delivers a sermon to Louis on the duties of a king and tells him to take the crown if he can fulfill those duties, and to refuse if he cannot. Louis, quaking with fear, accepts the crown but arouses his father's scorn and later proves to be indeed unworthy of rule. In *Huon de Bordeaux,* in a similar scene, Charles insists upon crowning his son Charlot, even though the barons, rather than accept the worthless youth as king, offer to administer the kingdom while Charles himself retains the royal dignity:

Nous vous aidrons vo terre a justicier,
Et se vous faites servir et aaissier;
Nous garderons vos pais et vos fies.[46]

Charles refuses the offer—which seems to have been made in good public faith by the barons, since Naimes, the type of the perfect advisor, had made it—and insists that Charlot rule alone. He tells his son:

Si m'ait Dix, tu tenras si franc fief
Comme Damedix, qui tot puet justicier,
Tient Paradis le regne droiturier.[47]

Charles eventually forces his son on the unwilling barons, but the prince is soon killed and the story takes up other themes.

Louis the Pious, the type of the *rex inutilis* in the *chansons de geste,* is frequently associated with William of Orange, the type of the noble hero. William possesses the *sapientia* and *fortitudo* that

45. Ed. E. Langlois, SATF (Paris, 1888), lines 20–26.

46. Ed. F. Guessard and C. Grandmaison, *Anciens poètes de La France* (Paris, 1860), lines 66–70.

47. Ibid, lines 101–03.

Louis lacks.[48] To heighten William's worth, Louis is frequently portrayed as ungrateful, vacillating, tyrannical, and totally helpless. In the chaotic world of these later *chansons* the individual hero often had to force his own law even against the king himself. The king frequently serves to reflect in his own person the disintegration of social and political order. And the individual hero becomes a destructive law unto himself as the bonds of society disintegrate about him.[49]

During the later twelfth century the representation of kingship in literature, as well as in political theory and law, underwent several striking changes. Among literary genres the heroic epics and the *chansons de geste* slowly gave way to the courtly romance. Literature reflected changes that took place on other levels of society as well. In the third quarter of the twelfth century a new period of historical interest joined the Carolingian background of the *chansons de geste,* the Burgundian background of the Germanic epics, and the antique background of the *romans* of Alexander, Troy, and Thebes. The new theme—the matter of Britain, as it was called—included the history of fifth- and sixth-century Britain and centered on Arthur and his role as temporary mainstay of the crumbling British culture of the period.[50] The matter of Britain did not, of course, completely drive out earlier literary techniques and interests. In the early Arthurian romances the king is still a periph-

48. See W. Goecke, *Die historischen Beziehungen in der Geste von Guillaume d'Orenge* (Halle, 1900). The most dramatic of these encounters occurs in the *Moniage Guillaume,* ed. W. Cloetta, SATF (Paris, 1906–11).

49. See R. R. Bezzola, "De Roland à Raoul de Cambrai," in *Mélanges Hoepffner* (Paris, 1949), pp. 195–213 (rep. in his *Les Origines de la littérature courtoise,* pt. II, vol. 2, BEHE, fasc. 313 [Paris, 1960], pp. 495–517). This is the best study of the social and political disintegration in the world of the later *chansons de geste.*

50. For the whole period, see Bezzola, *Les Origines.* On Britain, see P. Pickard, *Britain in Early French Literature* (Cambridge, 1956). Good recent studies are collected in R. S. Loomis, ed., *Arthurian Literature in the Middle Ages* (Oxford, 1959); R. S. Loomis, "The Arthurian Legend before 1139," in his *Wales and the Arthurian Legend* (Cardiff, 1956), pp. 179–220; Bezzola, *Les Origines,* pt. II, 2:527–48.

eral figure, as he had been in the *chansons de geste*.[51] A second theme retained from earlier literature is that of the fall of a race or the destruction of a people.[52] The political scope of the early romances is not great, but the structure of the society that one may glimpse through the narrative is considerably different from that of the later *chansons de geste.*

Writers who took up the new materials in the late twelfth century are perhaps best known for their exploration of human psychology in terms of chivalry and courtly love. They also tended to include theological themes in tales that ostensibly dealt with heroic adventure. They shifted the scenes of action from the isolated castle and the battlefield to the court and the forest of the romance world. Heroic action no longer received its praise from the grim world of anarchy, treachery, injustice and cruelty, which characterized the later *chansons de geste,* but from the reconciliation of the hero to the world of the court, which heightened, ordered, and gave meaning to the adventures experienced outside it. Finally, the matter of Britain was subjected most to the inclination on the part of thirteenth-century writers to integrate into a single narrative many themes and characters. These narratives became the prose-cycles of Lancelot, the Grail, and Tristan first, and later of Arthur himself and the theme of "the rise, flowering, and decay of an almost perfect civilization."

The most important single channel through which Arthurian material came into the hands of French poets was Geoffrey of Monmouth's *Historia Regum Brittaniae*.[53] Geoffrey's history de-

51. On the relationship between the figures of Arthur in the early romances and Charlemagne in the *chansons de geste,* see Erich Köhler, *Ideal und Wirklichkeit in der höfischen Epik,* Beiheft zur ZfRPh, Heft 97 (Tubingen, 1956), pp. 5–7; J. S. P. Tatlock, *The Legendary History of Britain* (Berkeley and Los Angeles, 1950), pp. 311–20.

52. For the theme in English historiography, see the brilliant study of Robert W. Hanning, *The Vision of History in Early Britain* (New York, 1966).

53. Text in E. Faral, *La Légende arthurienne* (Paris, 1929), 3:64–305; A. Griscom, *The Historia Regum Britanniae of Geoffrey of Monmouth* (New York, 1929). The most comprehensive study is that of Tatlock, *The Legendary History of Britain.* See the more recent comments of J. J. Parry

scribed in part the rise, decline, and temporary revival of British culture in the fifth and sixth centuries. Geoffrey's chief sources—Bede, Gildas, and Nennius—all discuss the decline of the Britons, sometimes with considerable vehemence. The uselessness of the Britons, for instance, was often linked to the degeneracy of some of their rulers. Perhaps the most striking of these is the infamous Vortigern, but other rulers often display an inclination for tyranny, drunkenness, lust, greed, and sodomy. In his depiction of Vortigern, Geoffrey used the motifs described above: the linking of a weak king with a strong and wicked queen, on the one hand, and with evil counselors, on the other. Indeed, the themes of sexual passion, bad counsel, and religious unorthodoxy in their relation to the *rex inutilis* are particularly noticeable in chroniclers' treatment of the theme of the fall of Britain.

Geoffrey's influence was not restricted to the writers of Arthurian romances. Subsequent legal and historiographical fashion were indebted to his work as well. His immediate influence, in fact, resulted in two translations of his Latin work into French by Wace and into English by Layamon. Both new versions altered and expanded their original.[54] Both, however, retained and elaborated

---

and R. A. Caldwell, "Geoffrey of Monmouth," in *ALMA,* pp. 71–93; Hanning, *The Vision of History in Early Britain,* pp. 121–72. On Geoffrey's later influence, see, e.g., Laura Keeler, *Geoffrey of Monmouth and the Late Latin Chroniclers, 1300–1500* (Berkeley and Los Angeles, 1946), and W. Ullmann, "On the Influence of Geoffrey of Monmouth in English History," in *Speculum Universale,* ed. C. Bauer et. al. (Munich, 1965), pp. 257–76.

54. Wace's *Brut,* ed. Ivor Arnold, *Le Roman de Brut,* 2 vols., SATF (Paris, 1938–40). See also Tatlock, pp. 463–82; Margaret Houck, *Sources of the Roman de Brut of Wace,* University of California Publications in English, vol. 5, no. 2 (Berkeley and Los Angeles, 1941); Charles Foulon, "Wace," in *ALMA,* pp. 94–103. The standard text of Layamon is that of F. Madden, but there is a new edition in preparation by G. L. Brooke and R. F. Leslie. Vol. 1, containing vv. 1–8020, has already appeared (EETS, Oxford, 1963). See also R. S. Loomis, "Layamon's Brut," in *ALMA,* pp. 104–11; Tatlock, pp. 483–533: Of particular interest are the recent studies of C. S. Lewis, "The Genesis of a Medieval Book," in his *Studies in Medieval and Renaissance Literature* (Cambridge, 1966) pp. 18–40, and Marie-Claude Blanchet, "Le Double Visage d'Arthur chez Layamon," in *Studi in onore di Italo Siciliano* (Florence, 1966), 1:71–84.

upon the themes of the weak kings of the Britons and the decline of the Britons as a people. Finally, both followed Geoffrey in giving a high place to Arthur. The twelfth-century vogue of legendary history provided a great impetus to poets as well as historians. To a certain extent the work of Geoffrey, Wace, and Layamon forms a prelude not to the romance of Chrétien but to the great historical prose cycles which began to appear in the first quarter of the thirteenth century. Although the figure of Arthur in these later romances is often that of a true *rex inutilis,* the Arthur of Geoffrey, Wace, and Layamon is a paragon of twelfth-century theories of kingship.

Arthur's reign marks for Geoffery the revival of the weak and degenerate insular Britons to the plane of their former glory. Whether or not Geoffrey alone was responsible for Arthur's twelfth-century reputation and his strong attraction for French poets need not be of concern here.[55] The greater adulation of that ruler in the works of Wace and Layamon, particularly that of Layamon, suggests that whatever works about Arthur were extant before and after Geoffrey, the *Historia* gave a high degree of uniformity to other fragmentary accounts and provided the historical background for later works.

Geoffrey's translators performed two invaluable services for the matter of Britain. They turned the Latin prose *Historia* into verse (in the case of Wace, in fact, into the standard octosyllabic French verse of the *chansons de geste* and the later romances of Chrétien), and they expanded Geoffrey's portrait of the great ruler who brought order out of the chaos of early Britain. In adapting Geoffrey's work to the vernacular idiom Wace and Layamon contributed to the contemporary atmosphere which was to be so noticeable in the later *romans courtois.* They also continued to transform sixth-

55. See Köhler, *Ideal und Wirklichkeit,* pp. 5–36; Karl Heinz Goller, *König Arthur in der englischen Literatur des späten Mittelalters,* Palaestra, Bd. 238 (Gottingen, 1963); R. W. Barber, *Arthur of Albion: An Introduction to the Arthurian Literature and Legends of England* (London, 1961); Charles Williams, "The Figure of Arthur," in C. S. Lewis, ed., *Arthurian Torso* (London, 1948), pp. 5–90.

century Britain into a replica of twelfth-century Anglo-Norman society and to change the figure of Arthur into that of a late twelfth-century Anglo-Norman ruler, They portrayed Arthur's greatness, to be sure, but in giving that ruler the traits of a contemporary king they drew a figure which could be easily adapted to the more restricted and ambiguous political confines of the later *romans.*

One instance of Arthur's position in this respect occurs in an episode, treated by all three writers, in which the general character of Arthur's rule becomes the subject of extensive comment. After Arthur has pacified Britain and firmly established himself as king, the Roman Emperor Lucius sends emissaries to Arthur demanding tribute. Cador, Duke of Cornwall, makes a brief speech on the subject of British sloth and effeminacy, and he is pleased that the Roman challenge may awake his fellow warriors from the pleasures of soft peace:

> Until now I have feared that the *otium* which the Britons have had during this long time of peace might make them *ignavos* and lose them their knightly fame in which they surpass other peoples. Indeed, when the practice of arms ceases and there is nothing but dicing and the pursuit of women and other meaningless activities, there is no doubt that *ignavia* will stain everything pertaining to virtue, honor, bravery, and renown. Five years have passed, during which we have given ourselves up to these vices, lacking the work of Mars. God, to free us from our *segnitia,* has inspired the Romans in this manner in order to restore our character to its original state *(ut ad pristinum statum nostram probitatem reducerent).*[56]

56. *Historia,* IX, 15 (ed. Griscom, p. 461). This passage has been discussed on several occasions by W. A. Nitze. See his *Lancelot and Guenevere, with T. P. Cross* (Chicago, 1930), pp. 83–87, in which Nitze examines these remarks in the light of Ovidian and Vergilian concepts of sloth and lethargy in love and in terms of the courtly reply which Wace *(Brut,* vv. 11044ff.) attributes to Gawain (see Nitze, "The Character of Gauvain in the Romances of Chrétien de Troyes," *Modern Philology* 50 (1952/53): 219–25). See also Nitze et. al., eds., *Le Haut Livre du Graal Perlesvaus* (Chicago, 1937), 2:202–03. The tradition of sloth in love, how-

Cador accuses not Arthur alone but all of the British warriors, and he implies that the warrior-virtues cannot survive in a world of peace. *Probitas* is constantly subject to the *segnitia* of degeneracy. Cador's speech presents the lay view of royal inadequacy only slightly changed by the historian's conventional rhetoric and only lightly touched by the ecclesiastical categories of royal inadequacy discussed in the first sections of this chapter. The warrior aristocracy of the *Historia,* like that of Germanic heroic literature, saw royal virtue from a military point of view. Although only five years had passed between Arthur's heroic pacification of Britain and the challenge of Lucius, Cador was aware of the difficulties that peace imposed upon an aristocracy and a king ill-equipped to live in the world Arthur had created.

Cador's speech is expanded by Wace and Layamon. In both instances the poets place emphasis upon the rhetorical exposition of the vices of peacetime, although both poets add a rebuttal by Gawain describing the virtues of peace. In Wace, Cador's speech and Gawain's response have the atmosphere of a courtly debate. In Layamon, on the other hand, the exchange takes on a darker and more ominous air, as if the English poet were unable to place such a discussion in the sophisticated setting given it by Wace, as if the issues at hand were too close to the life that Layamon knew for him to treat them lightly. Such elements as this, which becomes literally a *flyting* in Wace, Layamon, and the Vulgate *Merlin,* constituted the seeds for later Arthurian themes. Other sources, too, contributed elements that would serve to darken the picture of Arthur's reign given by Geoffrey. The Breton *lais,* for example, give the

---

ever, appears to have been largely independent of the theme of sloth attributed to the *rex inutilis.* See M. B. Ogle, "The Sloth of Erec," *Romanic Review* 9 (1918): 1–20, with a large collection of classical parallels. If the purely literary tradition of formalized sloth in love did not influence the concept of sloth in medieval psychology directly, such well-known instances as Aeneas's sloth in *Aeneid* IV, lines 256–76, 560–70, may well have illuminated both traditions. For Arthur's many political errors committed while in evil or misguided love, see below, chap. 5.

king a peripheral position.[57] The hagiographical sources dealing with Arthur often depict the king either as a tyrant who oppresses the saint or as a fool whom the saint puts to shame.[58] Finally, the general concern of poets with sexual passion, which was only partly expressed in the themes of courtly love, was to subject the figure of Arthur to treatments other than the purely heroic.

A continuing influence of the political atmosphere of the *chansons de geste* persisted in the *romans courtois.* Their central heroes were to remain for a long time individual knights serving shadowy kings whose peripheral character in the *chansons de geste* and in the earliest *romans courtois* was to retard to development of political themes in the newer genre. The ambiguous character of kingship in the legendary histories, in the *lais,* in hagiography, and in the earliest romances thus constituted a rich store for later writers. The weakness of contemporary real kings may have sharpened the criticism found in the early literary works. The nobility's realization of its own power and its own place in the changing political world of the late twelfth century, however, was to be expressed in far more subtle ways than that of indirect invective against contemporary monarchs. To be sure, such rulers as Robert, Philip I, Louis VI, and Stephen had their bad press. Yet it is doubtful that any considerable part of this press was to be found thinly disguised as fiction in the *chansons de geste* and the early romances.[59]

57. For the lais, see Horst Baader, *Die Lais. Zur Geschichte einer Gattung der altfranzösischen Kurzerzählungen,* Analecta Romanica, Heft 16 (Frankfurt a. M., 1966); E. Hoepffner, "The Breton Lais," in *ALMA,* pp. 112–21; Bezzola, *Les Origines,* pt. III, 1:269–312.

58. C. Grant Loomis, "King Arthur and the Saints," *Speculum* 8 (1933); Tatlock, pp. 179–80. For a possible historical parallel, see J. C. Russell, "The Canonization of Opposition to the King in Angevin England," *Haskins Anniversary Essays* (New York, 1929), pp. 279–90.

59. The figure of the *rex inutilis* in the courtly romances is discussed below, chap. 5. The role of the *chansons de geste* and the early romances as thinly disguised political propaganda is rarely as direct as Bezzola, for example, often suggests. See E. Köhler, "La Rôle de la "Coutume" dans les romans de Chrétien de Troyes," *Romania* 81 (1960): 386–97 (reprinted as "Die Rolle der 'Rechtsbrauch' [costume] in den Romanen des Chrestien von Troyes," in his *Trobadorlyrik und höfischer Roman* [Berlin, 1962], pp. 205–12).

The catalogues of vices and virtues, the conventional language of letters and documents, heroic literature, and legendary histories are some of the sources that influenced political terminology and contributed points of view from which royal inadequacy might be considered. Moral theology began to account for mental, as well as spiritual, states from the ninth century on, and its constant linking of such vices as *luxuria, tristitia,* and *acedia* with the chroniclers' themes of sexual passion, military inaction, and political lethargy gave a psychological dimension to political rhetoric such as that used by William of Malmesbury in the citation at the beginning of this chapter. The conventional protestations of inadequacy in private and public documents recognized honorific and pejorative aspects of that state, some of which were to reappear in later discussions of the *rex inutilis.* Other sources contributed more strictly lay views on the subject. This complex background to the topic of royal inadequacy accounts for some of the recurring themes that chroniclers and publicists continually associated with the figure of the *rex inutilis* before the thirteenth century.

The most important developments in medieval constitutionalism took place, however, not in historiography or literature but in practical political activity and in changes in the law. Other areas of thought were to add complexity and new points of view to theories of the *rex inutilis,* but the major discussion of the problem was to be undertaken by the canon lawyers of the late twelfth and early thirteenth-centuries.

3

Rex Inutilis and the Canon Lawyers, 1140–1243

The increased complexity and extent of royal government, the ideas of chroniclers, poets, and political theorists, and the growth of scientific jurisprudence enhanced the office of king in the twelfth and thirteenth centuries and began to surround it with some of the secular mystique that would grow into the *arcana imperii,* or "mysteries of state," of the fifteenth, sixteenth, and seventeenth centuries.[1] Within the scope of the changes from feudal monarchies to corporate states the figure of the king began to personify in part the concepts of public welfare and public law. Another area of thought, however, also contributed much to this development, although it did not set out to describe a specific theory of kingship or to deal in any comprehensive manner with purely secular problems. This was the large body of ecclesiastical jurisprudence, political theory, and juristic theology contained in the texts and commentaries of the canon law.

Under the influence of Gregory VII and his powerful successors canon law came to be something of a constitution of Christendom which dealt at great length not specifically with problems of *regnum* and *sacerdotium* but with the organization and structure of the *respublica christiana* at whose head was the pope.[2] The canonists thus approached kingship from several different points

1. A good study is that of E. Kantorowicz, "Mysteries of State: An Absolutist Concept and Its Late Medieval Origins," *Harvard Theological Review* 48 (1955): 65–91.

2. Brief reference may be made to two general studies dealing with the role of canon law in medieval society: A. M. Stickler, "Die Bedeutung der klassischen Kanonistik fur die Geschichtswissenschaft des Mittelalters," in

of view. Since the canon law was concerned primarily with the structure of the church, many decretists came to consider secular offices in terms of ecclesiastical offices and found parallels between ecclesiology and the administrative structure of territorial monarchies and the Empire. Some developed theories of monarchy out of their concern to define papal authority to intervene in secular affairs. Finally, some formulated a theory of kingship in analyzing the relation between the canon and Roman laws. Although the last two of these contributed much to the development of political thought, the first provides the best approach to the canonists' treatment of the *rex inutilis*. In the late thirteenth, fourteenth, and fifteenth centuries constitutionalist theories of resistance to the ruler borrowed much more from the canonists' analysis of kingship as an office than from the spectacular instances of papal depositions of temporal rulers or from the pattern of kingship found in the *Corpus iuris civilis*. The moral authority of the canon law was none the less legally complex for being moral. The canonists' approach to questions involving temporal authority was determined by their approach to purely ecclesiastical problems; that is, it derived from studies in the law, not from political theory. Because of its complex legal basis, canonist thought pervaded secular political theory in a form far different from that in which it had originally evolved.

Since the pontificate of Gregory VII the papal power of deposing temporal rulers had remained one of the most pressing questions in the relations between *sacerdotium* and *imperium*. Gregory himself, not only in the case of Henry IV but in his references to other deposition proceedings, had made the issue critical in the publicistic and canonical literature of the late eleventh and early twelfth centuries.[3] Although Gregory's contribution of texts to

---

Resumés des Communications, XIe Congrès International des Sciences Historiques, Stockholm, 1960 (Uppsala, 1960), pp. 98–100; Brian Tierney, "Medieval Canon Law and Western Constitutionalism," *CHR* 52 (1966): 1–17. A brief recent survey of canonistic studies may be found in Robert L. Benson, *The Bishop-Elect* (Princeton, 1968), pp. 10–22, 387–90.

3. Mirbt, *Die Publizistik im Zeitalters Gregors VII*, pp. 238–458; Ullmann, *The Growth of Papal Government*, pp. 262–310; Arquillière, *Saint Grégoire VII*, pp. 201–88.

Gratian's *Decretum* was not large, he did contribute one text which was for a long time to be the basis for canonists' discussions of the relations between the two powers. That text was *Alius item,* Gregory's citation of the case of Childeric III and Pepin in his letter to Hermann of Metz in 1081.[4] *Alius item,* as noted above, was included in several canonical collections of the late eleventh century. Gratian appears to have taken his version of the text (which he falsely attributed to Pope Gelasius I) from the *Panormia* of Ivo of Chartres.[5]

In including *Alius item* in the *Decretum,* however, Gratian does not appear to have been seeking particular texts illustrating the papal power of deposing evil or incompetent rulers. The text occurs in the second part of the *Decretum* as the third chapter of the sixth *quaestio* of the fifteenth *Causa.* The *Causae* were elaborate statements of hypothetical cases, each usually involving several points of law. These points were summarized by Gratian in the concluding lines of each *Causa* and became the *quaestiones* into which the *Causa* was subdivided. Each *quaestio* was then further subdivided into chapters which consisted of the texts proper as well

4. The text is C.15 q.6 c.3 *Alius item,* hereafter cited by opening words only. Ivo of Chartres, *Panormia,* V, 109, is in PL 161. 1235. Ivo used the section of the letter of 1081 which also contained Gregory's citation of the famous letter of Pope Gelasius I to the Emperor Anastasius, a text which Gratian included elsewhere in the *Decretum* as D.96 c.10 *Duo sunt.* Gratian attributed both texts to Gelasius. He was not, however, the last to do so. Hotman's *Franco-gallia* makes the same error of attribution four centuries later. The principles of interpretation of canonists' texts are laid down in A. M. Stickler, "Sacerdotium et regnum nei decretisti e primi decretalisti. Considerazione metodologiche di ricerca e testi," *Salesianum* 15 (1957): 575–612. The best general description of the canonist literature is that of A. Van Hove, *Commentaria Lovaniense in Codicem Iuris Canonici, Prolegomena* (Malines-Rome, 1945). The sources are surveyed in A. M. Stickler, *Historia iuris canonici: Institutiones academicae, I: Historia fontium* (Turin, 1950). The work of the decretists is catalogued in S. Kuttner, *Repertorium der Kanonistik (1140–1234); Prodromus corporis glossatorum,* Studi e Testi 71 (Vatican City, 1937; new ed. in preparation).

5. *PL* 161: 1235.

as Gratian's own *dicta* preceding and following the chapters.[6] The arrangement allowed Gratian to present a complicated legal issue, then to analyze its most important aspects, and finally to arrive at the "law" by citing ecclesiastical authorities through a careful process of selection and directed analysis.

The fifteenth *Causa* presents the case of a cleric who has committed a crime while of unsound mind. Other aspects of the case allow Gratian to raise such questions for discussion as whether or not crimes may be imputed to those of unsound mind, whether clerics may be condemned on the basis of a woman's confession, and whether a bishop may condemn a cleric without a synodal hearing. The sixth *quaestio* deals with the problem of forced confessions and their validity, a topic illustrated in a straightforward manner by the first chapter, whose rubric says, *Ministrorum confessio non sit extorta, sed spontanea.* The second chapter, however, moves from confessions to oaths and deals with the validity of false oaths and the papal power to absolve oath-takers from obligations they have been forced to take. The third chapter, *Alius item,* then deals exclusively with the papal authority to absolve from oaths. Within the broad limits of a case involving the means of trying a cleric, Gratian is able to discuss the wider question of oaths and the extent of papal power to dispense men from their consequences under certain conditions. The nature of the general heading under which *Alius item* found its place in the *Decretum* should explain both the wide range of topics that it served to illustrate in early decretist scholarship and the canonists' initial reluctance to use it as a basis for elaborate political theory.

Like other political texts in the *Decretum, Alius item* furnished the canonists with opportunities for the discussion of points of law, not all of which were directly concerned with relations between *sacerdotium* and *regnum.* Some canonists, for example, considered the text as simply a convenient point at which to discuss the dif-

6. Hence the standard abbreviations: C., q., c., D. The *dicta* of Gratian preceding and following some of the texts cited below are abbreviated respectively as d.g.a. and d.g.p.

ferences between oaths to *dignitates,* or offices, and oaths to individuals.[7] Those who considered the direct political aspects of the text often dealt with restricted aspects, such as the deposing authority exclusively—the question of whether pope or magnates really depose an unsuitable ruler.[8] Some dealt chiefly with the nature of the offense of Childeric and the penalty involved—whether incorrigible uselessness was to be considered the legal equivalent of tyranny and therefore to be punished by deposition, or whether it was a different offense entirely and merited a different treatment. Others added to these considerations such topics as defense of the *patria,* the individual moral character of rulers, and the parallel problems of royal and prelatal uselessness. Thus a brief text such as *Alius item* might serve as the starting point for many legal problems, not all of which shed light upon the figure of the *rex inutilis.*

In regard to the deposing authority, the earliest decretists generally upheld Gregory VII's view that a useless ruler should be deposed by the pope alone.[9] Others later revived, whether con-

7. E.g. Rufinus, *Summa Decretorum,* ed. H. Singer (Paderborn, 1902; rep. 1963), *ad* 15.6.3: "Hic sciendum est quod iuramentum fidelitatis fiunt aliquando intuitu personarum, aliquando dumtaxat intuitu dignitatum." Stephen of Tournai, Simon of Bisignano, Johannes Faventinus, and Huguccio of Pisa are among those who dealt with this aspect of the text. Individual studies of these canonists may be found in the *Dictionnaire de droit canonique,* 7 vols. (Paris, 1935–65).

8. See J. Juncker, "Die Summa des Simon von Bisignano und seine Glossen," *ZfRG,* K.A. 15 (1926): 326–500. Simon's gloss *(ad* 15.6.3 *ad v. deposuit)* reads: "Id est deponentibus consensit, vel subditos ab eius fidelitate absolvit, quod per cônsequentium fuit eum deponere." A fuller discussion of twelfth- and thirteenth-century canonist deposition theory is contained in the studies of J. A. Watt, O. Hageneder, and S. Mochi Onory.

9. The views of early decretists are discussed by S. Kuttner, "Bernardus Compostellanus Antiquus: A Study in the Glossators of the Canon Law," *Traditio* 1 (1943): esp. 279–92. See also S. Mochi Onory, *Le Fonte canonistiche dell' idea moderna dello stato* (Milan, 1951), and the numerous studies of A. M. Stickler. A survey of recent work to 1954 is B. Tierney, "Some Recent Works on the Political Theory of the Medieval Canonists," *Traditio* 10 (1954): 594–625. A bibliography of currrent work is printed in the annual "Bulletin of the Institute of Medieval Canon Law" in *Traditio.*

sciously or not, the older Carolingian idea of deposition by local magnates, clerical and lay, and approval alone by the pope. In spite of the political changes during the classical period of the canon law (1140–1340), these opposing views were maintained throughout later canonist discussions. In regard to the question of the *rex inutilis* there occurred still another instance of divided canonist opinion. Some canonists argued for the "Gregorian" solution that the *rex inutilis* should be deposed. Others, however, beginning with Huguccio of Pisa, maintained that uselessness was not the equivalent of tyranny and should not be punished by deposition.[10] To be sure, Huguccio admitted that Childeric had been *inutilis* and had been deposed, but chiefly by interpreting the text of *Alius item* in such a way that Childeric's uselessness became, in effect, an *iniquitas*. As Johannes Teutonicus, a later writer following Huguccio, put it, Childeric had been: "Non inutilis id est insufficiens, sed dissolutus . . . cum mulieribus et effeminatus."[11] Huguc-

10. For Huguccio, see G. Catalano, "Impero, regni e sacerdozio nel pensiero di Uguccio di Pisa," *Rivista di Storia del Diritto Italiano* 30 (1957): 93–139; A. M. Stickler, "Das Schwerterbegriff bei Huguccio," *Ephemerides Iuris Canonici* 3 (1947): 201–42: Stickler, "Sacerdotium et Regnum." Huguccio, while very influential, was not followed by all succeeding canonists. The legislation of Innocent III created a category of criminal negligence into which might be placed all princes who did not extirpate heresy, support ecclesiastical legal processes, or otherwise seem "useful" to the pope and the curia. Hence later glosses often used the Gregorian deposition thesis in connection with the pronouncements of Innocent III, as is the case in the *Summa* of Henricus Merseburgensis (Yale Law Library, MS no. 1, fol. 81^v; I am grateful to Dr. Peter Landau of the University of Regensburg for this reference): "Item notandum quandocumque aliquis secularis princeps fuerit inutilis dissolutus et negligens in heresi extirpanda, vel alia iustitia observanda non solum potest ab ecclesia excommunicari set etiam deponi, unde Zacharias papa deposuit Ludovicum [sic] regem francorum et praedecessorum pippini patris Karoli." The garbled version of the story should be noted. It was not uncommon. One source for the error as well as for the general thesis, may have been Tancred See Gaines Post, "Some Unpublished Glosses (ca.1210–1214) on the *Translatio imperii* and the Two Swords," *Archiv für katholisches Kirchenrecht* 117 (1937): 408–09.

11. Numerous editions of Gratian's *Decretum* have been used in the preparation of this study, all of which include the ordinary gloss of Johannes

cio's implication that there existed two kinds of *inutilitas,* of which one should be punished by deposition and one not, was the basis of many later canonist discussions of the problem and the result of earlier canonist thought on problems of ecclesiastical office. This earlier thought is to be found not only in glosses to *Alius item* but in glosses to many other texts in the *Decretum,* in *Notabilia, Casus, Quaestiones,* and *Summae:* all the literary forms which the canonists used during the late twelfth and early thirteenth centuries.

Huguccio's distinction between, as it were, two distinct kinds of royal *inutilitas,* of which one meant that the ruler was *insufficiens* and the other that he was *dissolutus* or *effeminatus,* was the result of his familiarity with the canon law concerning useless prelates and his recognition of the fact that the case of Childeric did not entirely fit the pattern which that law provided. On the one hand, the text made it perfectly clear that Zacharias had deposed Childeric because the king had been *inutilis.* On the other, Huguccio knew that prelates who were *inutiles* were definitely not to be deposed but to be given a coadjutor, as indicated by a number of texts in the first *quaestio* of *Causa* VII.[12] Like many other canonists, Huguccio considered temporal rulers as, in a sense, "equiparated" with higher prelates, not so much on theological as on juridical grounds. Indeed, the formula *prelatus vel princeps* became a canonist commonplace which arose, one may suspect, not from the ecclesiological disputes of the eleventh and twelfth centuries but from the lawyers' habit of finding analogies between all ranks of human society whose diversity had to be accommodated to the universality of the canon law. Although Huguccio's interpretation of *Alius item* hardly squared with the intentions of Gregory VII or, for that matter, of Zacharias, his approach to the problem of royal *inutilitas* reflects the scientific and encyclopedic character of twelfth-century canonical jurisprudence.

Teutonicus, from which this passage comes. Citations to this gloss will be to the part of the *Decretum,* not to pages of particular editions.

12. Other locations are C.7 q.i c1 *Scripsit;* C.7 q.1 c.4 *Pontifices;* C.7 q.1 c.6 *Sicut.* The best recent study on the medieval episcopate is that of Benson, *The Bishop-Elect.* See esp. pp. 346–63, 23–89.

Childeric, Huguccio notes, lived dissolutely, was effeminate, and neglected his duties. Charles, the father of Pepin, observed this and made it known to the pope, who in turn gave his permission that Childeric should be deposed and someone else elected in his place. Huguccio further notes that Childeric was not simply inadequate to administer the kingdom, in which case he would have had to be given a coadjutor, but because he "effeminatu et otio torpens cum mulieribus dissolute vivebat"[13]—an interpretation that inspired the neat perplexing distinction of Johannes Teutonicus mentioned above. Post has noted, "we must not worry about the historical accuracy of this version of the story."[14] In fact, of course, Charles Martel had nothing to do with the deposition of Childeric, and the canonists' scornful remarks about Childeric's dissolute life contrast sharply with Einhard's portrait of the *rex rusticus*.

The source for Huguccio's version of the Childeric deposition may have been Stephen of Tournai, who appears to have been the earliest canonist to state that Childeric was anything worse than the ineffective ruler described by the Carolingian chroniclers and later historians of the period.[15] Stephen's source for this version of Childeric's uselessness is obscure, since most eleventh- and twelfth-century histories do not depart from the judgment of Einhard to

13. Huguccio, *Summa ad* 15.6.3 *ad v. in istum.* (cited here from Mochi Onory, *Le Fonte canonistiche*, pp. 156f.): "Nota papa sententia non intulit, set de eius consensu et voluntate fuit depositus et electus, ut enim legitur in ystoria francorum, iste rex effeminatu et otio torpens cum mulieribus dissolute vivebat, quod videns quidam princeps militiae eius, id est carolus, pater pippini, pape totum significavit, et tunc dedit ei et aliis licentiam ut illum eiecerent et alium eligerent; quo eiecto alium silicet Pippinum filium Caroli, qui postea fuit pater Magni Caroli, regem fecerunt."

14. *Studies in Medieval Legal Thought*, p. 439.

15. Ibid., pp. 438–40. No contemporary sources suggest that Childeric had been guilty of these offenses. A twelfth-century standard version appears to be that of Godfrey of Viterbo, *Pantheon*, in *PL* 198.923–25. Stephen's remarks are printed in J. F. von Schulte, *Die Summa des Stephanus Tornacensis* (Giessen, 1891), pp. 221–22. The question of Stephen's source remains unsolved, since he too speaks of an "ystoria Francorum." I have suggested one possible source in *Studia Gratiana* 14 (1968): p. 286, n. 94.

any significant degree. Stephen's version, such as it was, accounted in Huguccio's eyes for the deposition of Childeric. By virtually ignoring the syntactic opposition in Gregory's statement: "Non tam pro suis iniquitatibus quam pro eo, quod . . . non erat utilis," Huguccio explained the deposition as the result of acts on Childeric's part which indeed strongly resembled, if they were not precisely called, *iniquitates*. Having disposed of the deposition itself, however, Huguccio had some observations to make concerning the other meaning of *inutilis*—that is, *insufficiens*. In his *Summa* he says: "His duabus de causis depositus fuit, unde non est questio quare illi non datus fuit coadiutor tunc enim illud locum habet cum quis innocens invenitur insufficiens administrationi, ut VII q.1 Quamvis, petisti, quia et VIII q.1 Si Petrus."[16] Huguccio here cites other canon law texts to support his thesis that a king who is not adequate to administer his kingdom should not be deposed but ought to be given a coadjutor. All these texts concern, however, incapacitated or inept prelates, not temporal rulers. Huguccio's bringing these texts to bear on theories of royal inadequacy constitutes the single most influential canonist contribution to medieval theories of the *rex inutilis*. The highly developed ecclesiastical theory of the *prelatus inutilis* was to sharpen and make explicit later theories of royal inadequacy.

These texts consist of a series of remarkably clear ideas on the nature of the episcopal office, the distinction between office and incumbent, and, more directly relevant for present purposes, the distinction between episcopal office as *administratio* and as *dignitas*.[17] Such aspects of office were not exclusively, of course, the creation of the twelfth-century canonists. As early as the fourth century there had occurred "the gradual disaggregation of the corporate ministry in a face-to-face fellowship. Thereupon the various orders of the clergy came to be thought of as the ecclesiastical

16. *Summa*, Admont Stiftsbibliothek MS 7, fol. 268r.

17. The studies of the medieval episcopal office useful for this distinction are: Benson, *The Bishop-Elect;* D. E. Heintschel, *The Medieval Concept of an Ecclesiastical Office* (Washington, 1956); P. Riesenberg, *The Inalienability of Sovereignty*. See also M. D. Chenu, "Officium: Théologiens et canonistes," *Etudes . . . LeBras*, 2:835–39.

counterpart of the succession of offices or the *cursus honorum* through which a magistrate normally advanced in the service of the state."[18] The influence upon the church of the administrative and constitutional structure of the Roman state extended to clerical costume, regalia, ordination ceremonies, and to the rhetorical convention of public and private documents.[19] Although not all churchmen approved the use of *famosum typum saeculi,* as an early church council described temporal elements, Roman administration, Roman diplomatic, and Roman legal ideas contributed significantly to the constitutional structure of the church in the fourth, fifth, and sixth centuries. During the pontificate of Gregory I many of these early influences became incorporated into the systematic directions which the papacy issued to the far-flung churches under its care. From Gregory's own register and from later collections many of them made their way further into the work of Gratian.[20]

Gregory I himself was not exclusively concerned with the spiritual suitability of prelates. He remarked, in a text which also found its way into the *Decretum:* "Notis, quia talis hoc temporis in regiminis debet arce constitui, qui non solum de salute animarum, verum etiam de extrinseca subiectorum utilitate, et cautela sciat esse sollicitus."[21] In a *dictum* preceding this text in the *Decretum* Gratian remarks: "Saecularium negotiorum opportet [praelati] habere solertiam." His rubric further notes: "Saecularium negotiorum imperiti non sunt in episcopos ordinandi." The complex

18. G. H. Williams, "The Ministry in the Ante-Nicene Church," in *The Ministry in Historical Perspectives* (New York, 1956), p. 29; see pp. 27–59.

19. See Theodor Klauser, *Der Ursprung der bischöflichen Insignien und Ehrenrechte,* Bonner akademische Reden, I (Klefeld, 1949); Kantorowicz, "Mysteries of State"; P. E. Schramm, "Sacerdotium und Regnum im Austausch ihrer Vorrechte. Eine Skizze der Entwicklung zur Beleuchtung des Dictatus Papae Gregors VII," *Studi Gregoriani* 2 (1947): 403–57.

20. Two recent studies of Gregory's influence are those of H. Hürten, "Gregor der Grosse und der mittelalterliche Episkopat," *Zeitschrift fur Kirchengeschichte* 73 (1963): 16–41, and Jean Gaudement, "Patristique et Pastorale: La Contribution de Grégoire le Grand au 'Miroir de l'Evêque' dans le *Decret* de Gratien," in *Etudes . . . Le Bras,* 1:129f.

21. D.39 c.1 *Petrus.*

character of a bishop's duties demanded that he be expert in both spiritual and temporal affairs. These demands constitute much of the background for later papal legislation in regard to episcopal deviations from the norm, both criminal and accidental.

The question of criminal deviation need not concern this study. The question of accidental deviation, however, was to bear directly upon later theories of the *rex inutilis*. In his *Summa* to *Causa* VII Rufinus noted two kinds of episcopal *inutilitas*, which probably form the basis for Huguccio's later distinction:

> Duo sunt que episcopos tanquam inutiles pontificatu ipsis adhuc viventibus privant, scilicet pravitas criminis et debilitas corporis. In superioribus igitur causis egit de criminum pravitate accusatione et condempnatione; nunc incipit agere de corporis debilitate, quo modo ea impeditus episcopus episcopatui possit supersedere et alium substituere.[22]

Further, in dealing with the first *quaestio* of *Causa* VII Rufinus lists seven causes which may authorize the removal of a bishop: "Episcopus removetur autem pro his septem causis: pro crimine, pro egritudine, pro senectute, pro vaga animi levitate, pro utilitate, pro necessitate, pro humilitate."[23] Of these seven reasons, only the second and third concern this study.[24] The concepts of *aegritudo* and *senectus*, however, are of particular interest. Although they are causes of prelatal *inutilitas* and may thereby lead to harmful consequences in body politic as well as in body ecclesiastic, they are normally not sins or crimes in themselves, but accidents. Whether *aegritudo* meant physical or mental illness, it rendered a bishop unsuitable for the *administratio* of his see. It may be con-

22. *Summa*, p. 285. This distinction probably formed the basis for Huguccio's later approach to C.15 q.6 c.3.

23. Ibid., p. 286.

24. The first, *pro crimine*, equiparates the prelate to the temporal *tyrannus*. The fourth, *pro vaga animi levitate*, derives from the vocabulary of vices and virtues. The fifth and sixth, *pro utilitate, pro necessitate*, refer respectively to administrative transfers and to the exigences of social disorder. The seventh, *pro humilitate*, refers to the prelate's retirement to the monastic life or to his becoming a penitent. For the application of this last principle to the papacy in the case of Celestine V, see below, chap 6.

venient to recall here the twelfth-century developments in the field of moral theology and psychology. Mental illness and mental deficiency began to meet the concepts of *acedia* and *tristitia* on a nearly common ground of terminology, and the work in this area of Hugh of St. Victor was known not only to theologians but to such canonists as Rufinus as well.[25] Thus both the juridical and moral problems that arose from the actions of irresponsible or incapable officials constituted problems to which lawyers and theologians of the twelfth and thirteenth centuries could apply articulate solutions drawn from the areas of psychology and law.

Some of these solutions are to be found in the texts which Huguccio used to clarify one meaning of *inutilis*. The first text, *Quamvis* (VII.1.14), consists of part of a letter sent by Gregory I to Etherius, Bishop of Lyons, outlining the procedure to be followed in the case of an insane prelate. In such cases, Gregory notes, the permanence or temporariness of the affliction should be determined. If the condition is permanent the chapter should elect a *coadiutor* who will administer the affairs of the diocese until the death or resignation of the incumbent, at which time he himself will be elected bishop. If the condition is temporary, or if the present bishop has lucid intervals, he should be asked to resign voluntarily. If he does so, another bishop is to be elected immediately. If he refuses to do so, a *coadiutor* is to be elected who will administer the affairs of the see during the terms of the bishop's illness or insanity.[26] Gregory further distinguishes between criminal offenses and those over which the offender has no control.[27] A number of preceding

25. For Hugh and Rufinus, see F. Merzbacher, "Recht und Gewaltenlehre bei Hugo von St. Viktor," *ZfRG* K.A. 44 (1958): 181–208; L. Prosdocimi, "Unità e dualità del popolo christiano in Stefano di Tournai e in Ugo di San Vittore," *Etudes . . . Le Bras,* 1:673–80.

26. See the comment in the *Summa Parisiensis,* ed. T. P. McLaughlin (Toronto 1952), p. 135.

27. See Gregory's register: *Gregorii Papae registrum epistolarum,* ed. P. Ewald and L. Hartmann, MGH *Epp.* I, *partes* 1–3 (Berlin, 1887–91), XI, 29 (p. 300): "Sed suggerendum est, ut, si is qui est in regimine aegrotat, dispensator illi talis requiratur, qui possit eas curam omnem agere et locum illius in regimine ecclesiae ipso non deposito, ac in custodia civitatis implere."

capitula in the same *quaestio* deal with this and related problems. A *dictum* of Gratian to VII.1.11 neatly sums up the doctrine: "Ecce his auctoritatibus patenter ostenditur quod episcopo vivente alius superordinari non potest, nec etiam pro eius aegritudine." One of the primary ecclesiological questions at issue in such cases was that of the canonical impossiblity of two bishops occupying a single see. Such dfficulties as these led to an analysis of the episcopal office, an attempt to distinguish between those powers which pertained chiefly to *administratio* and could be delegated and those which pertained to *dignitas* or *auctoritas* and could not.[28]

In the course of that analysis the popes and canonists developed the idea of an episcopal *curator, coadiutor,* or *dispensator,* a cleric of suitable character and ability, who could administer the affairs of the see during the prelate's periods of incapacity, because, as the glossators said, "Inutilitas praelati non debet redundare in damnum ecclesiae."[29] The prototype of the ecclesiastical *curator*

28. See now Benson, *The Bishop-Elect* esp. pp. 391–96. Relevant observations are those of the ordinary gloss to C.7 q.1 c.1 *Scripsit, ad v. curam omnem:* "Id est res administrare, sed quae spectant ad pontificale officium, vicini episcopi supplebunt. . . . Et est hic arg. quod coadiutor et administratores vel visitatores debeant habere liberam et generalem administrationem." Those things which the *curator* or *coadiutor* could do are usually termed *exteriora.* Those which pertained to the *pontificale officium* were chiefly consecrations and the imposing of holy orders. See, e.g., the *Summa Parisensis,* p. 133: "Si enim episcopus non possit administrare . . . vicini episcopi erunt sibi subsidio in consecrationibus et ordinibus."

29. As in, e.g., the ordinary gloss to C.16 q.6 c.6 *Si fortassis, ad v. non inutilis:* "Propter hoc quod praelatus inutilis factus, quasi diceret, inutilitas praelati non debet redundare in damnum ecclesiae." Gratian's rubric reads: "Inutilis sacerdos ecclesiam suam dignitate non privat." For a brief discussion of the history of the passage, see Walter Ullmann, "*Nos si aliquid incompetenter* . . . (Some Observations on the Register Fragments of Leo IV in the *Collectio Britannica*)," in *Ephemerides Iuris Canonici* 9 (1953): 279–87. Ullmann's observations on the historical applicability of such sentiments as those of Leo IV to the papacy may be well taken, but the case of Celestine V in 1294 uses ideas much like them. See below, chap. 6. The ordinary gloss to C.16 q.6 c.2 *Placuit, ad v. causae,* reads: "Quantum ad possessorium indicium etiam quia puniri debet in litis aestimatione si habet propria ad similitudinem eius quod de tutore dicitur C. de admi. tut. non ignotum [= *Code* 5.37.19] et C. unde vi meminerint

was the Roman law *curator,* who, like the *tutor, rector,* and *procurator,* was able to perform functions in private law which would normally be the exclusive right of the person in whose stead the *curator* acted. Roman law had worked out an elaborate system which regulated the rights, activities, and obligations of those who, like Labeo's "madmen, children, and cities," were unable to act in their own best interests.[30] Gregory's text, in fact, seems remarkably similar to a rescript of Justinian of the year 535 *(Code* V.70.6), a resemblance later noted by Pope Innocent IV.[31] The casus to Justinian's text in the *Glossa ordinaria* to the *Code* remarks:

> Cum quis furiosus est, aut perpetuo, aut ad tempus, primo casu curator administrare debet continue: nec eius cura finitur. Si autem dilucida habeat intervalla, an interim debeat cessare cura? Dicitur quod certum est, constitutum; sed in dilucido

[= *Code* 8.4.6], ut sicut factum tutoris non redundat in pupilli damnum: ita hec hoc delictum personae redundabit in damnum ecclesiae." Thus the *regula* from the *Code* of Justinian concerning tutors was adapted to the delicts of the ecclesiastical *persona,* as, for another example, in the ordinary gloss to C.16 q.6 c.2 *ad v. non inutilis:* "Propter hoc quod praelatus inutilis factus est, quasi diceret, inutilitas praelati non debet redundare in damnum ecclesiae." The principles of the Roman law for tutors gave juristic precision to a problem which had troubled the church first in the Donatist controversies and later in the Investiture dispute concerning reordinations. A theological development concerning the nature of sacraments thus found juristic expression in the norms of Roman law and was turned into a legal maxim of canon law. For the theological background, see N. M. Haring, "The Augustinian Axiom: *Nulli sacramento injuria facienda est,*" *Medieval Studies* 16 (1954): 87–117.

30. Cf. Riesenberg, *The Inalienability of Sovereignty,* p. 59: "When legists and theorists wished to enhance the imperial and regal office they did the same thing [as the Romans had done for women]: they ascribed special natures to the objects they wished to preserve, and based their protections on the same private law concepts, on the basis of which they protected the positions of women minors, and clerics in a hostile world." See also Kantorowicz, *The King's Two Bodies,* p. 374.

31. The standard work on Roman law in the Middle Ages, M. Conrat, *Geschichte der Quellen und Literatur des römischen Rechts* (rep. Aalen, 1963), does not cite Gregory's use of the Justinian text.

intervallo hae reditatem adire, vel contrahere potest sine auctoritate curatoris.

Many other passages in the *Institutes, Digest,* and *Code* deal at length with the legal status of *curators* and with the rights of their charges. All these constituted a convenient guide to Gregory I and his successors. If the private rights of individual Roman citizens could be protected to such a degree, how much more should those of prelates, who belonged to an *ordo,* possessed a *dignitas,* and fulfilled an *officium* infinitely higher than those of laymen, be protected? Gregory's text formed the groundwork for the doctrines of the other texts that Huguccio cited.[32]

The second of these texts, *Petisti* (VII.1.17), applied the Gregorian principle to the case of the *episcopus senex.* Boniface, Archbishop of Mainz, had asked Pope Zacharias that he be allowed to select a *curator* to assist him because of his advanced age and illness. Gratian's rubric tells us that this text illustrates the rule that coadjutors ought to be assigned to those *senectute gravatus.*[33] The third text, *Quia* (VII.1.18), describes a third condition which is the legal equivalent of *senectus* and *aegritudo*—that of *simplicitas.* Johannes, Bishop of Narni, asked Pope Pelagius for a coadjutor because he himself was incompetent to administer the affairs of his see and to maintain clerical discipline. He asked that a *presbyter*

32. For the rights of the insane in Roman law, see Carl Saas, *Die Behandlung der Geisteskranken im römischen Recht* (Zurich, 1911). For canon law, see S. Kuttner, *Kanonistische Schuldlehre von Gratian bis auf die Dekretalen Gregors IX,* Studi e testi 64 (Vatican City, 1935), pp. 85–109; R. C. Pickett, *Mental Affliction and Church Law* (Ottawa, 1952), pp. 1–70.

33. C.7 q.1 c.17: "Senectute gravato, coadiutor est dandus, qui morienti succedat." For a later striking example, cf. *Liber extra* 1.9.1 *Litteras tuas,* a letter from Alexander III to the Bishop of Lund, who had requested replacement because of his advancing age. The bishop, says Pope Alexander, should not consider resigning either because of *senectus* or *insufficientia,* because it would be better to have the church remain governed under his well-known name than under that of an unknown person, finally describing the *vigor devotionis* of the old bishop as being unaffected by his *corpore senescente.* For an earlier example, see Ladner, "Two Gregorian Letters."

be given him, "ut ea, quae sunt necessaria, competenti disponente sollicitudine fiant, nihil indecens fieri, vel inutile permittatur."[34] The *Summa Parisiensis* comments: "Iste multum erat simplex ut nesciret disponere saecularibus. Non tamen removetur, sed ei in subsidium adhibetur presbyter nomine Constituto ad ordinationem patrimonii, i.e., possessionis ecclesiae." All three of these cases fall under the general heading expressed by the rubric to *Quia:* "Non successor, sed coadiutor viventi episcopo datur."

The last text Huguccio cited was *Si Petrus* (VIII.1.1). It describes the obscure pattern of papal succession among the immediate followers of St. Peter: Linus, Cletus, and Clement. The text notes that although St. Peter constituted Linus and Cletus his *adiutores,* he did not transfer to them his *potestas pontificii, aut solvendi, aut ligandi,* but gave this to St. Clement. Linus and Cletus *ministrabant exteriora:* St. Peter *verbo et orationi insistebat.* The distinction between two aspects of the episcopal office, the (in this case) *potestas* and the *administratio,* occurs in a number of texts in the *Decretum,* the glosses to which often draw parallels between these aspects of ecclesiastical office and similar aspects of temporal offices.[35]

The canonical texts here cited by Huguccio all deal with the general principle that a living bishop could not be removed on grounds

34. C.7 q.1 c.18, *Casus:* "Iohannes episcopus Narniensis ecclesiae adeo simplex erat, quod res ecclesiae ministrante nesciebat." For a distinction between two kinds of *simplicitas* recognized by the canon lawyers, see, e.g., the ordinary gloss to D.39 c.1 *Petrus ad vv. Petrus . . . simplex est:* "Quaedam est simplicitas quae est contraria dolo, et illa est bona, ut 16 q.1 si cupis. Sed hic vocat simplicitatem negligentiam sive stultitiam, ut 36 dist. in princ. illa enim impedit promovendum, ut hic et arg. 74 dist. episcoporum. sed promotum non deiicit sed datur ei coadiutor, ut 7 q. 1 quia frater et 12 q. 2 vobis."

35. See esp. D. 22 c.1 *Omnes sive.* The *Summa "Antiquitate et tempore"* notes *(ad vv. terreni simul et celestis):* "Sed animadvertendum est, quod ius aliud est auctoritatis, aliud administrationis. Et quidem ius auctoritatis est ut in episcopo ad cuius ius omnes res ecclesiastice spectare dicuntur, quia eius auctoritate omnia disponuntur. Ius administrationis sicut in yconomo. Iste enim habet ius administrandi sed auctoritate caret imperandi" (cited by Stickler, "Imperator vicarius papae," p. 9, n. 21). Cf. Benson, *The Bishop-Elect,* pp. 56–89.

of inadequacy, but had to be given a *coadiutor.* Inadequacy, or *inutilitas,* consisted, among other things, of *aegritudo, senectus,* and *simplicitas.* The coadiutor was to possess the powers of *administratio,* but not those of *potestas* (here the equivalent of *dignitas*). The procedure developed by canonists derived from similar procedures in Roman law. The broad question of mental and physical competence occupied churchmen as well as Roman lawyers, since the constitutional structure of the church resembled that of Rome in many ways. No comparable developments occurred in the customary laws of the territorial monarchies until the procedure had been worked out by the canonists in the twelfth century. The relationship between the Roman law procedure for insanity and the canon law procedure for several kinds of inadequacy may account in part for the frequent conjunction of accusations of insanity and ineptitude in later ecclesiastical and political discussions of the *rex inutilis.*

The distinction between the spheres of authority of incumbent prelate and coadjutor was drawn, of course, in other areas of the law than those described above. In canon law, of particular interest is the canonists' discussion of D.21 c.7 *Nunc autem,* which describes an action taken by two Roman emperors reigning together. The text has generally attracted attention because it deals with the trial of a pope. However, the prospect of two emperors reigning simultaneously called for some explanation. Nothing was easier than to read back into the office of emperor the ecclesiastical distinction between *administratio* and *dignitas.* Hence, in the *Glossa ordinaria* to the text in the *Decretum,* Johannes Teutonicus remarked *(glo. ad v. Diocletiani):* "Nota simul duos fuisse Imperatores. Dic, quod erant duae personae, sed tamen erant loco unius. Sed contra, 7 q.1 in apibus. Sed forte unus habuit dignitatem: alter administrationem." Johannes rejected the first explanation, that two persons simply occupied one office, because he was familiar with the famous canonical text *In apibus* (VII.1.41):

> In apibus princeps unus est, grues unum sequuntur ordine letterario: imperator unus, iudex unus provinciae. Roma ut condita est, duos fratres simul habere reges non potuit et parricidio dedicatur. In Rebeccae utero Esau et Jacob bella

gesserunt: singuli ecclesiarum episcopi, singuli archipresbyteri, singuli archidiaconi et omnis ordo ecclesiasticus suis rectoribus nititur.

The words of St. Jerome became a rationale of ecclesiastical administration. Only one incumbent could enjoy a given *dignitas.* The increased legal sophistication of churchmen, however, evaded the full consequences of this idea by reserving a single *dignitas* but separating the *administratio* from it in certain cases. Later, of course, the question of delegated authority was to cause even more complicated divisions of power than this. In the course of the twelfth and thirteenth centuries questions of *libera administratio, libera potestas,* and *plena potestas* made the powers of the *curator* or *legatus* extremely complex. The legal actions which involved delegated authority, both in spiritual and temporal spheres, increased in scope and frequency and had to be dealt with not only by canon lawyers but by those responsible for royal minorities, by those who served in representative assemblies, and by those who acted in the king's stead.

By the late twelfth century, then, ecclesiastical law concerning episcopal inadequacy had been systematically and articulately defined in papal letters, conciliar canons, and the apparatus of legal thought which constituted the framework for the academic study of the *Decretum.* The greatest of the twelfth-century canonists. Huguccio, moreover, saw no difficulty in applying this ecclesiastical law to cases of temporal rulers. Whether he did so because he thought that such rulers were part of the ecclesiastical structure—that is, that they possessed a clerical character—or more simply because he saw a juridical analogy between the offices of prelate and *princeps,* need not concern this study. Such concepts as *dignitas, potestas, honor,* and *administratio* served to describe both spiritual and lay offices. Indeed, after the papal effort to diminish the sacerdotal character of the king between the late eleventh and early fourteenth centuries, the analogy continued to be drawn. During this period, as Kantorowicz has pointed out, the *lingua mezzo-teologica* of the royal jurists paralleled the *lingua mezzo-politica* of the theologians and canonists. If one does not seek an actual transposition of characteristics between the two orders, one may at least note a tendency common to both clergy and laity to discuss office and authority from a common legalistic point of view. As late as the fourteenth century, such lawyers as Panormitanus and Lucas de Penna could still comfortably discuss kingship in terms of a bishop's marriage to his see. And Andreas of Isernia could modify Nicholas I's description of the relation between a bishop and his church into: "The prince is in the *respublica* and the *respublica* is in the prince."[36]

Huguccio's contribution to the concept of the *rex inutilis* in canon law reflects both the broadened scope of legal thought in the late twelfth century and the increasingly abstract concepts of *regnum, praelatio,* and *episcopatum* applied to kingdoms or ecclesiastical units as administrative or corporate entities. The welfare, or *utilitas,* of these entities became the object of royal or episcopal activities. Although, to be sure, Huguccio's conclusions in regard to the two types of royal *inutilitas* were not adopted by all later canonists, they were influential upon Johannes Teutonicus, the author of the ordinary gloss to the *Decretum,* the standard commentary to which the decretalists would later turn. While up to Huguccio's own day *Alius item* had served as an illustration of the papal right to depose not only tyrannical but incompetent rulers, Huguccio opened up a new line of thought which, although not strictly in keeping with contemporary political practice, was consistent with other canonist ideas about the nature of public authority and governance. Between 1190 and 1243, however, this approach existed solely in the commentaries upon the *Decretum.* It remained for a political authority to test Huguccio's alternatives. This was not done until 1245. Then Innocent IV applied Huguccio's doctrine to the case of Sancho II of Portugal, brought to his attention in 1243 by the "clamores multiplices praelatorum et aliorum regni Portugalie."

36. Discussed by Kantorowicz in "Mysteries of State," pp. 79–83, and *The King's Two Bodies,* Index, s.v. "Marriage."

4

Sancho II of Portugal and Thirteenth-Century Deposition Theory

The universal character of the medieval canon law often gave universal legal significance to events which would not normally have exerted any appreciable influence upon the course of European history. In 1202, for example, the request of William, Lord of Montpellier, that Innocent III legitimize the Count's natural children elicited the decretal *Per venerabilem,* which not only disposed (unfavorably) of the Count's request but also laid down a series of observations on the relation between *sacerdotium* and *regnum* which remained "to the time of Hostiensis . . . the focus of the freshest canonist thinking about the principles of the relations of the two powers." In 1220 Honorius III found cause to complain of certain privileges granted by Andrew II of Hungary which the pope considered injurious to the *honor coronae.* Honorius's opinion, given in the decretal *Intellecto,* summed up a century of juristic theories concerning the inalienability of political authority and remained the starting point for future discussions of this increasingly important aspect of legal theory. In these and other incidents legal problems which might have remained isolated were worked into the articulation of a coherent structure of ecclesiastical jurisprudence having consequences not only in the papal administration of the *respublica christiana* but also in the increasingly more sophisticated public law of the territorial monarchies.[1]

1. J. A. Watt, "The Theory of Papal Monarchy in the Thirteenth Century: The Contribution of the Canonists," *Traditio* 20 (1964): 214–16; see pp. 179–318. Also published separately, New York and London, 1965. The fullest discussion of *Intellecto* is that of Riesenberg, *The Inalienability of Sovereignty.* Cf. Post, *Studies in Medieval Legal Thought,* pp. 415–33;

Another such case arose in Portugal in the second quarter of the thirteenth century. On July 24, 1245, Innocent IV issued the decretal *Grandi*, by which he deprived Sancho II of the governance of Portugal and appointed Sancho's brother Afonso, Count of Boulogne, guardian or *curator* of the realm. Afonso arrived in Portugal early in 1246 at the head of a crusading army, took Lisbon, and proceeded to enforce the terms of *Grandi* in the face of armed resistance on the part of his brother. Although Sancho had the support of some of the Portuguese nobility as well as that of Ferdinand III Castile and his son Alfonso, he was driven from his kingdom and forced to seek refuge in Toledo, where he died in 1248. Upon Sancho's death Afonso of Boulogne ascended the Portuguese throne as Afonso III.[2]

Sancho's case has not attracted the attention of many historians of thirteenth-century political theory. Some of this neglect may be explained by the peripheral status of Portugal in the wider world of European political affairs, by the overshadowing of Sancho's case by the more spectacular deposition of Frederick II, which had occurred a week earlier, and by the turbulent political conditions in England, Italy, and the Empire. However, Sancho's difficulties with his own nobles and prelates, the role of *Grandi* in papal political thought, and the subsequent interest which the decretal and its glosses generated in the territorial monarchies during the fourteenth and fifteenth centuries give the episode some importance for the

---

H. Hoffmann, "Die Unveräusserlichkeit der Kronrechte im Mittelalter," *DA* 20 (1964): 389–474. See the additional comments of Ullmann, *EHR* 76 (1961): 326, n. 1.

2. *Dat. Lugd.* IX *Kal. Aug. A.* III (1245). *Corpus iuris canonici,* vol. 2, cols. 971–74: *Liber Sextus* 1.8.2 *de supplenda negligentia praelatorum.* Berger, no. 1389. O. Raynaldi, *Annales ecclesiastici* (Colonia Agrippina, 1664f.), vol. 21, *ad. an.* 1245, no. 68. Mansi, vol. 23, cols. 652–53. Portuguese text in D. A. Caetano da Sousa, *Provas da historia genealogica da casa real portuguesa* (rep. Coimbra, 1946), 1:57–61; F. A. Brandão, *Monarchia Lusitana* (Lisbon, 1632), vol. 4: *Escritura* xxiii (= *Cronicas de De. Sancho II e D. Afonso III)* (Porto, 1946), pp. 358–61. J. Abranches, *Fontes de direito ecclesiastico portuguez* (Coimbra, 1895), hereafter cited as Abranches, followed by document no.

historian of constitutionalism and public law, particularly insofar as his work involves a study of changing concepts of kingship during the later Middle Ages.[3]

Innocent addressed *Grandi* to the "barons, communities, councils of cities and castles and of other places, and to all the knights and people constituting the realm of Portugal." The *arenga* consists of a series of observations on the aims and responsibilities of Christian kingdoms, the benefit to Christendom when these aims are fulfilled, and its grief when they are rent by discords, allow the ardor of devotion to cool, neglect justice, and permit evil to flourish. When these kingdoms are deflected from their proper courses, it is the duty of the pope to see to their reform, just as it is his duty to maintain good kingdoms in a state of prosperity.[4]

3. The only extensive discussions in recent years have been those of J. A. Cantini, "De autonomia judicis saecularis et de Romani Pontificis plenitudine potestatis in temporalibus secundum Innocentium IV," *Salesianum* 23 (1961): 407–80; G. Caspary, "The Deposition of Richard II and the Canon Law," *Proceedings of the Second International Congress of Medieval Canon Law,* Monumenta Iuris Canonici, Subsidia, vol. 1 (Rome, 1966), pp. 189–201. Brief notice is taken in P. Riesenberg, *The Inalienability of Sovereignty,* pp. 168–69; L. Buisson, *Potestas und Caritas. Die päpstliche Gewalt im Spätmittelalter* (Cologne, 1958), pp. 288–89; A. D. de Sousa Costa, *As Condordatas portuguesas* (Braga, 1966), pp. 11–15. After this study had been completed, I discovered another work which deals with similar materials: James M. Muldoon, "The Medieval Origins of the State: The Contributions of the Canonists from Gratian to Hostiensis" (Ph.D. Diss., Cornell University, 1965), esp. pp. 146–48, 171–73. I am grateful to Professor Muldoon for permission to read his work as well as for several discussions concerning this topic, and to Professors Caspary and Kuttner for permission to read "The Deposition of Richard II" in proof. Professor Caspary has been kind enough to discuss several points with me in correspondence.

4. The text of *Grandi* here cited is that of Friedberg, vol. 2, cols. 971–74: "Exultamus in Domino gaudio, quam christianae professionis regna sic salubri diriguntur statu . . . Vehementi autem dolore turbamur si quando regna ipsa . . . scinduntur discordiis, circa fidei cultum remisso devotionis ardore tepescunt, iustitiam negligunt, et in se ipsis permittunt illicita perpetrari . . . Nos convenit, ut christianorum regna quae in statu sunt prospero, incommutabiliter in illo regantur, et quae periculoso ruere dignoscuntur, reformatione laudabili reparentur."

The *narratio* summarizes the events in Portugal's recent history which led to the issuing of the decretal. Sancho, deluded by wicked counsel, had violated many ecclesiastical liberties, made numerous oppressions and exactions of churches and monasteries, and had permitted his officials to do the same. Certain prelates of the kingdom had appealed to Innocent's predecessors, and Gregory IX, after many admonitions, interdicts, and sentences of excommunication, had finally forced Sancho to promise to restore their original liberties and goods to those churches and monasteries whose rights he had violated. Sancho, however, not only neglected to keep his promise but increased his oppressions of the churches. Not only ecclesiastical but lay goods and rights were violated. Because of the king's negligence, criminals of all kinds were free to do as they liked without fear of punishment. Others were free to contract marriages within the prohibited degrees, to steal the goods of churches, and to create clear dangers to the faith, thus leading their own souls and the souls of others into the danger of heresy.[5]

The cause of this disorder was the king's own negligence *(negligentia)*, his idleness *(desidia)*, his acquiescence in wicked counsel,

5. "Ceterum castra, villas, possessiones et alia iura regalia, idem rex propter ipsius desidiam, suique cordis imbecillitatem deperire permittens, ac passim et illicite malignorum acquiescens consiliis . . . Terras insuper et alia christianorum bona in confinio Saracenorum posita non defendens, ea infidelibus devastanda, seu etiam occupanda ex animi pusillaninmitate relinquit. E licet a supradictis praelatis, ut ad corrigenda praemissa, pluraque alia nefanda, quorum seriosa narratio fastidium generaret, ardenter, ut tenetur, assurgeret, monitus fuit diligenter, idem tamen, eorum monitionibus obauditis, id efficere non curavit; propter quod nos episcoporum, abbatum, priorum et aliorum tam religiosorum, quam saecularium regni eiusdem conquestionibus et clamosis insinuationibus excitati, regem ipsum per nostras litteras ut praemissa corrigeret rogandum duximus attente." Cf. the remarks of Innocent's biographer, Nicholas da Curbio, *Vita Innocenti Papae IV,* in E. Baluze, *Miscellanea historia* (Lucca, 1761), 1:194–206, at chap. 20: "Rex Portugalliae Sancius, qui erat circa regni sui regimen multiplici negligentia et ignavia iam defectus, propter quod pupillo non iudicabat causa viduae ad ipsum non ingrediens deperiebat, Ecclesie destruebantur et monasteria, ipsum regnum et multipliciter quassabatur, meritis ipsius accusatis et examinatus in ipso consilio ad petitionem et instantium praelatorum ipsius regni."

and his pusillanimity. He neither defended nor in any way cared for those things which had been placed in his charge against the incursions of the Saracens. Because of royal indifference, many individuals, clerical and lay, had again appealed, this time to Innocent, to correct the evils of the realm. The pope had attempted unsuccessfully to force Sancho to act in two previous letters. From day to day the evils of the kingdom grew worse on account of Sancho's negligence and idleness. Innocent, therefore, wishing to relieve the kingdom from its adversities (in part, at least, because Portugal was a financial tributary of the papacy) decided to take the following steps. The Count of Boulogne, who would by law of the kingdom succeed to the throne if Sancho should die without heirs, is to assume the *cura et administratio generalis et libera* of the king himself as for that of the realm. Innocent adds the reservation that he does not intend by this action to deprive Sancho (or such legitimate issue as he may have) of the kingship *(regnum adimere)*—that is, of the royal dignity—but only of the administration, the governance, of the realm so that the kingdom may be saved by the providence of Afonso from the danger of destruction.[6]

The emphasis of Innocent's thought in *Grandi* falls heavily upon Sancho's inadequacy and upon the evil advantage that others have been able to take of the king's negligence and ineptitude and not on the criminal character of the king himself, as had been, for example, the case in the deposition of Frederick II. Sancho was not in Innocent's eyes a *rex iniquus* or *tyrannus,* a criminal ruler,

6. "Grandi non immerito . . . Mandamus, quatenus dilectum filium nobilem virum commitem Boloniensem, praefati regis Portugalliae fratrem, de devotione, probitate ac circumspectione multipliciter commendatum, qui eidem regi, si absque legitimo decederet filio, iure regni succederet, quique examinatae dilectionis affectu, quo vos et praedictum regnum prosequitur, magnanimitate ac potentia sibi plurimum suffragantibus, regnum ipsum maturius reformaturus firma credulitate speratur, praesertim quam ad curam et administrationem generalem et liberam regni eiusdem, tam pro saepe dicti regis quam ipsius regni utilitate . . . Per hoc non intendimus memorato regi vel ipsius legitimo filio, si quem habuerit, praedictum regnum adimere; sed potius sibi et eidem regno destructioni exposito, ac vobis epsis in vita ipsius regis per sollicitudinem et providentiam comitis consulere supra dicti."

but a *rex inutilis,* an inadequate one. Innocent's action against Sancho was determined by the direction of canonists' speculation on the nature of kingship and on the problem of royal inadequacy. Canonists' theories had been based in turn upon the general development of medieval political thought from the fourth to the twelfth centuries.

The charges listed in *Grandi* constitute a reliable, if strongly biased, approach to the study of Sancho's reign, since they are based upon the most copious source of evidence for the period, the large body of papal correspondence dealing with the realm between 1223 and 1245.[7] Although the papal correspondence provides a distinctly one-sided view of Portuguese history during the first half

7. I have traced 198 papal letters for Portugal during the period 1223–45, of which at least one-third deal with the relations between Sancho and the Portuguese higher clergy. The chief locations of these documents are listed above, n. 3. The best history of the period is that of A. Herculano, *Historia de Portugal* (9th ed., Lisbon, 1916–17), esp. vols. 4 and 5. There exists an unacknowledged English translation of parts of Herculano's history in E. McMurdo, *History of Portugal,* 2 vols. (London, 1888), but this work lacks Herculano's apparatus and often omits important passages without notice. There are no contemporary chronicles. Later chronicles are: Ruy de Pina, *Cronica do . . . D. Sancho II* (Lisbon, 1728); *Cronicas dos sete primeiros Reis de Portugal,* ed. C. de Silva Tarouca, in *Fontes narrativas da historia portuguesa,* no. I (Lisbon, 1952), 1:211–46; A. de Magelhaes Basto, *Cronica de cinco Reis de Portugal,* vol. 1 (Porto, 1945). For a general discussion of the chronicle sources, see Magelhaes Basto, *Estudios. Cronistas e cronicas antigas, Fernão Lopes e a "Cronica de 1419"* (Coimbra, 1959). No recent history supersedes that of Herculano. Sancho's reign is discussed in H. V. Livermore, *A New History of Portugal* (Cambridge, 1966), pp. 74–80 (hereafter cited as Livermore). The best study of the ecclesiastical problems of the reign is that of A. E. Reuter, *Königtum und Episkopat in Portugal im 13. Jahrhundert,* in *Abhandlungen zur mittlere und neuren Geschichte,* Heft 69 (Berlin-Grünewald, 1928) (hereafter cited as Reuter). For the earlier period, see C. Erdmann, *Das Papstum und Portugal im ersten Jahrhundert der portugiesischen Geschichte,* Abh. Akad. preuss. (Berlin, 1928). Cf. Miguel de Oliveira, *Historia ecclesiastica de Portugal* (Lisbon, 1940), pp. 80–96. The best guide to the history and literature of medieval Portugal is now A. H. de Oliveira Marques, *Guia do estudiante de historia medieval portuguesa* (Lisbon, 1964).

of the thirteenth century, it does provide an adequate background for a study of Innocent's action and its immediate political and legal consequences.

From 1185 to 1245 Portugal was the scene of a struggle between the monarchy and the lay and clerical magnates not unlike similar conflicts in other contemporary kingdoms. The king and his advisors attempted continually to strengthen the financial and judicial powers of the monarchy, and the magnates struggled to preserve intact their established rights and immunities. The political conclusion of this conflict was the deposition of Sancho, although the reigns of Sancho I (1185–1211), Afonso II (1211–23), and Sancho II (1223–45/48) all reflect parallel political disputes. In terms of the specific quarrel between king and clergy, Afonso III (1245/48–79) later encountered difficulties similar to those of the brother whom he had helped to remove. The problems which lay at the heart of Portuguese political difficulties in Sancho's reign were not, then, entirely new to Portugal, nor can they safely be attributed exclusively to Sancho's personal ineptitude. Several characteristics of Portuguese kingship, of the juridical position of the magnates, and of the political problems of the later part of Sancho's reign all served to aggravate the conditions that had developed in the twelfth century and culminated in *Grandi.*

The king of Portugal was the hereditary ruler of a territory which had declared itself an independent kingdom in 1139. In 1143 Afonso Henriques had declared his realm to be a financial tributary of the papacy, but papal recognition of a Portuguese kingdom did not come about till 1179.[8] The kings of Portugal were not anointed, nor were they crowned in a liturgical ceremony.[9] In the eyes of the

8. For early Portuguese kingship, see H. de Gama Barros, *História da administração publica em Portugal nos seculos XII a XV,* 2d ed. by T. de Sousa Soares (Lisbon, 1945–54), 1:149–372; 3:304–20 (hereafter cited as Gama Barros). Cf. A. Caetano do Amaral, *Para a historia da legislação e costumes de Portugal,* ed. M. Lopes de Almeida (Porto, 1945), 3:297, 315–20, 394.

9. The earliest papal communications with Portugal are discussed and printed in E. Erdmann, *Papsturkunden in Portugal,* Abh. Ges. Wiss. Göttingen, Neue Folge, Bd. 20.3 (Berlin, 1927). Afonso Henriques had

papacy, the clergy, and Portuguese laymen the king's chief role was that of a crusading warrior whose primary duty was to drive the Moors from the Iberian peninsula. Many subsequent conflicts between Sancho and his clergy hinge upon this conception of the kingship. Later accusations of inefficient generalship directed at Sancho carried more weight in Portugal than they might have else-

---

originally offered the pope a yearly tribute of four ounces of gold. There exists a falsified bull of Innocent II which confirms the gift (Erdmann, *Papsturkunden,* no. 32, pp. 19–23). In 1179 the king changed the tribute to one hundred ounces yearly in addition to a lump payment of one thousand pieces immediately (ibid., no. 81, pp. 254–55). Portugal's financial obligations to the papacy, noted by Innocent IV in *Grandi,* are the subject of numerous papal letters of the late twelfth and early thirteenth centuries. In 1190 Clement III reminded Sancho I of the tribute which the king had evidently neglected to pay (ibid., no. 124, pp. 342–43; *QE* 25–26). In 1198 Innocent III wrote to Sancho I citing earlier papal letters of Lucius II, Clement III, and Alexander III in the decretal *Serenitatem regiam (QE* 29–30; *Potthast* 103; cf. A. Luchaire, *Les Royautés vassales au Saint Siège,* vol. 5 of his *Innocent III* (Paris, 1908), pp. 8–10. Later in the same year Innocent III wrote again *(In eminenti sedis,* in *QE* 31; *Potthast* 447), and again in 1209 *(QE* 35). The problem is the subject of two letters of 1212 *(Potthast* 4432; *QE* 72). In 1218 Honorius III mentions the annual tribute as being two marks of gold *(QE* 72; *Potthast* 5663). All questions concerning payment appear to have been settled during the reign of Afonso II. For the general aspects of the tribute, see W. E. Lunt, *Papal Revenues of the Middle Ages,* in *Columbia Records of Civilization: Sources and Studies,* no. 19 (New York, 1934), 1:57–64. See also D. Mauricio, "Portugal e o censo a Santa Se," *Broteria* 21:98–107.

Not until 1428 did Portuguese kings receive papal permission to be anointed. The bull of Martin IV is discussed by Gama Barros, 3:312, n. 2. The study of P. Merea ("A Aclamação dos nossos reis," *Revista dos Centenarios,* no. 16 (Lisbon, 1940), has been revised and expanded with a useful bibliography under the title "Sobre a aclamação dos nossos reis," *Revista Portuguesa de Historia* 10 (1962): 411–17. However, after the pontificate of Gregory VII, coronation and anointing appear to have had much more effect in the eyes of subjects than in those of the church. See Kantorowicz, *The King's Two Bodies,* pp. 318–28, and B. C. Keeney, "The Medieval Idea of the State: The Great Cause, 1291–2," *University of Toronto Law Journal* 8 (1949–50): 48–71.

where. For the king of Portugal crusading was a raison d'être; failure there meant ultimate failure as a Christian ruler.[10]

The apparent unity of purpose which the crusading ideal gave to the kingdom did not contribute greatly toward the unification of dissident political elements into a whole. Although the amount of royally owned territory and royally controlled justice was greater in Portugal than in any kingdom north of the Pyrenees, the extent of land and judicial power outside the king's hands was considerable. The king could demand such tribute as the *colheita* (free maintenance during his visits to most castles and towns), monopolize coinage, and command extraordinary services and restrictions of local privileges for the purpose of the Crusade. His power, however, was continually weakened by the magnates' vigorous efforts to maintain their own established rights and their equally vigorous resistance to the royal *inquirições,* inquiries into the origins and legitimacy of many titles, land rights, and jurisdictional preserves.[11]

The clergy derived its great strength from its extensive territorial and jurisdictional rights and from its position as director of the spiritual life of a crusading kingdom. It constituted far more a political than a moral opposition to the king. It had exercised its strength in earlier conflicts with Sancho I and Afonso II from which it had emerged victorious.[12] The brevity of these reigns, the pattern of misfortunes associated with each of their ends, the fact of

10. As late as the fifteenth century, kings of Portugal cited their military successes as their chief attributes. See F. M. Rogers, ed. and trans., *The Obedience of a King of Portugal* (Minneapolis, 1958), a letter from King John II to Innocent VIII.

11. The royal actions against the clerical and lay magnates consisted chiefly of *inquirições,* investigations into the legality of claimed rights and immunities similar to the English *Quo Warranto* proceedings. For the nobles, see Gama Barros, 3:13–289, 341–496; for the clergy, ibid., pp. 13–289, and Reuter, passim.

12. See, for some general remarks, Reuter, pp. 8–20. For the disputes of 1211 see the papal letters *Graves oppressiones* (*QE* 26–37 and *Potthast* 4001) and *Si diligenter* (*QE* 39 and *Potthast* 4187). For a recent study, see A. D. de Sousa Costa, *Mestre Silvestre e Mestre Vicente, juristas das contendas entre D. Afonso II e suas irmas* (Braga, 1967).

Sancho's minority in 1223, and the precedent of crippling concessions that both of his immediate predecessors had made to the clergy constituted severe handicaps to successful rule at the outset of Sancho's majority.[13]

Portugal also suffered from the extent of allodial lands entirely outside the royal control in the hands of the powerful nobility. The king, strengthened by none of the ties of feudal land tenure, was forced to depend almost entirely on the good will and personal loyalty of the *ricos homens,* with whom he filled the offices of court.[14] The role played by this powerful nobility during the reign of Afonso II and the minority of Sancho II is indicative of the extent to which the king's freedom of action was limited, not by constitutionalist theories of kingship *sub lege,* but by the actual resources of power outside royal control.

Sancho's reign has had two distinct schools of interpreters. Most of the papal correspondence, documents from the reign of Afonso III, and some modern historians put the case for the legitimacy of the deposition in the strongest possible terms. For these, "Sancho ruled badly in every conceivable way ... [He] neglected the welfare of his subjects; clerics, widows, and children went unprotected. ... Churches, monasteries, and the nation's defenses fell into disuse and ruin. ... [Sancho] presented an extreme case, in the sense that his ineptitude for rule was so acute."[15] On the other hand, some contemporary sources and other later historians suggest that Sancho was the unwitting victim of clerical avarice and papal political ambitions. Herculano, the greatest historian of medieval Portugal, is chief among the latter. Finally, there is a body of literature of the genre known as the *cantigas de escarnho* (satirical broadsides

13. Herculano, 4:161–80; Reuter, pp. 16–24. A letter issued by Honorius III (Pressutti 5135) takes Sancho and the kingdom under the protection of the Holy See. Two other letters of the same date (October 22, 1224; Pressutti 5136, 5137) announce the appointment of friar Gonsaldo as Apostolic Nuncio to Portugal during Sancho's minority and notify others in Portugal of the papal action.

14. Discussed briefly in Livermore, pp. 67–69.

15. Riesenberg, *The Inalienability of Sovereignty,* pp. 168–69.

somewhat resembling the Provençal *sirventes*), which frequently evinces great sympathy for Sancho's cause.[16]

Neither of these positions seems now to be entirely tenable. Sancho's opposition cast its charges into a recognizable rhetoric of malfeasance whose terms had been shaped by jurists, chroniclers, and publicists between the ninth and the thirteenth centuries and would remain in use till the end of the Middle Ages. His supporters, notably Herculano, tend to read back a distinct anticlericalism into the contemporary sources and to ignore the real problems of public law inherent in the two sets of conflicting claims. Sancho was certainly guilty of unwise and imprudent political behavior and of characteristic royal high-handedness, but he was far from being, on the one hand, the inept cipher described in the papal correspondence or, on the other, the heroic victim of papal visions of world monarchy.

The first of *Grandi's* charges, that Sancho had violated legitimate ecclesiastical liberties, set the dominant tone for the papal correspondence throughout the king's reign and illuminates what was perhaps the chief cause of Sancho's troubles. At the very outset of his reign Sancho had been forced to make immense financial reparations to Estevam Soares, Archbishop of Braga, in order to lift the interdict placed upon the kingdom during his father's lifetime and to be able to bury his father in consecrated ground.[17] The cause

16. Cf. Carolina Michaelis de Vasconcellos, "Em Volta de Sancho II," *Lusitania* 2 (1924): 7–25. There is a new edition of these *cantigas* by M. Rodrigues Lapa, *Cantigas, d'escarnho e de mal dizer: Dos Cancioneiros medievais galego=portugueses* (Coimbra, 1965). Brief notice of this literary suport is taken by A. J. Saraiva, *Historia de cultura em Portugal* (Lisbon, 1950), 1:310–12, and A. E. Beau, *Die Entwicklung des portugiesischen Nationalbewusstseins* (Hamburg, 1945), pp. 41–42.

17. Sancho's character undergoes several distinct changes in the papal correspondence between Honorius III and Innocent IV. The letters of Honorius often picture the king as an active oppressor of the church (cf. Pressutti 4683). In 1222 Honorius had written to Afonso II threatening him with outright deposition: "Alioquin nos non solum praedictas sententiae faciemus frequentius publicari . . . verum etiam crescente contumacia tua severius contra te . . . procedemus, terram tuam exponendo regibus

of the interdict and of Afonso II's excommunication had been, characteristically, an earlier dispute between the old king and the archbishop concerning royal encroachments upon the financial and jurisdictional preserves of the higher clergy.[18] The *Concordata* of 1223, the instrument of Sancho's agreement with Soares, resembles the acts of the Cortes of 1211, which had consisted chiefly of similar concessions that Afonso II had made to the clergy at the outset of his own reign.[19]

Between 1223 and 1228 and again between 1232 and 1240 Portugal witnessed periods of growing antagonism between king and clergy interrupted briefly by successful military campaigns against the Arabs and concluded by temporary reconciliations between political opponents whose underlying enmity only left the way open for further conflicts. After 1240 Sancho's failure to continue his crusading efforts and his increasingly intransigent attitude toward the claims of the higher clergy and the nobility gave his opponents no alternative that they could perceive other than that which resulted in a joint effort to bring about his downfall. Between 1241 and 1245 the efforts of most of the Portuguese higher clergy and of a large part of the nobility were directed to this end. The appearance of Afonso of Boulogne as a likely candidate for the Portuguese throne and the far-reaching concerns of Innocent IV for the political stability of Christendom resulted in the promulgation of *Grandi* and in the three years of intermittent warfare required to enforce its terms upon the kingdom.

The first of these periods of heightened antagonism may be said to begin with the reconciliation and concessions of 1223. Sancho's

---

et principibus occupandam" (*Potthast* 6860; *QE* 82). For the early thirteenth-century context of such papal threats, see O. Hageneder, "Das päpstliche Recht der Fürstenabsetzung," *Archivum Historiae Pontificiae* 1 (1963): 71; see pp. 53–95. Gregory IX deals far more with the depredations of the royal officials than with the criminal character of the king himself.

18. Reuter, pp. 11–20; Herculano, 4:1–160.

19. The Concordata of 1223 is printed in Gabriel Pereira de Castro, *De Manu Regia,* a work which I have been unable to consult. See also *QE* 89–93; Herculano, 4:162–67; Reuter, p. 23.

difficulty in observing these terms is reflected in the papal registers dealing with this period. The registers indicate a large number of complaints on the part of the clergy against the exactions of royal officials,[20] on the part of the monastic orders against the exactions of the secular clergy,[21] and on the part of the bishops of Lisbon and Oporto against the exactions of the king.[22] These complaints indicate not only the absence of a centralized judicial authority but the presence of numerous local centers of power, each armed with rights and immunities and bent on serving its own interests, often in the name, but in the name only, of serving the king. The crusading campaign of 1226 did not lessen the antagonism appreciably, and in 1228 the complaints and cross-complaints had become so widespread that Gregory IX sent Jean d'Abbeville to Portugal as papal legate with authority to listen to all complaints and to work out a solution to Portugal's difficulties. The legate's efforts at medi-

20. See Pressutti 4664, 4665, 4672, 4674, 4678; Auvray 71; *QE* 94; 100–01. Most of these complaints concern royal judges claiming jurisdiction in ecclesiastical territories, diocesan clerics who leave their benefices in order to serve the king, and royal officials' *(praetores, alvaziles, et maiordomos ac alios regis Portugalensis satellites)* exactions of goods and money.

21. The question of the rivalry among secular clergy, the religious orders, and the military orders is extremely involved. Sancho favored the military orders, giving them immense grants of land and jurisdiction, and invited a number of religious orders into the kingdom. These groups generally supported him, and the role of the secular clergy as middlemen between papal financial claims and the kings served to alienate them further from royal favor. Herculano and Almeida *(Historia de la Igreja em Portugal* [Coimbra, 1910–22], vol. 1) cite an otherwise unknown papal letter of December 17, 1226 (Almeida, *Igreja,* 1:393), reflecting some of this rivalry. Other documents are: Abranches 74, 77, 79, 80; *QE* 101, 101–02, 102 (Auvray 169); Abranches 84, 86, 88, 95 *(QE* 105), 91, 92.

22. Pressutti 4664, 4665, 4666, 4667, 4672, 4673, 4679, 4683, 4684, 6141 *(QE* 94), 6188 *(QE* 95–97); Raynaldi, *ad. an.* 1227, no. 10; *Potthast* 7656, 6187 *(QE* 97–98); Auvray 70 *(QE* 99–100). The lack of a centralized administration reflects Portugal's separation of centers of real power. The wealth and power of the king could not make headway against the entrenched liberties of the clergy and the nobles, although elsewhere—e.g. England and France—such centralization had begun much earlier.

ation and ecclesiastical reorganization appear to have been, for a time, at least, successful.[23] The *Cortes* of 1228 proclaimed a new crusading campaign, inaugurated a resettlement program in the newly rehabilitated see of Idanha-Guarda, and witnessed another temporary reconciliation between king and clergy.

The second period, although it in a sense duplicates the events of the first, is characterized by a greater intensity on the part of each side and by the rise of new clerical opponents of the king. Pedro Salvadores succeeded Martinho Rodrigues in the see of Oporto, and Silvestre Godinho, who had succeeded Estevam Soares in the archiepiscopal see of Braga in 1228, began to complain of royal activities even more vociferously than had his predecessor. Johannes Falbertus (João Rolis) succeeded Sueiro Gomes in the Lisbon episcopate. The election of Johannes illustrates both the character of Sancho's new opponents and the extreme seriousness of the steps which both sides began to take. In 1234 Sueiro of Lisbon died. His successor, D. Paio, lived only a few months and was in turn succeeded by Johannes, papal physician, dean of the Lisbon cathedral chapter, and a strong supporter of clerical privileges. Johannes's rival in the episcopal election, Sancho Gomes, obtained royal support and urged the king to prevent Johannes from entering his new office.[24] On one occasion the royal forces, commanded by Ferdinand of Serpa, the king's brother, pursued Johannes's friends into a church. When his own soldiers refused to violate their sanctuary, Ferdinand turned a troop of Moslem mercenaries after his quarry. The mercenaries killed Johannes's friends, destroyed his goods, and desecrated the church into which they had fled. This royal offense, coupled with another quarrel between Sancho himself and Pedro Salvadores, more

23. Cf. the letter of Gregory IX of July 13, 1232 (Auvray 829) concerning the legate's suspension of 1,786 clerics of illegitimate birth from their benefices. For the mission generally, see Reuter, pp. 27–29; Herculano, 4:190–205; Almeida, *Igreja,* pp. 397–98.

24. For Silvestre, see the studies of Sousa Costa (above, n. 26) and I. da Rosa Pereira, "Silvestre Godinho, Um Canonista portugues," extract from *Lumen* (1962). For the dispute see Reuter, pp. 32–33; Herculano, 4:274–86; Auvray 1525, 1664, 1669, 1670, 2019 (= *Potthast* 9495), 2388–90, 2476, 4976–77, 4994, 4995, 4997, 5002–03, 5005–11, 5316 *(QE* 135–38); *QE* 123–24.

than outweighed Sancho's crusading successes in 1228 and 1232. The punishment leveled against Ferdinand of Serpa and Sancho and their humble acceptance of it indicates both the psychological and juridical disadvantages at which they stood.[25]

By 1240 Sancho and Ferdinand of Serpa had again made peace with the pope and the Portuguese prelates, although Ferdinand's acceptance of an unusually harsh penance appears to have alienated the brothers permanently.[26] The interdict and excommunications were lifted and a new crusading effort was planned. This settlement, however, was to be no longer-lasting than the others. The Crusade failed to materialize, and Sancho, unwisely antagonizing his clerical opponents, married Mecia Lopes de Haro, daughter of the Lord of Biscay. The clergy considered this marriage a direct affront, since Sancho and Mecia Lopes were consanguineous within the fourth degree. Besides the ecclesiastical difficulties which the marriage presented, there arose a number of political problems centered on the marriage, and one may see the years between 1241 and 1245 as the period in which political and ecclesiastical opposition to Sancho began to coalesce. The marriage was the first, but not the only, step in the process.[27]

The clergy were not the only ones in Portugal who concerned themselves with Sancho's marriage. The king's brother, Afonso of Boulogne,[28] who, according to Herculano, had harbored at his court those Portuguese nobles who fled from Sancho's disfavor, appears from this period on to have worked actively with the Portuguese clergy for the removal of Sancho. Whether Afonso was, as Herculano claims, a permanent center of political opposition to his broth-

25. Herculano, 4:345–47; Reuter, pp. 29–32, 34.

26. Ferdinand's oath is in Auvray 4996. For the new truce, see Reuter, pp. 34–36; Auvray 5210 (= *QE* 140–41; Abranches 5367 (= *QE* 141; Brandão, *Monarchia Lusitana,* vol. 4, fol. 144; *Potthast* 10989; Abranches 112).

27. For Mecia Lopes, see Herculano, 5:12–13, 281–88. Her depiction in the sources is far closer to that of the characteristic wicked queen than to an individual description. Cf. Johannes Mariana, *De rebus Hispaniae* (Mainz, 1519), pp. 545–46.

28. Afonso, apparently by the patronage of Blanche of Castile, had married the heiress of Boulogne in 1238 (Reuter, pp. 36–38).

er since his marriage to the heiress of Boulogne in 1238 is not entirely demonstrable. However, Afonso is designated as the major complainant in Innocent IV's decretal annulling the marriage in February 1245.[29] The cause for Afonso's role in the actions against Sancho after 1241 may well have been his concern that the marriage, valid or not, might produce an heir whose claims to succeed Sancho would, according to Portuguese custom, be considerably stronger than his own.[30] Moreover, the connections between Afonso of Boulogne and Innocent IV, on the one hand, and Blanche of Castile, and Louis IX of France, on the other, although never thoroughly traced, may have given Afonso support as great as that offered by the Portuguese nobility and clergy.[31]

Sancho's failure to carry out his crusading plans also counted heavily against him. Indeed, his earlier military successes had stood him in good stead with Rome and had on occasion served as a buffer between his own high-handedness and the clerical wrath which had plagued him since his succession.[32] Some of the narrative sources and some of the papal correspondence strongly imply a progressive mental and physical dilapidation on the part of the king, partly from the supposed magical powers of his new wife. Apocryphal as these suggestions probably are, they provide an imagina-

29. The decree of invalidation is *Sua nobis dilectus filius* of February 12, 1245 (Berger 995; *QE* 144).

30. For the terms of succession, see Gama Barros, 3:297. In this commentary on *Grandi* Innocent IV was to note briefly this aspect of the case *(Apparatus super libros Decretalium* [Venice, 1481], fol. 45r *ad v. regni):* "Speciale est in regno quam reges non possunt privare nec dum filios nec fratres vel alios consanguineos ex stirpe parterna descendentes a regno sola voluntate." For the general development of juridical thought in Portugal, see. M. J. de Almeida Costa, "Para a historia da cultura juridica medieva em Portugal," *Boletim de Faculdade de Direito* 25 (Coimbra, 1960): 253–76.

31. The subject has never been thoroughly studied. See E. Berger, *Saint Louis et Innocent IV* (Paris, 1893), p. 150.

32. Sancho's campaigns are discussed briefly in C. Selvagem, *Portugal militar* (Lisbon, 1931), pp. 86–90. For papal defense of Sancho see, e.g., the bulls of October 1232 (Auvray 926) and, more important, of August 1234*(QE* 121; Abranches 105).

tive dimension to the very real political problems that the king was unable to solve. The figures of evil queens and wicked counselors are familiar motifs in medieval and Renaissance political rhetoric, but the political difficulties they always imply are real enough. However technically inaccurate these charges were, they were a characteristic response to what thirteenth-century men considered bad governance.

After 1241 ecclesiastical and political opposition to Sancho began to coalesce. Afonso's opposition to the marriage, the articulate hostility of a new generation of clerical opponents (and perhaps their greater legal skill), and the failure of Sancho's later advisors to measure up to the diplomatic and legal ability of the earlier great chancelors, Mestre Julião and Mestre Vicente, all contributed to a unified opposition which made it even less likely that the king might reach a political settlement on terms less disastrous than those of 1223 or 1228.[33] Moreover, in 1241, another event took place which probably hastened Sancho's downfall. Frederick II intercepted a papal fleet off Pisa and scattered the prelates who were proceeding to Rome for general council. Among those who escaped Frederick and fled to Rome were some of Sancho's most persistent opponents. The prolonged stay of these prelates in Rome suggests to Herculano that this was the period in which the plans for the deposition were laid, and that from the autumn of 1241 on, Sancho's removal was a question of direct concern to the prelates, to Afonso and his French supporters, and to the pope himself.[34]

The coincidence of a concerted opposition after 1241 and a simultaneous decline of Sancho's personal and political powers constitutes a neat but hardly verifiable picture. The official descriptions of Sancho's ineptitude and lethargy are belied by his earlier crusading victories, by the vigor with which he pursued his exactions,

33. The careers of these two great chancellors remain to be studied in full. See the remarks of Post, *Studies in Medieval Legal Thought,* p. 485, and Sousa Costa, above. For Mestre Vicente, see now S. Kuttner, "Emendationes et notae variae: I: 'Wo war Vicentius Hispanus Bischof?' " in *Traditio* 22 (1966): 471–74.

34. A letter from the prelates to Gregory IX is in *QE* 141–42. See also Reuter, pp. 34–36.

and by his effective resistance to Afonso between 1245 and 1247. These descriptions, however, did reveal one important fact: in not having pursued the Crusade, Sancho abandoned the one course of action which might have saved him. With support for his Crusade gone, Sancho forfeited his strongest claim, not only to a status higher than that of his clergy, but to any right to rule at all. Sancho's political bad judgment, his inability to control large influential segments of the nobility and the clergy, and his inability to hold his own in the battle of charges and countercharges reflected in the papal correspondence resulted in the portrait drawn in the *narratio* of *Grandi.* In general, that portrait was the result of a political breakdown within the kingdom not unlike those which took place in other contemporary realms. But unlike some wiser and more fortunate rulers, Sancho was able to profit neither from scientific jurisprudence of recent legal scholarship nor from the factionalism within the ranks of the nobility.

Between 1241 and 1245 Sancho remained militarily, but not politically, inactive. He continued his attempts to control clerical jurisdiction and to arrogate to himself more and more governmental power. With the accession of Innocent IV, however, Sancho's opposition found a willing pope. Between February and July of 1245 four papal letters were issued for Portugal, each of which constituted one step in the process of removing Sancho from the throne. The first of these, the letter of annullment, mentions Afonso of Boulogne as complainant and declares the marriage invalid.

The second, dated March 20, is the decretal *Inter alia,* directly addressed to Sancho, which describes the state of Portugal in terms that were to be echoed almost verbatim in *Grandi.*[35] The letter

35. The full text is given only in Raynaldi (above, p. 136, n. 2), *ad annum* 1245, no. 6 (vol. 21, tome II, pp. 318–19). *Dat. Lugduni* XIII *kal. ap. ann.* II, *Illustri Regi Portugalliae . . . Inter alia desiderabilia.* See above, nn. 6, 7: "Inter alia desiderabilia cordis nostri salutem fidelium, quorum regimini, licet immeriti, Deo praesumus disponente, principaliter affectantes grandi gaudio exultamus in Domino, cum ea nobis de ipsis fidelibus referuntur, per quae suarum profectus provenire dignoscitur animarum; et vehementi dolore turbamur, si nos illa de eis audire contigat, quae ipsis et aliis pravo exemplo salutis afferunt detrimentum: unde tanto laetitia majori replebimur, si cultui virtutum insistens studeas te ante oculos reddere divinae maiestatis acceptum, quanto plures ex hoc et

further states that if Sancho's outrage continue, they will put the well-being of both the kingdom and the soul of the king in great danger.[36] Before allowing this to happen, says Innocent, he will

---

a malo retrahere et ad exercitum bonitatis inducere comprobaris. Sane non sine gravi turbatione mentis audivimus, quod post clamores et querelas multiplices praelatorum et aliorum regni Portugalliae contra te super conculatione libertatis ecclesiasticae, aliisque oppressionibus ecclesiarum eiusdem regni depositas, et admonitiones frequentes tibi propter hoc a Rom. pontificibus nostris praedecessoribus et provisiones super iis a felicis recordationis Gregorio Papa praedecessore nostro inter te et quosdam ex praelatis ipsis, ac promissiones a te in hac parte super articulis certis factas; tu circa malefactorum ipsus regni audaciam reprimendam sic negligens inveniris."

36. The letter ends: "Caeterum castra, villas, possessiones et alia iura regalia deperire permittens personarum tam ecclesiasticarum, quam saecularium, nobilium et ignobilium, occisiones nefarias, dum religioni non parcitur, nec sexui, vel aetati; rapinas, incestus, raptusque monialium et saeclarium mulierum; rusticorum et clericorum, ad negotiatorum tormenta gravia, quae ipsis a nonnullis regni praefati pro extorquenda ab ipsis pecunia infliguntur; ecclesiarum et coemeteriorum violationes et incendia, fractiones treugarum, et alia enormia, quae a tibi subjectis libere committuntur, scienter toleras: quin potius tot tantisque malis, dum ea praeteris impunita, consentire videris, et pandis aditum ad pejora. Terras insuper et alia Christianorum bona in confinio Sarracenorum posita non defendens, ea infidelibus occupanda relinquis. Et licet a supradictis praelatis, ut ad corrigenda praemissa pluraque alia nefanda, quorum coenosa narratio fastidium generaret, ardenter, ut teneris assurgeres, monitus fueris diligenter; tu tamen eorum monitionibus obauditis, id hactenus officere neglixisti. Nos igitur eidem regno super tam miserabili statu paterno condolentes affectu, et cupientes ipsum a tot respirare angustiis, totque oppresionibus relevari; serenitatem regiam monemus, rogamus, et hortamur attente in remissionem tibi peccaminum iniungentes, quatenus prudenter considerans, quod si omnipotens Dominus tuam super iis negligentiam ad tempus forte sustineat, postremo tamen si in te, ac tuis contemnas errata corrigere, illam et hic impunitam non deseret et in futuro nihilominus ulciscetur gravius; sic ad corrigenda praemissa solerter et ferventer exurgas, ut culpas subditorum tuas per reprobabilem patientiam non efficias: sed in te ac ipsis proberis odire malitiam et diligere bonitatem; et de persona tua grata de caetero auctore Domino audiamus. Quod si forte, quod non credimus, fueris circa haec corrigenda remissus, neguaquam tolerare sedes Apostolica poterit, quin super iis ad salutem tuam dictique regni commode remedium adhibeat opportunum: et nihilominus venera-

take steps to correct them. He appoints the bishops of Oporto and Coimbra and the Dominican prior to urge Sancho to make the necessary reforms and to report to the pope at the Council of Lyons if the king should prove intractable. The brief period between the promulgation of *Inter alia* and that of *Grandi* leads Herculano and others to conclude that the former was simply a technical ultimatum which the pope knew perfectly well Sancho could not carry out.[37] Innocent, says Herculano, issued *Inter alia* simply in order to add a necessary charge of contumacy to the final decree of deposition.

The third document, the decretal *Cum zelo fidei,* was addressed to the Count of Boulogne and granted to him and his soldiers the customary crusading indulgences for his forthcoming campaign against the Moors.[38] Herculano regards this document to be one further example of papal duplicity, a political move disguised as a crusading privilege.[39] The final document is *Grandi.* As noted above, Sancho did not carry out Innocent's instructions, and the pope, considering the merits of Afonso, transferred to him the care of the realm, yet allowed Sancho to retain the *regnum,* or *dignitas.* In September 1245 Afonso went to Paris, where he concluded a formal agreement with the Portuguese clergy similar to those of 1211, 1223, and 1228,[40] by now almost a necessity for a new

---

bilibus fratribus nostris Portugallensi et Coimbriensi episcopis, ac dilecto filio priori fratrum Praedicatorum Coimbriensium litteris nostris iniungimus ut te ad id monentes attente, et efficaciter intendentes, qualiter super hoc faciendum duxeris, et de ipsorum circa te in hac parte processu, nos in concilio a nobis proximo celebrando certificare procurent."

37. Herculano, 5:19–53.

38. Herculano, 5:30–46. The letter is *Potthast* 11625; *QE* 146–47; Brandão, *Monarchia Lusitana,* vol. 4, fol. 156v; Abranches 121. Cf. the earlier crusading privilege, *Terra sancta Christi dispersa* of January 1245 (*QE* 143; Abranches 120; cf. *Potthast* 11491, 11516, 11517).

39. Herculano, 5:30–46.

40. For the agreement at Paris, see Herculano, 5:49–60; *QE* 153–57; Brandão, *Monarchia Lusitana,* vol. 4, fol. 278 (= Cronicas de *D. Sancho II,* pp. 363–64); Ruy de Pina, *Cronica do . . . D. Sancho II,* pp. 7–9; Caetano da Sousa, *Provas* (above, n. 3), I, doc. no. 26; A. H. de Sousa Costa, *As Concordatas portuguesas* (Braga, 1966), p. 15; idem, *Cronicas dos sete primeiros reis de Portugal,* pp. 218–22; Livermore, pp. 78–79.

Portuguese ruler. Although Sancho and his allies put up a spirited resistance to Afonso's forces, the king had no choice by 1247 but to withdraw from the kingdom, "omni spe depulsus regni obtinendi, Toleti consenuit, viventi vectigalia Regis [Ferdinand III] liberalitate donata."[41] Until his death Sancho continued to use the title *Dei Gratia Rex Portugalliae;* at the same time, Afonso re-

41. Mariana, *De rebus Hispaniae,* p. 546. For Ruy de Pina, Sancho was "a disgraced king . . . in life and death an example of human infelicity." In 1735 Caetano da Sousa had Sancho neatly deposed "by the three estates of the realm *com injuria de magestade" (Historia genealogica da casa Real portuguesa* [rep. Coimbra, 1946], 1:100). Many scholars, including Mansi, long thought that *Grandi* and *Ad apostolice* had both been pronounced during the Council of Lyon. In Mansi, vol. 23, *Grandi* is in fact printed among the *additiones* to the Council. The question of conciliar deposition had apparently been bruited about long before Mansi, however, since Johannes Andreae took note of it in his *Apparatus* to the *Liber Sextus (ad.* 2.14.2 *Ad apostolice):* "Et sine sententia vel licentia consilii, sententia papae sufficeret imperatorem, et quemcumque alium. 15.6.3 alius, ibi non dicitur quod in concilio facta fuerit depositio: enim ipse habet plenitudinem potestatis." The deposition of Frederick II took place at the first and third sessions of the Council. See Hefele–Leclerq, *Histoire des conciles* (Paris, 1913), 5:1633–79, and P. Pouzet "Le Pape Innocent IV à Lyon—Le Concile de 1245," *Revue de l'Histoire de l'Eglise de France* 15 (1929): 281–318. For Innocent's views of his own authority, see M. Pacaut, "L'Autorité pontificale selon Innocent IV," *Le Moyen Age* 66 (1960): 85–120, and the recent studies of J. A. Watt, "The Theory of Papal Monarchy in the Thirteenth Century" and "Medieval Deposition Theory: A Neglected Canonist Consultatio from the First Council of Lyons," in *Studies in Church History,* vol. 2, ed. G. J. Cuming (London, 1965), pp. 197–214. The case of Sancho, however, was not part of the council's business in any case. See S. Kuttner, "Die Konstitutionen des ersten allgemeinen Konzils in Lyon," in *Studia et Documenta Historiae et Iuris* 6 (Rome, 1940): 70–131. Kuttner's distinction between the conciliar and nonconciliar legislation of Innocent contradicts the brilliant but quite false picture drawn by Herculano (5:46) of Innocent haughtily waving *Grandi* and *Ad apostolice* under the noses of the assembled prelates and peremptorily including them as conciliar canons. For further Innocentian legislation, see P.-J. Kessler, "Die Novellengesetzgebung Innocent IV," *Zeitschrift der Savigny Stiftung für Rechtsgeschichte, Kanonistiche Abteilung* 31 (1942): 142–320; 32 (1943): 300–83; 33 (1944): 56–128. For further comments, cf. Walter Ullmann, *Medieval Papalism* (London, 1949), pp. 201–07.

ferred to his own capacity in official documents as that of *curator, governador,* or *visitator* of Portugal.[42]

The issues at hand in the case of Sancho and Innocent's disposal of them sharply illustrate some of the difficulties of public law in the early thirteenth century. Innocent's concern, as he himself notes, is for the *utilitas* of the king and kingdom, for the *necessitas* of the kingdom, and for its *status,* not merely spiritually, but in a distinct temporal sense as well. The solutions which the pope proposed for Portugal's difficulties reveal certain conceptions of kingship and papal jurisdiction, an analysis of which may serve to shed some light on Innocent's view of the character of the temporal state and its relation to papal *plenitudo potestatis.*

At first glance, Sancho's difficulties with his clergy and nobles do not appear to differ significantly from those of other contemporary and near-contemporary rulers such as John of England, Frederick II, Otto IV, and Sancho's own father, Afonso II. All of these rulers were excommunicated, and all were deposed or threatened with deposition by Innocent III, Honorius III, Gregory IX, or Innocent IV. It is not unlikely that Sancho's offenses, seen exclusively in the light of the papal correspondence of the early part of his reign, might have merited for him the fate of Frederick II. Yet Innocent IV went to great pains to point out that Sancho was not technically deposed. Innocent's decision, as the remainder of this study will show, was consistent with some earlier canonist political thought, although in practice it was to invoke principles which were to prove unworkable. The practical political difficulties involved in separating the *administratio* of a kingdom from the royal *dignitas* were effectively to prevent such an approach from evolving into a successful theory of kingship. The military defeat of Sancho in 1247 marked a limited success for Innocent's principles, but neither

42. E.g. in both of Sancho's wills. In the first, written early in 1245, he disposes of the kingdom; in the second, written in 1248, he does not. His title is the same, however, in both. These wills may be found in Brandão, *Monarchia Lusitana,* vol. 4, fol. 278 (= *Cronicas,* pp. 363–65), and in Caetano da Sousa, *Provas* (vol. 1, nos. 24–25). For Afonso's titles, see Gama Barros, 3:316, and F. Almeida, *Historia de Portugal* (Coimbra, 1910), 1:452–56.

Grandi nor the declaration of the English barons in 1308 that the Crown might be separated from the person of the king would ever become a clear-cut, generally accepted alternative to deposition.[43]

Innocent outlined his own view of papal authority in cases of negligent kingship in his remarks on his own decretal *Ad apostolice,* the instrument of the deposition of Frederick II, which Innocent as a canonist glossed among the decretals in the *Liber extra* of Gregory IX. In his *Apparatus* Innocent asks: "But what if another king is negligent, or another prince who has no superior? We say then that [the pope] succeeds to his jurisdiction, not because [that king] holds his kingdom from [the pope], but because of the plenitude of power which [the pope] has because he is the vicar of Christ."[44] The problem of royal negligence here allows Innocent to outline concisely the distinction between legal-political superiority and judicial *plenitudo potestatis.* The pope may act, not because he is the legal superior, the ultimate monarch or lord of negligent rulers, but because he is empowered by virtue of his vicariate of Christ to act extraordinarily, as Maitland once remarked, as "an omnicompetent court of first instance for the whole of Christendom."[45]

In the late twelfth and early thirteenth centuries canonists

43. Both the English barons' declaration of 1308 and *Grandi* represent essentially abstract conclusions concerning the character of royal authority. Although such terms as *administratio, regnum, corone,* and *person* were capable of being the subjects of abstract political discussion during the period, their meaning was never sufficiently defined to enable them to stand as concrete political realities. For the text of the barons' declaration, see H. G. Richardson and G. O. Sayles, *The Governance of Medieval England* (Edinburgh, 1963), pp. 466–69.

44. Ed. cit. above, p. 150, n. 30 *(X. 2.2.9 ad v. vacante).* Cf. Watt, "Theory of Papal Monarchy," pp. 275–76.

45. "William of Drogheda and the Universal Ordinary," in F. W. Maitland, *Roman Canon Law and the Church of England* (London, 1898), pp. 100–31. The most recent discussions of the problems of *plenitudo potestatis* are those of J. A. Watt in "The Use of the Term *Plenitudo potestatis* by Hostiensis," *Proceedings of the Second International Congress of Medieval Canon Law* (cited above, p. 137, n. 3), pp. 161–88; R. L. Benson, "Plenitudo Potestatis: Evolution of a Formula from Gregory IV to Gratian," *Studio Gratania* 14, Collectanea Stephan Kuttner IV (1967): 195–217.

began to give considerable attention to the different occasions upon which these extraordinary papal judicial powers might be used. They compiled lists of these instances which grew in length and complexity as scholarship and speculation on the canon law became more comprehensive and papal decretals began to incorporate the results of earlier canonist thought. Among the starting points of such speculation was Innocent III's decretal *Per venerabilem,* briefly noted above.[46] Papal intervention in the affairs of temporal rulers was, however, similar to the more strictly ecclesiastical question of the rights of ecclesiastical judges to intervene in lay judicial affairs. The occasions on which such intervention was permissible comprehend the specific political occasions described by Innocent III, Tancred, Hostensis, and others. In the middle of the thirteenth century Goffredo da Trani provided a particularly comprehensive list in his *Apparatus* to the *Liber extra* of Gregory IX:

> There are, however, certain causes in which jurisdiction belongs to the ecclesiastical judge . . . such as causes between servants or farmers of the church . . . causes of penitents . . . causes of wretched persons . . . causes concerning the feudal rights of the church . . . causes of travelers or pilgrims . . . causes concerning the theft of ecclesiastical property . . . causes concerning spiritual affairs or things connected to spiritual affairs . . . causes in which the secular judge is negligent . . . causes in which the secular judge is suspect . . . or during a vacancy in the empire . . . or because of the temporal jurisdiction which the Church possesses in temporal affairs or because of custom . . . also in causes concerning doweries . . . or in causes involving ecclesiastical crimes.[47]

To be sure, other Innocentian decretals further developed the judicial role of the papacy in temporal affairs. The most influential of

46. See above, pp. 135–36. See also Watt, "Theory of Papal Monarchy," pp. 211–36, and B. Tierney, "*Tria quippe distinguit iudicia* . . . A Note on Innocent III's Decretal *Per venerabilem,*" *Speculum* 37 (1962): 48–59.

47. Gottofredus de Trano, *Apparatus super titulis Decretalium* (Venice, 1491), fol. 28v. For discussions of other similar lists, see Watt, "Theories of Papal Monarchy," p. 290; Tierney, "Tria quippe . . .," pp. 52–53; W. Ullmann, *Medieval Papalism* (London, 1949), pp. 102–09.

these was probably *Novit,* which laid down the famous principle of papal intervention *ratione peccati.*[48] In a sense the decretal activity of Innocent III constitutes the framework which supported the attempts of thirteenth-century canonists to describe the function of papacy in precise legal terminology, to complete the development of the idea of *christianitas* in its politico-legal aspects.

Within this characteristic of legal thought the case of Sancho illustrates a number of justifiable grounds for papal intervention. Sancho had created *causae miserabilium personarum.* He and his officials had also been *raptores rerum ecclesiae* and were doubtless *suspecti* as judges. Sancho himself was a *judex negligens,* and his case technically was disposed of during a vacancy of the Empire. In one sense Portugal was a *feudum ecclesiae,* and there may even have been some question of customary ecclesiastical jurisdiction in Portuguese temporal affairs, since the canon law had been publicly declared legally binding on all subjects of the King of Portugal at the *Cortes* of 1211.[49] More important, however, was the general canonist theory that the papal authority to depose or otherwise correct temporal rulers extended not only to those guilty of *quolibet peccatum* but to those who were *minus utilis* as well.[50]

During the second half of the thirteenth century the response to *Grandi* contributed further to the clarification of ideas of public law and kingship. The canonists, including Innocent himself, generally approved of the action taken, although at least one of them appears to have maintained that Innocent should have deposed Sancho outright.[51] Contemporary political response, however, appears to have been just as uniformly unfavorable. Both Alfonso of Castile and Frederick II took the occasion provided by the publication of *Grandi* to criticize papal conduct severely. As late as the sixteenth century, in fact, no less a political thinker than Jean Bodin

48. Cf. Watt, "Theories of Papal Monarchy," pp. 218–19, 296–300.

49. Reuter, pp. 11–13.

50. Cf. Johannes Teutonicus, *Glo. Ord.* D. 40 c. 6 ***Si papa, ad vv. a fide devius:*** "Sed pro quo peccato potest Imperator deponi? Pro quolibet: si est incorrigibilis unde deponitur, si est minus utilis, ut 15 q. 6 alius."

51. Bernardus Compostellanus Junior. See Riesenberg, ***The Inalienability of Sovereignty,*** pp. 168–69. See below, p. 164, n. 60.

was to note some of the political problems that the decretal raised.[52]

Although Innocent failed to include *Grandi* in his own first two collections of his decretals, he did include it in the so-called *Collectio* III, a list of incipits indicating those of his decretals which he wished included in an official lawbook,[53] and he commented on it in his discussions of some of his decretals in his *Apparatus* to the *Liber extra.* In 1298 *Grandi* was included in Boniface VIII's official collection, the *Liber sextus,* under the title *De supplenda negligentia praelatorum (VI,* 1, 8, 2). Partly as a result of its delayed appearance in Innocent's collections, *Grandi* was often omitted in early canonists' discussions of Innocent's decretal production.[54]

52. Jean Bodin, *De republica libri sex latine* (I cite the edition of Frankfurt, 1641), 1:187–88. Bodin may have gotten his information from Mariana, but the case of Sancho had been discussed by a number of fourteenth-century canonists, some of whose works had been printed in the early sixteenth century (e.g. Johannes Andreae, Johannes Monachus, Geminianus, Antonio a Butrio, et al). Baldus had also discussed the text briefly *(Repertorium in omnia consiliorum* [Venice, 1580], vol. 1: *Consilia* I, *cons.* 271, no. 3, fol. 81v). Philippus Probus, a sixteenth-century canonist, had used the text as the basis for a long *additio* on the subject of whether inheritance or election was the proper way for kingship to be acquired *(Johannes Monachi glos. in sextum Decretalium* [Venice, 1585]: *Additiones Probi,* fols. 121r–v). In 1614 Melchior Goldast cited the gloss of Innocent IV verbatim and applied it to the figure of the emperor: *Politica imperialia* (Frankfurt, 1614), pt. II, p. iv.

53. The literary history of Innocent's decretal collections has been traced by Schulte, "Die Dekretalen zwischen den Decretales Gregorii IX und Liber VI Bonifacii VIII," in S.B. Wien 55 (1867), and "Beiträge zur Literatur über die Dekretalen Gregors IX, Innocenz IV, Gregors X," in S.B. Wien 68 (1871). It has been more recently and thoroughly traced by S. Kuttner, "Decretalistica," *Zeitschrift der Savigny-Stiftung für Rechtsgeschichte, Knonistische Abteilung* 26 (1937): 471–89, and by P.-J. Kessler, cited above, p. 155, n. 41. *Grandi* was included under the title *"De supplenda negligentia prelatorum":* Guido de Baysio, *Archidiac. super Sexto Decretalium* (Venice, 1577), fol. 41r: "Hec dec. ponitur sub rubrica ista, quia reges etiam prelati nuncupantur, ut 11 q. 3 praecipue." The early fourteenth-century decretalist Boatinus remarks (Oestrr. Bibl. Wien, Cod. 2129, fol. 124v): ". . . supplenda negligentia prelatorum ecclesiasticorum ista sola loquitur in supplenda negligentia prelatorum secularium."

54. Kessler, following Kuttner, suggests that Innocent had withheld *Grandi (Collectio* III, chap. 7) and *Ad apostolice (Collectio* III, chap. 23)

However, in the ordinary gloss of Johannes Andreae to the *Liber sextus* and in his *Novella,* the decretal became a well-known canonical text.[55]

Innocent himself discussed several aspects of the decretal in his *Apparatus:* the law of succession in Portugal, the *libera administratio* of the curator, the *utilitas regis et regni,* and the role of the pope when there exists no *iudex superior* from whom justice may be obtained.[56] Of these four topics, the third is most important for this study:

> Nota causas iustas dandi curatorem regibus. . . . si nesciunt suum regnum defendere vel in eo iustitiam et pacem servare maxime religiosis personis locis et pauperibus. Et etiam quod plus est si nesciunt perdita recuperare. Et idem quod diximus in regibus servandum est in ducibus comitibus et aliis qui habent iurisdictionem super alios. Aliis autem privatis non datur curator nisi sint furiosi vel prodigi. C. de cur. fur.[57]

Innocent's repetition of *nesciunt* suggests strongly the ruler's own incompetence, his lack of *scientia regnandi.* Further, Innocent purposely draws a parallel between *nescire* and *furiosus vel prodigus* [*esse*] in the Roman law concerning the assigning of *curators.* A ruler who lacks the *scientia* to govern properly merits the same treatment as a citizen who is unable to govern his own private affairs.

Nor was Innocent capricious, as Herculano and others have sometimes suggested. In his *Apparatus* to *Ad apostolice* Innocent noted the problems involved in taking public action against rulers: "Est enim memorandum de hac sententia depositionis que non debet

---

from his earlier collections precisely because of their powerful political implications. He also suggests the subsequent use made of *Ad apostolice* (*Grandi* also appears to have been used) in the deposition of Adolf of Nassau in 1298. See also Caspary.

55. *Novella in sextum* (Venice, 1499; rep. Graz, 1963), pp. 75–76.

56. Innocent's topics, particularly that of the manner of succession to the Portuguese throne, attracted the attention of all later commentators.

57. *Apparatus ad* X 1.10.1 *Grandi, ad v. utilitate.*

ferri nisi urgente multa necessitate et multis causis et criminibus et infamiis manifestis contra imperatorem clamantibus."[58] In other part of his commentary on the same decretal he remarks at greater length:

> Bene facit papa quod non solum multa crimina sed etiam multa genera peccatorum subiecit sententiae depositionis imperatoris. Magna enim causa subesse debet depositioni imperatoris. Non est simile eius ad depositionem clericorum, qui per quolibet peccato deponi possunt . . . Imperatores et alii principes de periculis et periculum est causa quare aliquid detrahitur rigori.

Fully aware of the implications of papal deposition not only in the immediate political and social circumstances surrounding the act but in the history of canonist commentary as well, Innocent refrained from deposing Sancho outright precisely because his case did not appear at all points to be identical to that of Frederick II. Yet the *publica utilitas* of Portugal was doubtless in great danger, at least according to Innocent's sources of information. The previous history of relations in Portugal between *regnum* and *sacerdotium,* the threats of Honorius III and Gregory IX, and the articulate complaints of influential Portguese clergy contributed toward forcing Innocent's hand. Alongside the *rex iustus* and the *tyrannus,* there emerged the *rex inutilis,* guilty of no sin except ignorance and inadequacy, for whom a new course of action had to be instituted. Innocent found his grounds for that action in the history of the *praelatus inutilis,* in Huguccio's remarks on *Alius item,* and in Roman private law.

Innocent's point of view was taken up and expanded in Johannes Andreae's ordinary gloss to the *Liber sextus.* In his comment on *Ad apostolice* Johannes notes *(VI* 2.14.2, *ad v. privamus):*

> Propter crimina ergo deponit Papa Imperatorem, ut hic. Idem cum est inutilis 15.q.6 alius et dat coadiutores ipsis male administrantibus supra, eodem lib. de sup. negl. prael. grandi. Per negligentiam ipsorum iurisdictionem assumit, supra de

58. *Apparatus ad* X 2.14.2 *Ad apostolice, ad v. sempiternam.*

> foro competente licet. Compellit ipsos iustitiam facere, 23 q.5 admnistratores, et ius canonicum etiam debitus casibus observare, supra, eodem lib. de foro competente, c.2 de iureiurando licet, infra .j. de sent. excom. decernimus. Unum enim oportet esse principatum ad quem omnes recurrant, 7 q.1 in apibus, qui fil. sint. legi. per venerabilem.

Johannes here makes the distinction between a ruler's crimes *(propter crimina)* and his "uselessness" *(cum est inutilis)* and appears to add a third category *(male administrantes)*. His remarks on the first two categories reflect the older canonist response to the deposition of Childeric III because "tantae potestati non erat utilis." In this case one should consider *inutilis* to mean not *insufficiens* but something close to criminal negligence, as it had for Huguccio and Johannes Teutonicus earlier.

Watt has said, in regard to Innocent IV's remarks on the decretal *Licet* of Innocent III:

> If, then, there is no other superior to whom recourse might be had in this crisis, the pope would act as that superior in an act of prerogative power held in virtue of his *plenitudo potestatis* as vicar of Christ. He would supply this deficiency, just as he would any other defect of law if for lack of a higher authority justice would be denied anyone or peace endangered.[59]

No pope, however, may act *motu proprio* in such cases; an appeal to him must be made. Innocent's own remarks reveal his awareness of the implications of papal *plenitudo potestatis* when it is used in cases such as those of Frederick II and Sancho II. Johannes Andreae repeated Innocent's remarks concerning the gravity of deposition in his own *Apparatus* (VI 1.8.2, *ad v. gravissima):* "bene dixit: quia maxima causa subesse debuit imperatoris depositioni. Nec est similis depositioni clericorum, qui pro quolibet peccato deponi possunt, 81 dist. c.1." The pope's authority to act and the nature of the action which he took ought not to be considered separately. Innocent IV was well aware of the separate areas of jurisdiction of spiritual and temporal judges, and his meticulous legal reasoning

59. "Theory of Papal Monarchy," p. 276, cf. Cantini, p. 479.

in the cases of Sancho and Frederick reveals the solicitude, if not the political sophistication, of the greatest of the medieval lawyer-popes.

When Johannes Andreae came to comment on *Grandi* proper, he had a less substantial history of canonist commentary on the decretal than had Johannes Teutonicus, for example, on *Alius item.*[60] Nevertheless, his work had substantially the same effect. In a *notabilium* to *Grandi* he sums up the general significance of the text:

> Nota primo principalem effectum huius cap. videlicet quam si ille qui praeest alicui communitati sit negligens et remissus, potest superior sibi dare coadiutorem qui in iure vocatur curator. Nota ulterius conditionis requisitas in coadiutorem, et in illo, qui praeest alicui communitati: quia debet esse devotus erga Deum, circumspectus, plenus oculis, et bonus mundanus . . . sed glossa ista debet intellegi, quod adiutor istius regis successisset in regnum, si rex ipse nullos habet filios.

60. The comments of Bernardus Compostellanus Jr., Guido de Baysio, and Johannes Andreae were the most substantial outside of the remarks of Innocent himself. Other early glosses—e.g. those of Petrus de Sampsona, Zenzelinus de Cassanis, Bernardus Raymundus, and Pierre Bertrand—are considerably slighter. In the later fourteenth century the comments of Guillelmus de Monte Landuno, Lapus Tactus, and particularly Johannes Monachus treated the text at greater length. The description of Sancho by Bernardus Compostellanus became the standard approach to the historical king (MS Vat. Pal. Lat. 629, fol. 263r): ". . . apparet quod iste rex negligens erat et remissus circa regnum et subditos eius prodigus erat et dissipator sive dilapidator ut dicitur circa finem .c. ibi destructioni exposito unde debuit privari regno, quia propter negligentiam removentur prelati . . . et propter dilapidatio deponuntur prelati . . . et ita non debuit ei dari curator sed potius debuit privari regno duabus rationibus et hic ad finem devolvi ordine geniture cum filium non habet . . . dicas quod licet rex sit negligens et remissus aut etiam prodigus sive dissipator precipue cum per successionem regnum sibi defertur propter hoc non debet privari regno sed dari debet sibi curator exemplo furiosi vel prodigi . . . [curator] qui curam debet habere tam regis quam regni sicut curator furiosi vel prodigi . . . et quia papa possit deponere talis propter delicta sua probatur infra de re. iudi. ad apostilice in fi. xv q. vi alius."

Sancho, Johannes goes on to note, "dissipator erat et negligens." The Count of Boulogne, on the other hand, was "devotus, circumspectus, magnanimus et potens."[61]

Guillelmus Durantis and Guido de Baysio *(Archidiaconus)* both had some observations to make concerning *Grandi* and its implications. Although Durantis considers *Alius item* an instance of deposition by the pope alone, on account of the ruler's iniquities, he notes that *Grandi* has become the standard treatment for *reges inutiles:* "Deponit [Papa] imperatorem propter ipsius iniquitates, ut ext. de re iud. lib. 6 [= VI 2.14.2 *Ad apostolice*], et etiam reges 15. q.6 alius, et dat eis curatores ubi ipsi sunt inutiles ad regendum: et extr. de sup. neg. prel. grandi lib. 6 [=VI 1.8.2]."[62] In Durantis's view *Ad apostolice* and *Alius item* are parallel texts which concern respectively the deposition of emperors and kings, both for iniquities or crimes. *Grandi,* however, is the standard approach for kings who are inadequate (=*inutiles)* to rule. *Inutilitas* is not, as it had been for Rufinus, Tancred, Alanus, and others, a sufficient cause for judicial deposition.

The most significant dissenting voice among the canonists appears to have been that of Bernardus Compostellanus *junior.* With-

61. The qualities of the *curator* attracted the attention of a number of commentators, none of whom rose much above the customary level of juridical panegyric. Two instances, however, may deserve notice. An anonymous commentator of the fourteenth century contrasted the *magnanimitas* of the *curator* with the *pusillanimitas* of the king (MS Vat. Pal. Lat. 8071, fol. 124r *ad v. magnanimitate):* "magnanimitas est rerum dificilium et terribilium spontanea et rationabilis aggressio et est contra pusillanimitas." Lapus Tactus and Johannes Andreae cite Seneca's letters and Cicero to illustrate the ideal virtues of *curators* and kings, reflecting perhaps the beginnings of canonist's use of classical literature.

62. *Speculum iudiciale,* I *de Legato,* 6, 17. Guido de Baysio (see above, p. 160, no. 53) remarks: "Hic assignat diversas causas quare isti comiti commisit curam et administrationem regni. & sic est arg. hic, quod datio tutoris et cure et coadiutoris, fieri debet cum causae cognitione & hanc commissionem fecit, quia ipse rex erat valde negligens et male administrabat iura regni. et quia negligebat defensionem ecclesiarum, monasteriorum, et aliorum piorum locorum, et personarum ecclesiasticarum."

out, however, entirely disagreeing with Innocent's action, Bernardus maintained that he should have deposed Sancho outright—that is, removed the *dignitas (=regnum)* as well as the *administratio* from the incompetent king.[63] Thus Bernardus's view seems to be quite close to that of Gregory VII and an influential group of late twelfth- and early thirteenth-century canonists, and it may have suggested to Johannes Andreae the distinction between the *rex inutilis* and the bad administrator. Bernardus Raymundus, the author of an early *Apparatus* to the *Liber Sextus,* agrees with the assigning of a *curator,*"ubi rex superiorem non habens negligens est et remissus."[64]

Besides his commentaries as a canonist, Innocent IV found other opportunities to discuss *Grandi* and its implications. Alfonso of Castile, an ally of Sancho who had been given territories and incomes in Portugal, wrote several letters to Innocent complaining of the Count of Boulogne's mishandling of his commission. The damage caused by the count's activities, Alfonso claimed, was greater by far than that which he had been called in to correct. Alfonso's repeated complaints resulted in several further letters from the pope, including one to the Count of Boulogne in which Innocent expounded at greater length on the duties of curators.[65] More serious, however, was the opposition of Frederick II. Frederick's letters following his deposition are remarkable documents in which the emperor used all the political pressure he could bring to bear on his fellow rulers in order to sway royal and aristocratic opinion away from the papal cause.[66] To the King of Castile, Frederick

63. See Bernardus's text, cited above, n. 60. The later decretalist Geminianus noted the two opinions *Geminianus super Sexto Decretalium* [Venice, n.d., fol. 76v]: "Gl. super verbo regis oppo. quod propter duo hic occurrentia in tex. *potius debebat deponi quam dari sibi coadiutor.* Fl. format contrarium, et fol. Et idem querit an propter crimen debeat deponi: et dicit quod sic in fin. glos."

64. University of Pennsylvania, MS Lat. 114, fol. 20v.

65. For the correspondence, see Berger 1932, 8027; *Potthast* 12177, 12512, 12513; *QE* 163–64, 181; Herculano, 5:66–68. For the Castilian point of view, see A. Ballesteros-Beretta, *Alfonso X El Sabio* (Madrid, 1963), pp. 74–77.

66. *Petrus de Vineis Epistolae,* ed. S. Schard (Basel, 1566), esp. I.2 and I.21 (pp. 99, 152–72).

used the case of Sancho to illustrate the danger to other kingdoms of Innocent's greed for power:

> Vos tamen, quorum in hoc non minus vestra causa quam nostra nunc agitur . . . Verum cum istae Romanae Sedis antistites ab ea forsitan devians pietate, quam praedicat quocunque; modo poterit (licet contra nos suum posse non valeat) tam in Imperio quam in regnis nostram nitatur offendere majestatem, motus nostros arcere non possumus, quin causam nostram et aliorum injuriam viriliter tueamur. Requirimus igitur, et adfectionem vestram rogamus attente, quatenus, diligentius advertentes, qualiter summus pontifex suis viribus qui nihil habere debet, cum gladio non contentus, in alienam messem falcem praesumptuosus inmittit: et ut non longe petatur a nobis examplum: qualiter in regno Portugalliae honoris sibi usurpavit dignitatem, curas vestras et animos excitetit.[67]

Neither Alfonso's nor Frederick's protests, however, effected any change in Innocent's legal arrangements. Frederick lent Sancho no assistance, and Alfonso, engaged upon his father's Crusade, could not swing the military balance in Sancho's favor with the aid he did send.

In 1245 the public law of the *respublica christiana* was strengthened by the addition of a legal process for cases of royal inadequacy. The figure of the *rex inutilis,* familiar in practice, if not always in theory, from 751 on, became the object of a legal definition made not by those who suffered from the consequences of inept rule but by one who felt himself entrusted with the duty to remedy all defects of law by virtue of an authority which men had come to regard as being judicial as well as theological. If the writings of

67. Ibid., I.16 (pp. 133–36). See also F. Graefe, *Die Publizistik in der letzten Epoche Kaiser Friedrichs II* (Heidelberg, 1909), p. 288, n. 70. One of the rubrics of Johannes Monachus's discussion of *Grandi* in his gloss (*Ion. Mona. glos. in sextum Decretalium* [Venice, 1585], fol. 120v: *Summarium,* no. 4: "Falcem in messem alienam non debemus ponere") must surely have been inspired by Frederick's accusation and its circulation.

Huguccio and others created a juristic contingency existing only in theory, Innocent IV gave full legal meaning to that contingency by his action against Sancho II.

Innocent, however, solved only the judicial, not the political, problems connected with the *rex inutilis.* History, seen under the aspect of law, must also take into account the men who effect (and are affected by) changes in that law. The elaborate legal scholarship contained in *Grandi,* in Innocent's *Apparatus* to *Grandi,* in his letters to Alfonso of Castile, and in his other political decretals fell on unprepared political ground in the kingdom of Portugal. *Grandi,* indeed, contained the results of the most articulate legal tradition that Europe had seen since the age of Justinian, but few territorial monarchies were capable, in 1245, of profiting fully from that tradition. The reign of Afonso III reveals how little *Grandi* contributed toward solving the real problems of Portugal.

A little-known episode from the end of Sancho's reign may illustrate these problems as effectively as any document discussed thus far:

> When Sancho II departed from Castile, he left behind as *alcaide* of Coimbra a certain Martim de Freitas. The Count of Boulogne laid heavy siege to the castle, but neither his promises nor his power were able to reduce the people within, who, in spite of great hardships, resisted for a long time until news was brought to them of Sancho's death at Toledo. The faithful *alcaide* asked for and received security from Afonso of Boulogne and passed through the ring of besiegers. He directed his way to the ancient capital of Spain and ordered that Sancho's tomb be opened, that he might see with his own eyes that the king truly was dead. Having assured himself that the sad event had indeed taken place, he placed in the hands of the dead king the keys of the castle whose care had been entrusted to him. Then, taking the keys again, he returned to Portugal and gave them to Afonso, opening the gates of the city to the besieging army. The prince, struck with admiration at such loyalty, asked Martin to retain the office of *alcaide.*

> The knight, however, far from accepting, cursed any of his descendants who might ever presume to receive from any king the castle which had once been in his charge.[68]

Mariana remarks: "Viri fidem atque constantiam omnibus seculis praedicandam. Lusitani generis et sanguinis propriam laudam."[69]

The legal authority of the Count of Boulogne and the personal fidelity of Martim de Freitas illustrate the two political poles which many kingdoms had to reconcile in the twelfth and thirteenth centuries: that of impersonal public law and that of private fidelity. Each of these repeatedly articulated its own claims, sometimes in legal decisions, sometimes in heroic gesture. The legal history of the *rex inutilis* is inextricably bound up with a series of specific local problems, like those of Portugal. It must be considered at least as much in terms of them as in terms of the general history of law. 1245 did not see the final date in the process of reconciliation, but neither did it quite see, as Herculano claimed, "Uma grande obra de trevas, de corrupção, e de hypocrisia."[70]

68. This version may be found in Herculano, 5:73–74. Cf. Mariana, *De rebus Hispaniae*, pp. 546–47.

69. Mariana, p. 547.

70. Herculano, 5:36.

5

Rex Inutilis in the Arthurian Romances

Legal changes in the medieval idea of the *rex inutilis* paralleled changes in the literary representation of royal inadequacy. The *chansons de geste* had celebrated the ethos of the individual warrior against a background of chaos, infidelity, and injustice. The individual knight moved against a different background, a world of unreality centered on the court, not the battlefield. William of Orange and Raoul de Cambrai fought historically recognizable enemies on a familiar landscape, dark, treacherous, and unfriendly. Lancelot, Yvain, and the other Arthurian knights fought no Sarracens; they fought other knights in a ritual combat whose aim was psychological honor, not political victory. The battles of the *chansons de geste* were supplanted by the *adventures* of the romances. The weakness of a Louis the Pious and the impotence and irascibility of Charlemagne gave way before the curious hesitations and sexual passions of Arthur and the mysterious illnesses of the *Roi-Mehaignié* and the *Roi-Pêcheur,* the Maimed King and the Fisher King.

Arthur's first appearance in twelfth-century literature had been that of a hero, the conquering ruler of the Britons against anarchic elements in British society and, more directly, against Saxon invaders and the rulers of territories outside his realm of Logres. Certain aspects of legendary history, hagiography, and the tradition of the weak kings in the *chansons de geste* and its underlying social and political inspiration, however, made the figure of Arthur potentially less heroic than he had originally appeared. The figure of the *Roi-Mehaignié,* whose career touches elements of kingship quite different from those usually associated with Arthur, is the prototype of the ruler whose physical integrity is closely, but obscurely, bound up with that of his realm. These two rulers, whose depiction is far more complex than that of the kings in the *chansons de geste,* comprise in their combined careers many twelfth- and thirteenth-century views of royal incapacity. Yet it is not enough to say of them, as some scholars tend to do, that they were uniformly *rois fainéants.* The complexity of kingship in the courtly romances is nearly as great as that found in the plays of Shakespeare.

The *romans courtois* were influenced by a variety of literary genres, although they appear to describe a narrowly-constituted society and to reflect the taste and ideals of a small segment of the aristocracy. Not only the increasingly more comprehensive view of man and his place in the world as reflected in moral theology, but the influence of antiquity and the classical conception of the hero gave to the courtly romances a breadth and a degree of sophistication quite different from those of the *chansons de geste.* Yet, for all their concentration upon the individual hero and his psychological as well as physical state, the romances did not neglect the problems of collective action and collective welfare. Paradoxically, the individual knight ultimately achieved his greatest *aventure* in terms of his own inner obligations and his relation to society. If, as Kohler remarks, "the individual knight becomes the true bearer of responsibility for order . . . his *aventures* succeed one another in an ascending gradation of order until [they reach] the supreme exploit, which results in effecting the liberation of an entire community," the community, eventually no less than the individual knight, becomes an institution of some concern. Indeed, if one compares the narrow, abstract community of the *Chanson de Roland* with that of the Arthurian kingdom in Malory, the latter seems much closer to many aspects of courtly society, in spite of its sophisticated unreality.

The figure of Arthur in the early romances possesses the most admirable qualities of the few respectable kings in the *chansons de geste* and of the twelfth-century kings described in contemporary panegyric and historiography. The greatest of royal virtues is *largesce:*[1]

1. E. Köhler, "Quelques Observations d'ordre historico-sociologique sur les rapports entre la chanson de geste et le roman coutrois," in *Chanson de Geste und Höfischer Roman,* Heidelberger Kolloquium, 30 Jun., 1961

... largesce est dame et reine
Qui totes vertuz anlumine.

largesce
... est de si grant hautesce
Que totes vertuz enlumine,
Si est appelee: Reine
Sur totes les autres vertuz.[2]

Largesce, which refers to the king's general function as a provider of adventures as well as goods, shelter, food, and justice, is one of several royal virtues, some of which are derived from the ecclesiastical treatises on kingship and some from contemporary political practice:

Je suis rois, ne doi pas mantir,
Ne vilenie consantir,
Ne faussete ne demesure:
Reison doi garder et droiture.
Ce apartient a leal roi
Que il doit maintenir la loi,
Verite, et foi et justise.[3]

The king must possess not only the virtues of a good knight:

(Heidelberg, 1963), pp. 21–30. In the same collection see also Hans Robert Jauss, "Chanson de geste et roman courtois au XIIe siècle," pp. 61–77. The general question of transition from epic to romance has been widely debated. Particularly useful for this study have been the contributions of E. Hoepffner, "La Chanson de geste et les débuts du roman courtois," in *Mélanges . . . Jeanroy* (Paris, 1928), pp. 422–37; Southern, *The Making of the Middle Ages,* pp. 219–57 (as well as the criticism of Southern's views by E. Vinaver in "From Epic to Romance," *BJRL* 46 [1963/64]: 476–503).

2. Chrétien de Troyes, *Cliges,* vv. 193–94; *Perceval,* vv. 1145–50. For the author, see Jean Frappier, "Chrétien de Troyes," in *ALMA,* pp. 157–91. See, for the popularity of these passages, John B. Fox, *Robert de Blois, Son Oeuvre didactique et narrative* (Paris, 1950), pp. 47–56.

3. Chrétien de Troyes, *Erec,* vv. 1793–99. See also H. Euler, *Recht und Staat in den Romanen des Chrestien von Troyes* (Marburg, 1906).

proesce, raisons, largesce, and *sens,*[4] but those of Christian kingship as well. Since negative, or preventative, virtues in the citation from Chrétien's *Erec* above seem to accord more closely to feudal concerns than ecclesiastical ones, they emphasize the king's role as protector, as a maintaining, rather than a creating, force in courtly society. The romance kingdom of Arthur was not one in which warriors battled pagan opponents as much for political as for theological reasons, but one whose daily life was oriented toward lay, rather than clerical, concerns. In much of Chrétien's work Arthur embodies these aims more than any other ruler, in some aspects more than he had in Geoffrey, Wace, or Layamon.

Aside from their description in such rhetorical set-speeches as the one cited above, royal virtues had more complex aspects. The character of courtly society in the romances demanded that the king often step aside when challenged or insulted and permit another to redress the wrongs done him, to accomplish the *aventure.* The romances of *Erec, Cligès, Lancelot,* and *Yvain* have as their subjects the adventures of individual knights, not those of Arthur. The king's court constitutes a frame of reference for their adventures in the forest, a center to which they always return and from which their prolonged absence often causes considerable alarm.[5] In such a world the king often appears helpless as much from literary convention as from any political bias on the part of the poet or his audience.

A striking aspect of such royal helplessness is illustrated by the ruler's relation to custom, *coutume.* Custom and customary law are the mainstay of the royal power. In an age which looked to the past for its ideals, and which viewed time as a corrupting element in the experience of individuals and of society, custom was the only vehicle of preserving as much of the past as it was possible to keep. As Köhler remarks, "Le droit traditionnel, toujours un droit coutumier, constitue le principe ordonnateur du royaume et la légitimation de la position du roi."[6] Proper observance of custom

4. Cf. W. A. Nitze, "The Character of Gauvain in the Romances of Chrétien de Troyes," *Modern Philology* 50 (1952/53): 219–25.

5. Cf. Kohler, *Ideal und Wirklichkeit,* pp. 66–88.

6. See particularly Kohler, "Le Rôle de la coutume."

maintains the order of the kingdom. Violations of custom, or the discovery of wicked customs, threaten that order and must be either abolished or rectified. Custom, in one of its srtiking manifestations, that of *aventure,* also provides the raison d'être for the knights of Arthur's court. They journey into the world outside the court partly, at least, to prove the superior order and legitimacy of that court over the perplexing and often hostile world of the forest. When, through the fault of the king or of his knights, custom ceases to be upheld (usually through a failure of *largesce),* the court loses its virtue and the king his usefulness. The role of the king (not only Arthur, but other rulers in Chrétien's works whose lack of vigilance has caused wicked customs to arise) is to provide the medium through which the knights balance the potential anarchy inherent in the structure of the society over which he rules by performing their proper function, accepting and experiencing *aventure.*

Aventure, coutume, marvels, and knights-errant are not, then, extraneous to, but an essential part of, the political world of the romances. In Chrétien's *Lancelot,* for example, the knight Meleagant insults Arthur and carries the queen, Guinevere, to his realm of Gorre, where he has imprisoned many other folk of Arthur's realm. The ritual which Lancelot eventually follows to win back the queen and the captive subjects of Arthur is intricate and informative. The king himself is powerless. In fact, the opening scenes give Arthur a conventional powerlessness which strongly differs from the king's success at other times, even in other works of Chrétien. The offense itself bears with it the ritual that will erase it. Not the direct political action of a William of Orange but the ritual *aventure* of Lancelot redeems the exiles from Gorre.

In Chrétien's unfinished *Perceval* Arthur's court, although it is the center of the world, possesses the same characteristics. Perceval's mother has deliberately raised her son in a world of antichivalry and done everything in her power to keep from him any information of the world of knighthood. Perceval discovers knights, however, and makes his way to Arthur's court, arriving there immediately after Arthur had been challenged by the Red Knight. Perceval cannot believe that the state of dejection he witnesses could possibly be that of Arthur's court, about which he had heard so much. The challenge to the king disrupts all aspects of court life and reflects, in the chaos it causes, its importance for the order of society. The political world of Chrétien's romances is expressed symbolically through social ritual, not through narrative description. Chrétien's concern for the psychological experience of his characters leads him to depict all human activity in terms of ritual gesture rather than social action, since his interest is centered in the individual knight rather than the social collective.

From Arthur's powerlessness in the opening scenes of *Lancelot* and the first court scene of *Perceval,* it is no great distance to the most striking instance of royal inadequacy in all of the early romances—that depicted in the first scenes of the *Perlesvaus,* a prose romance of the first quarter of the thirteenth century.[7] The *Perlesvaus* stands somewhere between the verse romances of Chrétien and the prose Vulgate cycle. It is one of the first courtly romances to reveal traces of clerical authorship, and its association of the hero's adventures with the conversion of Logres from the "old law" to the "new law" (from Judaism and the Old Testament to Christianity and the New Testament, but rendered as a personal reform on the part of individual knights) gives it a historical atmosphere at once remote from the timelessness of the verse romances and close to the approaches to the conversion of Britain given by Bede, Gildas, and Nennius.

The romance begins with a description of the former glory of Arthur's kingdom:

> L'autoritez de l'excriture nos dit que apres le crucefiement Nostre Seigneur n'avanca rois terriens tant la foi Jesu Christ com fist li rois Artuz de Breteigne, par lui e par les buens chevaliers qui reperant estoient dedenz sa cort. Li buens rois Artuz, apres le crucefiement Nostre Seigneur estoit si com ge vos di; e estoit rois poissanz e bien creanz en Dieu; e molt avenoient de buennes aventures en sa cort, e avoit la Table

7. Vol. 1, ed. W. A. Nitze and T. A. Jenkins (Chicago, 1932); vol. 2, ed. W. A. Nitze et al. (Chicago, 1937). Good discussions are those of Nitze, in *ALMA,* pp. 263–73, and R. S. Loomis, "Some Additional Sources of the Perlesvaus," *Romania* 81 (1960): 492–99.

> Ronde, qui estoit garnie des meilleurs chevaliers du monde. Li rois Artuz apres la mort son pere mena la plus haute vie e la plus cointe que nus rois menast onques, si que tuit li prince e tuit li baron prenoient essanple a lui de bien faire.[8]

Arthur is singled out as having advanced the Christian faith (the main theme of the work) and of having as an implied reward *aventures,* the Round Table, and the best knights of the world. Arthur, however, began to decline from his former greatness:

> Li rois Artuz fu .x. anz en tel point com ge vos di, ne n'estoit nus rois terriens tant loez comme il, *tant que une volentez delaianz li vint,* e commenca a perdre le talent des largesces que il soloit faire. Ne voioit cort tenir a Noel, ne a Pasques, ne a Pentecoste. Li chevalier de la Table Reonde, quant il virent son bienfet alentir, il s'en partirent e commencierent sa cort a lessier. De trois .c. e .lxx. chevaliers q'il soloit avoit de sa mesniee, n'avoit il ore mie plus de .xxv. au plus. Nule aventure n'avenoit mes a sa cort. Tuit li autre prince avoient leur biensfez delaiez por ce q'il veoient le roi maintenir si foiblement. La roine Guenievre en estoit si dolente qu'ele savoit conroi de li meisme.[9]

The *volentez delaianz* which causes Arthur to cease to hold court, to lose his knights, and to cease to have *aventure* parallels, as Nitze pointed out, the *segnitia* described by Cador in Geoffery, Wace, and Layamon. Although the sequence appears hurried, the events which occur during Arthur's decline parallel those which occurred during his rise to fame in the preceding sentences. The emphasis upon a series of key terms, each of which is particularly significant in the vocabulary of courtly romance, compensates to a certain extent for the lack of further causal explanation.

The brevity of the description of Arthur's fall, the crowding of important events one upon the other, and the persisting image of the king's *otium* serve a structural as well as a stylistic function. The whole romance will describe the circumstances of the fall of the

8. *Perlesvaus,* 1:59–60, lines 58–77.
9. Ibid. Italics mine. See also 2:201–05.

court and, more important, of the role of the court in redeeming its lost status. These concerns become evident immediately after the opening lines, when Guinevere exchanges the following words with Arthur:

> J'e veu a tel jor com hui est, que vos aviez si grant plente de chevaliers en vostre cort que a paines le poist on nonbrer. Ore en i a si poi chascun jor que ge en e grant vergoigne, ne nule aventure n'i avient mes; se e grant poor que Dex ne vos ait mis en obli.

Arthur anwers:

> Certes, dame, dist li rois, ge n'e volente de fere largesce ne chose qui tort a honeur; ainz m'est mex talenz muez en floibece de cuer, e par ce se ge bien que ge pert mes chevaliers e l'amor de mes amis.[10]

In view of the courtly importance of *aventure, largesce, don,* and *coutume,* Arthur here convicts himself of having violated all of the main requirements of a romance-king. The cause of his loss of honor is the mysterious *volentez delaianz,* the opposite of the *volentez de fere largesce.* It is, in fact, a kind of negative willing which takes the form of inaction, and certainly, as far as the romance writers were concerned with the mental states of their characters, a psychological aberration.

The symptoms of Arthur's behavior were not unique to the courtly romances. Nitze, for example, has pointed out in this and in another context the resemblance between Arthur's present state of mind and the vice of *acedia. Acedïa,* as discussed above, functioned in the twelfth century to describe psychological as well as spiritual states. Yet Arthur's *volentez delaianz,* however close it might be to the classical symptoms of the vice, is at best only loosely connected with it in the passage at hand. Since there was relatively little concern with a systematized psychology among medieval writers before the thirteenth century, such phenomena as Arthur's inability to act might have been explained from among a

10. Ibid., 1:26.

number of different approaches to human action in general. The first, and most obvious, standard is that illustrated by Cador in his exchange with Gawain, the fighting man's rough contempt for any kind of life except that of the battlefield. The second, deriving from twelfth-century poets' concern with love and sexual passion, had its origins in classical literature, particularly Ovid, and is represented widely in courtly literature as the stupor or sloth of the lover. Neither of these, however, bears as strongly as *acedia* on the figure of Arthur. Yet Arthur's "acedia" deviates from the vice at certain key points. If it had been identical with the vice, there were certain well-recognized means of ridding oneself of it: manual effort, spiritual studies, even, according to some writers, an effort at *hilaritas* might serve to release the sufferer. Further, Arthur obviously knows no way of avoiding the *floibece de cuer* (a close vernacular approximation of the *taedium cordis,* or *pusillanimitas* used by theological writers) and has to be told what to do.

Before he ceased to hold court, he had been overcome by the *volentez delaianz,* a psychological condition which made him lose all interest in his most important functions. An Arthur who loses interest in his knights and his court in the romances might only be compared with a king in the *chansons de geste* who was reluctant to defend or maintain his kingdom. The ruler in the *chanson de geste* was a lord of warriors; Arthur is the lord of knights and *aventure.* The syntax of the passage emphasizes chiefly the temporal aspects of Arthur's fall from greatness to lethargy and does not suggest anything about the king's character that might account for an incipient predisposition toward the affliction from which the king suffers. Arthur's state of mind, first described in a brief, swiftly moving narrative, then restated in direct discourse, is ultimately explained by a hermit whom the king encounters during a visit to the chapel of St. Augustine. Arthur, who had been sent to the chapel on the advice of Guinevere, whose dream had told her of the means to cure her husband's lethargy, wanders through the opening scenes of the romance bewildered and appalled but unable to break out of his indifference to *honor.*

The hermit contrasts Arthur's former glory with his present disgrace:

> Si vos en mescharra molt durement, se vos ne remetez vostre afere a point o vos l'aviez commencie; car vostre corz estoit la sovrainne de totes les corz, e la plus aventureuse; or est la pis vaillanz.

The hermit continues:

> Molt puet estre dolenz qi d'onneur vient a honte, mes cil ne puet avoir reproche qui mal li face, qui de honte vient a honeur; car l'oneurs en coi il est trovez le resqeut ades. Mes blasmes ne puet rescorre l'omme s'il a guerpie honneur por honte, car la honte e la vilenie en coi il est pris le juge mauves.[11]

The king, who has fallen from *honneur* to *honte* through his lethargy and indifference to courtly life must amend his conduct by upholding the Law, which had been renewed by the *Saint Prophète.* By doing so the king will rectify his fall from honor to shame. The curious mélange of courtly and religious life in these passages is striking. The chief effect of the two areas of experience and values which the author unsuccessfully attempts to bridge is to heighten the spiritual-psychological mental attitudes of the characters in their purely courtly activities and to impart to the political fortunes of Arthur an air of mystery which had been absent from the verse romances of Chrétien.

The hermit then tells the king of a *granz doleurs* which has come about through the failure of a knight who stayed for a time at the castle of the *riche roi Pescheur* and saw there *li sainz Graauz,* to ask the question:

> de coi ce servoit, ne cui on en servoit; por ce qu'il ne le demanda, sont totes les terres de guerre escommeues, ne chevaliers n'encontre autre en forest q'il ne qeure sus ocie s'il puet, e vos meismes vos en perceveroiz bien ainz que vos partez de ceste lande.

Arthur leaves the hermit and meets a girl who describes the court of Arthur as the worst in the world. After a series of dangerous

11. Ibid., pp. 37–38.

adventures, Arthur is about to leave the forest when a voice announces:

> Artu, li rois de la Grant Breteigne, molt puez estre joiex en ton cuer de ce que Dex m'a envoie a toi. E si te mande que tu teignes cort au plus tost que tu porras; car li siecles, qui enpiriez est par toi e par le delaiement de ton bienfet, en amendra molt.[12]

Arthur returns home, announces to all that he will again hold court, and assembles a great number of knights from all over the world, who are astounded that Arthur has regained his desire to hold court and, presumably, to distribute *largesce.* At the great court at Penzance three damsels appear and finally complete the story of Arthur's lethargy. The *roi Pescheur* had fallen into a *dolereuse langeur,* caused by the failure of a knight to ask the proper questions concerning the *sainz Graauz.* The results of this failure are the lethargies of both kings and the disorder into which the world has been thrown. Arthur resolves to send knights to find the grail and announces the beginnings of the quest.

Arthur's lethargy, it may be noted in passing, is different from the *langeur* of the Fisher King. Arthur is able, as soon as he leaves the hermit's forest, to resume his royal activities as if no impediment had ever existed. His *volentez delaianz* has been remedied by a ritual observance revealed to the queen in a dream, not by an individual act of will on his own part. The king's own psychological state had been a consequence, just as his failure to hold court had been a consequence, of a state of mind which the author can only describe as having "come over" him. This obscure lethargy, however, is only with difficulty to be completely identified with the theologians's *acedia.* It shares the mental symptoms of *acedia* and probably represents a stage in the development of medieval psychology. But the inner defect is here removed by reference to an external ritual sequence, an *aventure,* into whose terms the mental state has been obscurely translated. Arthur's lethargy, then, is something more complex than Cador's dislike of peace or the

12. Ibid., pp. 44–45.

lover's sloth, something more, even, than the old vice of *acedia,* although it borrows elements from all of these. Moreover, the king, so he is told, is not personally responsible for what has happened to him, since his lethargy is the result of actions over which he had had no control. Finally, his personal lethargy results in the diminishing of the welfare of the kingdom, the *felicitas regni,* although it is not the primary cause of that loss.

In brief, the problem of royal weakness or inadequacy acquires a new dimension in this romance. It is restricted neither to the exigencies of literary convention nor the attitudes of a feudal aristocracy. It partakes of the general crisis in society, to which it is linked by analogy, not by causal relationship, and which centers on the mysterious Fisher King and includes a wider world of which the two kingdoms are only a part. The subsequent treatment of these two kingdoms and their rulers in the prose romances, from *Perlesvaus,* the continuations of Chrétien's *Perceval,* and Wolfram von Eschenbach to the Vulgate and post-Vulgate prose cycles and Malory, reveals the increasing preoccupation on the part of the authors of romances with the political, as well as the social, aspects of the *royaume aventureux.*

Chrétien's *Perceval* and the prose *Perlesvaus* also represent the entry into European literature of the Fisher King, a figure whose progressively stronger association with the court of Arthur and whose literary characteristics make it perhaps the most striking illustration of royal incapacity in Western literature. Few literary themes from any period have attracted as much attention from contemporary readers or later scholars as has that of the quest. Although the theme has many forms and a long history, the medieval quest was usually connected with the grail and was to be fulfilled by the greatest knight in the world. The grail, whose properties and form also vary considerably, was located in the grail-castle, presided over by the Fisher King, who was sometimes identified with, sometimes associated with, the Maimed King.[13] The hero's discovery of the

13. A recent survey of the many views of the Fisher King is that of Frederick W. Locke, *The Quest for the Holy Grail* (Stanford, 1960). See also R. S. Loomis, *Celtic Myth and Arthurian Romance* (New York,

castle and his asking the proper questions of its inhabitants not only proved him to be the best knight in the world but also cured the king and restored the land surrounding the castle, *la terre gaste* or wasteland, to fertility and its people to concord. The theme was not, in its earliest stages, closely bound up with the well-being of Logres, Arthur's kingdom, but often became so in later romances. Even before this association, however, the Maimed King and the Fisher King had become well-developed figures in their own right, embodying the elements of many literary traditions and reflecting attitudes to kingship not always dealt with in the Arthurian romances proper.

The Maimed King-Fisher King first appears in the Arthurian romances in Chrétien's *Perceval.* This ruler provides hospitality to the wandering knight, who, after witnessing a strange procession in which the grail is included, fails to ask his host the grail-question, "cui on en sert," whom one serves with it. Perceval's failure prevents the healing of the king and causes the wasting of the land. The remainder of the romance (which Chrétien left unfinished) provides Perceval with more information concerning his host and his error, and it describes his attempts to rediscover the grail-castle and redeem his earlier failure.

Three scenes in Chrétien's work serve to inform Perceval more fully of the nature of his quest and of the character of the Fisher King. The first occurs shortly after Perceval leaves the grail-castle. He encounters a girl to whom he describes his adventure and the Fisher King:[14]

1927), pp. 177–86; Helaine Newstead, *Bran the Blessed in Arthurian Romance* (New York, 1939); R. S. Loomis, *Arthurian Tradition and Chrétien de Troyes* (New York, 1949), pp. 389–93; W. A. Nitze, "The Fisher King and the Grail in Retrospect," *Romance Philology* 6 (1952/53): 14–22; Marx, "La Légende arthurienne et le graal," pp. 182–204; R. S. Loomis, *The Grail: From Celtic Myth to Christian Symbol* (New York–Cardiff, 1963); L. Olschki, *The Grail Castle and Its Mysteries* (Berkeley and Los Angeles, 1966). Physiological aspects of the Maimed King are surveyed in C. Brunel, "Les Hanches du Roi Pêcheur," *Romania* 81 (1960): 37–43.

14. Chrétien de Troyes, *Le Roman de Perceval,* ed. W. Roach, Textes Littéraires Français (Geneva, 1956). Cited hereafter by line numbers.

Pucele, par le Salveor,
Ne sai s'il est peschiere ou rois,
Mais molt est sages et cortois. (vv. 3496–98)

The girl then tells him of his host:

Biax sire,
Rois est il, bien le vos puis dire;
Mais il fu en une bataille
Navrez et mehaigniez sanz faille,
Si que puis aidier ne se pot,
Qu'il fu ferus d'un gavelot
Parmi les quisses ambesdeus
Qu'il ne puet sor cheval monter. (vv. 3507–15)

The king, she says, fishes only because he needs diversion and has, in fact, many servants, as befits a rich king. When she discovers that Perceval has failed to ask the proper question, the girl grieves. If Perceval had asked, she says,

Que tant eusses amende
Le buen roi qui est mehaigniez
Que toz eust regaaigniez
Ses membres et terre tenist
Et si grans biens t'en avenist. (vv. 3586–90)

After other adventures Perceval goes on to Arthur's court, where he is again upbraided for having failed at the grail-castle, this time by the Loathly Messenger, an ugly damsel, who tells him that besides the continuing illness of the king, his neglect has also caused the land to be laid waste:

A mal eur tu te teusses,
Que se tu demande l'eusses,
Li riches rois, qui or s'esmaie,
Fust ja toz garis de sa plaie
Et si tenist sa terre en pais,
Dont il ne tendra point jamais.
Et ses tu qu'il en avendra
Del roi qui terre ne tendra
Ne n'iert de ses plaies garis?

Dames en perdront lor maris,
Terres en seront escillies
Et puceles desconseillies,
Qui orfenines remandront,
Et maint chevalier en morront;
Tot dist mal esteront par toi. (vv. 4669–83)

In this speech it is clear that there is no implied relation between the physical integrity of the ruler and that of his land, but that there is a political relation between a king *qui terre ne tendra* and a series of other calamities whose character is not essentially different from those frequently described in ecclesiastical political rhetoric. There is nothing magical about the wounded ruler but the duration of his illness. Had Perceval cured him, the king would have reigned well (note the emphasis on *terre tenir* in the speech of the first girl as well). Now, the prolongation of the king's incapacity causes the firmness of his rule to slip and the disasters to occur. Perceval finally learns the whole history of the king from a hermit. The Fisher King is Perceval's uncle, the brother of the hermit and of Perceval's mother. The old king, whom Perceval had also seen at the grail-castle, is the Maimed King's father, who has survived for twelve years upon nothing but a host brought to him in the grail.

Thus far, this is the first appearance of the Fisher King. Leaving aside many of the complex literary and theological questions which have arisen with these adventures, this study will concentrate upon two main questions. First, to what extent is the depiction of a physically incapaciated ruler recognizable in terms of contemporary lay and clerical views of kingship? Second, what is the relation between the physical integrity of the king and that of his land, not only in these and other literary works, but in thirteenth-century political thought as well? When the excommunicated Emperor Henry IV was on route to Canossa, so some sources tell us, peasants touched the king's garments in order to ensure themselves of a good harvest.[15] To what extent did such beliefs exist among the

15. The episode is noted by Marc Bloch in *Feudal Society,* trans. L .A. Manyon (Chicago, 1961), p. 381.

audiences of the courtly romance? To what extent do the romances depict kingship as a supernatural institution?[16]

The Fisher King in Chrétien's poem has become, through no fault of his own, incapable of ruling his kingdom because of a wound vaguely described as having been received *en une bataille.* His being unable to hold his realm *(tenir sa terre),* as the Loathly Messenger makes clear, is disastrous to the kingdom. The disasters have occurred, however, as a consequence of the impaired abilities of the king, not through any process of supernatural sympathy between king and kingdom. The land is laid waste by Perceval's failure to ask the question, not by the wounding of the king. Historically, at least, Chrétien is on strong ground. In 887 the East Frankish nobles, led by Arnulf of Carinthia, had deposed the Emperor Charles III partly because that ruler's illness had impaired his ability to govern. Other Western rulers had lost political power, if not their kingdoms, through having been blinded or otherwise maimed, and, in Byzantium, at least, the physical integrity of the ruler was a necessity, hence the occasional blinding of a candidate for the imperial throne. All these rulers, except perhaps Louis the Blind of Arles, had lost their kingdoms. Chrétien's Fisher King retains his. Although the land suffers from his inability to rule, no one even speaks of deposing him, for clearly it is only by *his* restoration that the land will prosper.

16. The literature on sacral kingship is very large and not always particularly relevant. Studies of value are those of James G. Frazer, *Lectures on the Early History of Kingship* (London, 1905); E. L. A. Meyerowitz, *The Divine Kingship in Ghana and Ancient Egypt* (London, 1960); K. Czegledy, "Das sakrale Königtum bei den Steppenvolkern," *Numen* 13 (1966): 14–26: S. H. Hooke, ed., *Myth, Ritual, and Kingship* (Oxford, 1958); A. R. Johnson, *Sacral Kingship in Ancient Israel* (Cardiff, 1955); I. Engnell, *Studies in Divine Kingship in the Ancient Near East* (Uppsala, 1943); A. M. Hocart, *Kingship* (London, 1927); idem, *Kings and Councillors* (Cairo, 1960); F. Taeger, *Charisma. Studien zur Geschichte des antiken Herrscherkultes* (Stuttgart: vol. 1, 1957; vol. 2, 1960); H. Hoffman, "Die Begriffe 'König' and 'Herrschaft' im indischen Kulturkreis," *Saeculum* 4 (1954): 334–39; Marc Bloch, *Les Rois thaumaturges.* Less convincing are the studies of Margaret Murray. See now also John W. Perry "Reflections on the Nature of the Kingship Archetype," *Journal of Analytical Psychology* 2 (1966).

Among the changes which the twelfth century witnessed in regard to theories of kingship, none was more important than the strengthening of the monarchy by enhancing the legitimacy of governance and by promulgating the doctrine that kings could be deposed only for the gravest of crimes, and then only with the authority or approval of the papacy. One case that occupied the attention of both East and West in the twelfth century and that provided an instance of royal incapacity in which the ruler retained the kingship although fatally ill was that of Baldwin IV of Jerusalem. Baldwin's illness, leprosy, was, moreover, frequently linked by historians with the sins of his subjects.[17] The prospects of Baldwin's reign had been destroyed by his illness, although he was a popular ruler and retained the crown of Jerusalem as long as he was able. In a recent study Helen Adolf has suggested the influence of Baldwin's case upon Chrétien's conception of the Fisher King in *Perceval.*[18] Her suggestion that Baldwin was the prototype of the Fisher King deserves careful consideration. That a ruler should be severely incapacitated and yet retain his kingship would have been a new but not totally unfamiliar idea in the last quarter of the twelfth century. That the ruler of a kingdom in which all Christians had, at least in theory, a great concern, should be so stricken must have made a considerable impression on late twelfth-century Europe. One may suggest without establishing a causal relationship between the real and the literary ruler that a reader's response to the one would be colored by his knowledge of the other.

Dr. Adolf's discussion of Alexander III's decretal *Cor nostrum* of 1181, a letter to the princes of Europe describing the desolation of the kingdom of Jerusalem and the condition of the king, suggests strongly that there were other means besides those of sympathetic

17. See J. L. LaMonte, *Feudal Monarchy in the Latin Kingdom of Jerusalem, 1100–1291* (Cambridge, Mass., 1932), pp. 30–38. Of particular interest is Alexander III's decretal of 1181, *Cor Nostrum (PL* 200. 1294–96), in which the pope paints a portrait of Baldwin's sufferings to the whole world.

18. Helen Adolf, "A Historical Background to Chrétien's Perceval, *PMLA* 58 (1943): 597–620, later expanded into a full-length study, *Visio Pacis: Holy City and Grail: An Attempt at an Inner History of The Grail Legend* (State College, Pa., 1960).

magic by which the condition of the ruler might be considered in terms of the desolation of his realm. The theological basis of twelfth-century ecclesiastical political thought, moreover, provided just such a means: a moral-historical medium through which the divine judgment expressed itself in terms of individual or social prosperity or misfortune. The disasters of the second Crusade, as well as the new invective that was directed at many of its leaders, are further evidence that the increased scope of royal activity in the eleventh and twelfth centuries created new categories of royal success and failure, of suitability and unsuitability, and thus new dimensions for the consideration of royal conduct. Whatever his attitude toward the case of Baldwin IV, Chrétien modeled his Fisher King closely upon a pattern of traits which Baldwin shared. Both rulers retained their royal dignity, even though their doing so brought disaster upon their realms. The twelfth-century ruler, literary or historical, was not easily separated from his office, *dignitas,* or *regnum.* The cases of Baldwin IV and the Fisher King reflect not archaic aspects of kingship but the most current twelfth-century conceptions of the royal office.

Chrétien's story was continued several times during the half-century following its first appearance.[19] Several of these additions contained matter dealing with episodes upon which Chrétien did not touch. There also began to appear histories which linked the events in Chrétien's *Perceval* with the events surrounding the passion and death of Christ and the coming of Christianity to Britain. Before a complete history of the grail appeared, however, another Perceval story was written, based upon Chrétien and one of his continuators. It was the last major Arthurian romance written before the conflation of individual stories into the great prose cycles, the *Parzival* of Wolfram von Eschenbach.[20]

19. For the additions, see A. W. Thompson, "Additions to Chrétien's Perceval—Prologues and Continuations," in *ALMA,* pp. 206–17; W. Roach, "Transformations of the Grail Theme in the First Two Continuations of the Old French Perceval," *Proc. Amer. Phil. Soc.* 110, no. 3 (1966): 160–64; also D. D. Owen, "The Development of the Perceval Story," *Romania* 80 (1959): 473–92.

20. Bibliography in the notes to Otto Springer, "Wolfram's Parzival," in *ALMA* pp. 218–50, the best discussion of the work. Ed. cited here is

Wolfram's great poem presents a far more detailed grail-world than does Chrétien's. Those who live at the grail-castle, *Munsalvaesche,* belong to a distinct order, that of the *Templeisen,* not unlike many of the military orders of the poet's own day. The work of the order is to serve the grail, which here is a gem of considerable size possessing evident, but ambiguous, theological significance. The king of the order, Amfortas, lives in agony, however, because he has been wounded grievously in the genitals and can neither die nor be cured until the chosen grail-knight asks the question that will heal him. Besides Amfortas, there is another maimed king at the castle, Amfortas's grandfather, Titurel, a figure who parallels the king in Chrétien's *Perceval* who subsisted only upon the host. In a series of episodes which correspond approximately to parallel scenes in Chrétien, Parzival learns the story of the grail-castle and of his own place in its history.

Amfortas had received his wound not, as had Chrétien's king, *en une bataille,* but in a tournament in which he had fought for a lady in violation of the rules of his order. His passion, like that of Arthur in some romances, had caused him to neglect his royal duties. His wound, caused by a poisoned spear, is ghastly and is portrayed far more realistically than that of any of the other *rois mehaigniés.* Trevrizent, the hermit who tells Parzival the story, describes the wound in great detail, and his account of attempts to cure it reads like an encyclopedia of legendary pharmacology.

Besides the realistic wound and the expanded account of its cause (some philologists derive Amfortas's name, in fact, from the Latin *infirmitas),* Wolfram has added a more complex account of Amfortas's kingship. The king's rule, even after his wound has incapacitated him, is never questioned. Amfortas continues to rule, however, not because he is worthy of the kingship, but because

---

that of H. Leitzmann, 3 vols. (Halle, 1903–11). Of great use have been the studies of H. B. Willson, "The Grail King in Wolfram's *Parzival,*" *Modern Language Review* 55 (1960): 553–63; H. Kolb, *Munsalvaesche. Studien zum Kyotproblem* (Munich, 1963); D. Blamries, *Characterization and Individuality in Wolfram's Parzival* (Cambridge, 1966), pp. 266–82; W. J. Schroder, *Der Ritter zwischen Welt und Gott* (Weimar, 1952).

there is no one else available. Trevrizent, his brother and presumably the next in line, had renounced knighthood when Amfortas had been wounded and was therefore not eligible to accept the crown. Parzival, the moral successor to Amfortas, is the king's legal successor as well, since he appears to be the only living member of the grail-dynasty except for the maimed king and the hermit. Although Amfortas had been elected (and Parzival himself would be elected, not only through divine selection but by the members of the order), the grail-kingship had long become a customary adjunct to the Titurel dynasty.[21]

The *Templeisen,* however much above the world of earthly chivalry their order stands, are nevertheless human beings and are subject to human failings. Their king, however good and worthy he had been at his election, must also suffer from the consequences of his human weakness. The poet's linking of the eternal wound to the king's mistaken choise of *amor* over *diemuot* is another instance of the literary technique which couples royal neglect with sexual passion. Yet Wolfram is unique in associating this destructive passion with the figure of the Fisher King himself. In the other romances and in the prose cycles the royal figure most closely associated with the theme is Arthur. Wolfram's emphasis upon the family relationships among his characters, his geographical consistency, and his references to the history and customs of his own immediate surroundings give the *Parzival* a unity and a coherence often lacking in the work of Chrétien and his successors.

Amfortas is a recognizable thirteenth-century royal figure whose description is not inconsistent with that of contemporary kings. He succeeds to the kingship of the *Templeisen* by succession and election. His neglect of his duties had made him unfit to rule, and his wound makes him physically incapable of ruling. If there is a single striking difference between him and a contemporary *rex inutilis* it is the fact that his incapacity is prolonged indefinitely: he is not subject to the effects of time, to deterioration or healing, as would be a historical ruler. He continues to rule because there is

21. Wolfram's other romance, *Titurel* (ed. K. Bartsch, Leipzig, 1890), further illuminates the theme of Grail-kingship.

no suitable successor. His physical incapacity is a consequence of his inner *inutilitas,* just as his wound is a *contrapasso* of his sin. His useless rule is prolonged partly because of his own sin and partly because of the sins of other members of the order. His character, which is worthy in all other respects, represents perhaps the increasing twelfth-century realization that the king is at the same time an individual human being and a transcendental medium through which divine and human laws are transmitted to his people and in which is embodied the power and majesty of the order. His failure in *diemuot,* which reflects his *hochvart (superbia),* is the unique dilemma of the ruler not only in the world of the grail-order but in the less dramatic and less coherent world of the tracts for the instruction of princes, legal scholarship, and historical kingship.

Wolfram's depiction of Amfortas, however close to problems of some historical *reges inutiles,* did not markedly influence subsequent representations of the Fisher King. The future of this figure lay with the Chrétien tradition as it was taken up by other hands, chiefly those of Robert de Boron and his continuators, the compilers of the first works which attempted to connect the individual themes of the romances dealing with the matter of Britain into larger cycles. The works of Robert himself, the *Joseph, Merlin,* and, perhaps, a *Perceval,* became the basis for subsequent treatments of the Arthurian and grail legends.[22] To the prose versions of Robert's works there were added the parts of the prose *Lancelot* to form, between 1220 and 1230, the largest single romance cycle, the Vulgate. Later, probably between 1230 and 1240, the whole Vulgate was reworked into the post-Vulgate *Roman du Graal.*[23] Thus the tradition of tales and motifs which had entered courtly literature

22. Pierre le Gentil, "The Work of Robert de Boron and the Didot-Perceval," in *ALMA*, pp. 251–62, and Mary E. Griffin, "A Reading of Robert de Boron," *PMLA* 80 (1965): 499–507.

23. The whole Vulgate, ed. H. O. Sommer, 8 vols. (Washington, 1909–16). There is a new edition of parts of the work in progress by Elspeth Kennedy. Other editions of individual sections have also appeared. See J. Frappier, "The Vulgate Cycle," in *ALMA,* pp. 294–318, and A. Micha, "The Vulgate Merlin," in *ALMA,* pp. 319–24.

with Chrétien grew slowly into a comprehensive epic history of Arthur's kingdom and the advent of Christianity to Britain.[24]

The representation of the Fisher King in the *Perlesvaus,* the early prose romance which is so unique in its treatment of Arthur,[25] is quite distinct from those of Chrétien and Wolfram and closer to the figure depicted in what is probably a version of Robert de Boron's *Perceval,* the so-called *Didot-Perceval.*[26] In the *Perlesvaus* the Fisher King is not wounded at all, but suffers from a mysterious *langor,* which may parallel the *volentez delaianz* of Arthur. Both the king's *langor* and the wasting of his land are the results of Perlesvaus's failure to ask the question, and the lethargy appears to have strong theological overtones, since the well-being of the Fisher King in the romance symbolizes the accomplishment of the New Law, Christianity, in Britain. Yet there is another meaning of *langor* which also fits the case of the king. In English and canon law *languor* was the tecnhical term relating to the condition of a defendant who had taken to his bed for a year and a day in order to avoid been brought to court.[27] That two such diverse notions might have been simultaneously linked in the mind of the author of the *Perlesvaus* is not impossible. The connotations of both terms suggest psychological as well as legal inaction. The strong theological orientation of the romance ties the lethargy of the Fisher King to that of Arthur and to the "si granz mescheances a la Grant Breteigne que totes les illes e totes les terres en chairent en grant

24. Much of the following is indebted to the study of Fanni Bogdanow, *The Romance of the Grail: A Study of the Structure and Genesis of a Thirteenth-Century Arthurian Prose Romance* (Manchester and New York, 1966).

25. Useful here are the studies of J. Neale Carman, "The Relationship of the *Perlesvaus* and the 'Queste del Saint Graal,'" *University of Kansas Humanistic Studies* 4, no. 2 (Lawrence, Kan., 1936); idem, "The Structure of the *Perlesvaus,*" *PMLA* 61 (1942): 42–83; Margaret Schlauch, "The Allegory of Church and Synagogue," *Speculum* 14 (1939): 448–64.

26. Ed W. Roach (Philadelphia, 1941). See esp. lines E 1922f. and E 198f.

27. For the law dealing with essoin, see, e.g., Glanvill, *De legibus et consuetudinibus regni Angliae,* ed. G. Woodbine (New Haven, 1932), I, c. 18 (p. 47). See also Woodbine's note, pp. 192–93.

doleur." The *langor* of the Fisher King and the *volentez delaianz* of Arthur are effective literary devices because they derived from the most sophisticated psychological vocabulary that the twelfth century possessed. These afflictions, as Carman notes, are close to the theological *pigritia* and represent the view of kingship which an ecclesiastic might take. Their political overtones, however, are none the less noticeable. The conception of royal inadequacy is more complex in this romance because the author was concerned with another area of moral judgment than exclusively that of chivalry.

The second question asked at the beginning of this section deserves some further consideration. As has been noted, these early romances indicate little concern for the supernatural sympathy between the physical integrity of the king and that of his kingdom. One group of scholars, however, has suggested another approach to this question. Weston and others, relying upon the parallel structure of certain parts of Celtic folklore, literature, and mythology, have suggested not only that the Celtic material constituted a source for the Arthurian romances, but that particular fertility-myths account for the obscure origins of the Fisher King.[28] It may be useful to consider this point in the light of twelfth-century ideas of kingship, particularly in view of the anecdote concerning Henry IV cited above.

The theme of the wasting of the Fisher King's realm as a consequence of the king's wounding is by no means uniformly presented in these romances. The circumstances in Chrétien and Wolfram do not, in fact, indicate that the infirmity—or sterility—of the king is the cause of any comparable phenomenon in the realm.[29] The addition to Chrétien called the *Elucidation* gives an account of the wasting of the land which is completely unrelated to the maiming of the king.[30] None of the "theological" versions of the story—those of Robert de Boron and the *Perlesvaus*—link the

28. See, e.g., Jesse L. Weston, *From Ritual to Romance* (Cambridge, 1920), chap. 9.

29. For the Waste Land, see W. A. Nitze, "The Wasteland; A Celtic Arthurian Theme," *Modern Philology* 43 (1945): 58–61; Loomis, *Arthurian Tradition and Chrétien de Troyes,* pp. 389–91.

30. Ed. A. W. Thompson (New York, 1931), vv. 95–100.

sterility of the land causally with the king's affliction. In brief, those instances of the early romances which described the suffering of the realm as well as that of the maimed king make the blighting of the land the result of either the king's political incapacity (Chrétien), the sorrow and sins of his subjects (Wolfram), or an unrelated event *(Elucidation)*. The relation between the maiming of the land and that of the king is analogical, not causal.

In the Vulgate and post-Vulgate cycles the wounding of the king and the blighting of the land are closely tied together, but almost uniformly as parallel disasters inflicted by God upon the people. The two events are linked in these later works by the Dolorous Stroke, a blow inflicted upon a blameless king by an unworthy man sacrilegiously wielding a sacred weapon.[31] The blighting of the land, which sometimes occurs before, sometimes simultaneously with, the Dolorous Stroke, is not therefore a sympathetic response on the part of the land to the misfortune of its ruler. The miraculous events of the romances, moreover, are not very dissimilar from comparable events in hagiography or historiography. Whatever elements these romances may have ultimately borrowed from other sources have been filtered through the medium of twelfth-century Christianity and through the political sensibility of the twelfth- and thirteenth-century literary public. Celtic and other legendary material enriched the courtly romance with its imaginative scope. It did not, however, reinforce any unorthodox consistent belief on the part of the twelfth-century poet and reader in the supernatural sympathy between king and kingdom. Instead, it provided a dimension in which the individual humanity of the ruler might be explored to a greater degree.

As Loomis once remarked of the entire grail legend, one may say of the Fisher King that there was not one but a multitude, "each a medley of incoherent motifs."[32] In the early courtly ro-

31. E. Vinaver, Introduction to M. Dominica Legge, *Le Roman de Balin, A Prose Romance of the Thirteenth Century* (Manchester, 1942), pp. ix–xxx; idem, "The Dolorous Stroke," *Medium Aevum* 25 (1956): 175–80; Bogdanow, *The Romance of the Grail*, pp. 129–37.

32. *Arthurian Tradition and Chrétien de Troyes*, p. 372.

mances there is no one Fisher King whose history is consistent and whose relationship to Arthur and his kingdom is uniformly clear. The representation of these rulers reflects not only the intermittent interest on the part of authors in the institution of kingship but the relationships which they saw between kingship and theology, on the one hand, and knightly codes, on the other. From the grim, realistic wounds of Amfortas to the mysterious quasi-legal *langor* of the king in *Perlesvaus,* the representation of royal incapacity varied according to the design of each author and to his concern—or lack of concern—with actual historical circumstances. In the subsequent prose cycles, however, the figures of the Fisher King and Arthur were drawn progressively closer together, their final destinies inseparably linked, and their inadequacy and majesty removed from the courtly and the theological planes to that of historical epic. Their reigns are related in terms of time and space. Their histories, made thus consistent and contiguous, begin to loom over the individual adventures, less ominously in the *Lancelot,* more so in the *Roman du Graal* and in Malory.

The material in Geoffrey of Monmouth's *Historia* concerning the fall of Britain was metamorphosed into an account of the rise, flowering, and fall of Logres, the *roiaume aventureus.* In a sense the kingdom itself became the subject of *aventure.* The combination of the history of the grail and that of Arthur's reign resulted in an epic history of the Britons and was inspired partly by literary interest, by a change in the relationship between romance and history, and possibly by contemporary ideas of a Breton revival.[33] The history of the grail, extended back in time to the first days of Christianity, and that of Arthur, magnified out of its original place in the history of the struggle between Britons and Saxons to that of a heroic kingdom on the eve of its destruction, constituted the background for the prose Vulgate, whose chief hero was, of course, Lancelot. Even simply as background, however, these two elements contributed to the unity of what would otherwise have been another sequence of individual adventures.

33. Bogdanow, *The Romance of the Grail,* pp. 197–221; D. de Séchelles, "L'Evolution et la transformation du mythe arthurien dans le thème du Graal," *Romania* 78 (1957): 182–98.

The increasing stress placed upon the relation between *aventure* and kingdom, rather than upon the relation between *aventure* and individual knight, may be seen most clearly in the shift of knightly criteria which supplanted Lancelot as the best knight in the world by Galahad, the celestial-chivalric savior of the grail kingdom. In terms of kingship the earlier manner of depicting royal inadequacy —as purely personal shortcomings on the part of the ruler, a technique for which the name "courtly politics" might not be entirely inappropriate—gave way to a repeated emphasis on the welfare of the whole kingdom, and scenes occur in the later prose cycles which deal more and more frequently with purely administrative matters. The political atmosphere of the Vulgate and the post-Vulgate cycles eventually became the theme of what Bogdanow has termed the "New Arthuriad." It is also the theme which recent writers on Malory have professed to see in his *Morte Darthur.*[34] In the later prose cycles the dilemma of the *rex inutilis,* the social consequences of his failure seen in political rather than in moral terms, is developed. The contrast between the ruler's virtue (represented by the enhancing of his character and his majesty) and his shortcomings (represented either by his wound or by the sudden appearance of the consequences of an old, forgotten sin) often results in a tension which governs much of the sweep of these narratives. To be sure, the older, "courtly" criticism of the ruler still survives in the Vulgate and in some later individual romances.[35] The theme of the *rex inutilis* becomes a tragic one; the exploration of human failure and its consequences becomes the norm, not the exception, in the prose romances, and the canvas upon which failure is depicted becomes that of history rather than that of timeless *aventure.* Because the *rex inutilis* becomes a tragic, rather than a pathetic, figure, paradoxically, his *inutilitas* becomes less personal and acquires

34. E.g. D. S. Brewer, "the hoole book," in J. A. W. Bennett, ed., *Essays on Malory* (Oxford, 1963), pp. 41–63; Charles Moorman, *The Book of King Arthur: The Unity of Malory's Morte Darthur* (Lexington, Ky., 1965).

35. Hans Schnyder, "Aspects of Kingship in 'Sir Gawain and the Green Knight,'" *English Studies* 40 (1959): 289–94.

meaning from its consequences rather than from the character of the individual who is *inutilis.*

For the purposes of the following discussion the prose Vulgate, the chief object of this study, will be considered as consisting of two parts. The first is composed of the prose *Lancelot* proper (containing three parts: the *Enfances,* the *Charette,* and the *Agravain*), the *Queste del Saint Graal,* and the *Mort Artu.* The second part consists of the complete Vulgate, which prefaces the *Lancelot-Queste-Mort* sequence with two preliminary works, the *Estoire del Saint Graal* and the *Estoire de Merlin.* The last two of these, though written after the *Lancelot,* deal with earlier periods and are usually placed first in the manuscripts. They will be considered here as providing mainly supplementary material to the others.

The *Enfances (Lancelot,* Part I)[36] opens with a description of the death of King Ban and the loss of Benoyc, his kingdom, to Claudas, a rival ruler. The story of the death of Ban and the triumph of Claudas emerges out of a welter of feudal chaos, treachery, and avarice that strongly resembles the atmosphere of some of the later *chansons de geste.*[37] Although there are isolated instances of heroism and loyalty, the overwhelming impression is one of unrelieved disaster. Arthur had neglected to come to Ban's aid, thus breaking the bond of fidelity between them. The very opening of the work, then, presents political disorder and hints at a weakness of Arthur. Claudas is perhaps the most complex figure in the whole work. He attacks and kills Ban without just cause, conducts a brutal war, and pursues Ban's wife, child, and nephews with a vengeance. He is, on the other hand, honorable within a limited feudal code, careful to observe the conventions of warfare, and a brave fighter. He does not quite match the type of the *tyrannus,* although he is the least majestic of the rulers in the work.

From the opening scenes of war and treachery the scene shifts to

36. Sommer, vol. 3.

37. See the excellent study of E. Kennedy, "Social and Political Ideas in the French Prose *Lancelot,*" *Medium Aevum* 26 (1957); 90–106; F. Lot, *Etude sur le Lancelot en prose* (Paris, 1918); E. Kennedy, "King Arthur in the First Part of the Prose *Lancelot,*" in *Medieval Miscellany presented to E. Vinaver* (Manchester–New York, 1965), pp. 186–95.

Arthur's court, to which Claudas goes in disguise. The peace, splendor, and wealth which abound at Arthur's court contrast sharply with the disorder of the opening scenes of the work. But the court does not exist in isolation. A friar reproaches Arthur with having failed to come to the aid of King Ban and for thus sharing the responsibility for his death and for the disherison of his children.[38] Claudas returns to his kingdom and is immediately met wth a parallel reproach. In his mistreatment of Ban's son, Lancelot, and his nephews, Bors and Lionel, he has revealed himsmelf a *felon,* a far more serious charge than that brought against Arthur. The Lady of the Lake pointedly contrasts Claudas's *felonie* with those qualities of kingship which Claudas lacks: he is not *sage, courtois,* or *debonnaire.* The subsequent Claudas-scenes are filled with technical legal discussions of the king's obligations, at once more like the rough equality of the *chansons de geste,* but far more technically concerned with difficult points of feudal law.

The sharp conflicts in these portraits of kingship are revealed again in Arthur's behavior when his own kingdom is invaded by Galehaut.[39] He insists upon meeting the invading army before his allies come up in order to spare his people suffering. On the other hand, he easily gives way to total despair when the battle swings against him, is persecuted by ominous dreams, and greatly fears the loss of his *honor.* At the moment of his greatest fear he is reminded of his failure to aid King Ban.

The final significant element of Arthur's weakness is that of his inordinate and unreasonable sexual passions, reflected in the episode of the enchantress Camille and the war with the Saxons, which brings the *Enfances Lancelot* to a close.[40] In this episode the king's passion for the woman is linked closely to his negligent conduct of the war. He eventually achieves victory only after he has repudiated his paramour. These elements all contribute to the ambiguous picture of Arthur introduced in the *Enfances.* His forgetfulness of his vassals, his overactive conscience, the fear of losing *honor,* his ex-

38. Sommer, 3:29–47. See also Frappier, in *ALMA,* pp. 296–302. The friar's speech is Sommer, 3:45–47.

39. Sommer, 3:215–21.

40. Sommer, 3:406–27. See also Lot, *Etude,* pp. 67, 182.

cessive *amor de siecle* which has kept him from *humilité* (rather parallel to the *amor-diemuot* contrast in Amfortas), and thus from *droiture,* and finally his sexual passions have impaired his military prowess. On the other hand, his court is splendid, he is genuinely concerned for the welfare of his people, and he exceeds contemporary historical standards by wearing his crown at five, instead of three, feasts: Easter, Ascension, Whitsuntide, All Saints, and Christmas.

The *Charette (Lancelot,* Part II)[41] deals chiefly with the love affair between Lancelot and Guinevere, but also provides a parallel affair between Arthur and the False Guinevere.[42] Again Arthur's sexual passion impairs his ability to rule, this time in more complex ways than those described in Part I. During the king's stay with the False Guinevere at Carmelide, for example, his barons, fearing him dead, decide to elect a new king: "Il ne pooient souffrir que la terre fust sans seignor."[43] They elect Gawain, who is extremely reluctant to ascend the throne. Upon Arthur's return his dishonor is great and his uselessness is severely chastised by Amustans, in a scene which parallels those between Arthur and the friar and between Arthur and the *preudhons* in the earlier parts of the work. The rehabilitation process of the king may be said to reflect contemporary concern for royal humiliation as expressed in such historical episodes as in the festive crowning of Richard I after returning to England from his captivity.[44]

Besides the episode of the False Guinevere, other scenes in the work throw light upon other aspects of kingship. Perhaps the most striking of these aspects is that of delegated royal authority and the necessity of kingship as an institution. Besides Gawain's election to the kingship, there occurs another episode in the *Charette* in which the question of delegated authority takes an important

41. Sommer, vol. 4.

42. Sommer, 4:10–16, 44–79. Background for this episode is provided in the Vulgate *Estoire de Merlin,* Sommer, 2:300–01, 308–16; Lot, *Etude,* p. 67.

43. Sommer, 4:51; cf. pp. 73–78.

44. Gervase of Canterbury, *Opera Historica,* ed. W. Stubbs, RS (London, 1879), 1:524–27.

place. After Lancelot has reconciled Arthur and Galehaut, the latter decides to spend some time at Arthur's court before his own coronation.[45] He does not, however, simply leave his kingdom of Sorelois, but calls an assembly of his greatest barons and discusses the question of who would be suitable to rule in his absence. The care with which the discussion is carried out reflects the thirteenth-century concern for the powers and the character of those holding such delegated authority and the necessity of their support from the other barons:

> Mais por ce que mes terres sont lees et espandues et grandes et iou ne porrai mie dez ore mais en avant estre si souvent comme iou ai este . Si me couvient querre .i. preudomme ancien et loial qui hache le tort et aimece droiture . si il baillerai mes terres et il menra a chief mes besoignes et mes afaires a son pooir et a mon onour.[46]

Galehaut only reserves to himself the final power of appointment and asks the barons particularly to elect someone suitable, "Car la terre est morte et destruite ou il a bailleu couuoiteus qui lait entre mains." The Barons eventually choose Baudemagus, king of Gorre, and their choice is ultimately vindicated.

Kingship in the *Agravain (Lancelot,* Part III)[47] is depicted chiefly in terms of the great war between Arthur and Claudas, which brings to a conclusion the themes that opened the *Lancelot.* During Arthur's stay in Gaul, however, other aspects of kingship are prominent. The first is the question of Arthur's legal right to wage war at all. In a dispute between the king and Frolle of Alemaigne, Arthur justifies his war on Claudas and upon Gaul by citing the complicated series of alliances which bound Faramon, the King of Gaul in King Ban's time (and the historically eponymous ancestor of the Frankish kings), and Arthur's father, Uter-

45. On knights-errant in the romances, see, besides the studies cited above, C. E. Pickford, *L'Evolution du roman arthurien en prose vers la fin du moyen âge d'après le manuscrit 112 du fonds français de la Bibliothèque Nationale* (Paris, 1960), pp. 215–95.

46. Sommer, 4:37–38.

47. Sommer, vol. 5.

pendragon. On the way to Benoyc, Arthur makes a point of conquering Frolle personally and then investing Lancelot with the kingship of Gaul and Benoyc, instead of letting Lancelot represent him in the battle with Frolle. This episode suggests that, in the mind of the author, if Lancelot had fought and defeated Frolle, even as Arthur's representative, he would have had a legitimate claim to the kingship of Gaul based on right of conquest. The third is the depiction of Claudas, who refuses to flee and desert his subjects until all hope has been lost.

Perhaps the most striking aspect of kingship here is the prolonged discussion of the respective merits of kingship and chivalry which takes place after Claudas has been defeated and Bors, Lionel, and Lancelot have been offered the kingship of Gannes, Benoyc, and Gaul respectively. Bors refuses the kingship, however,

> Car si tostes que iou aurai le roiaume si me conuendra laissier cheualerie ou iou voelle ou non. Et ce nest nulle honor a moi ne a vous . . . quar certes plus u aueroie doneur se iou estoie poures cheualiers et boins que se ie estoie malvais roys recreans . . . quar ce sera pechies morteuls se vous de si haute cheualerie et de si grant proece lostes pour devenir roy. Quar a coronne ne puet il [Hector] mie falir sil vit longement. Mais se il laisse cheualerie orendroit il ne le recouerra iamais.[48]

The great distinction between knight and king which runs through the *Lancelot* is here drawn especially sharply. Bors's first point is that *cheualerie* is practiced only by *cheualiers,* not by kings, not even by kings who wish to continue *cheualerie.* He refuses Lancelot's offer because he would rather be a good knight than a bad king, and because it would be a mortal sin to give up chivalry for kingship. A knightly career is the best training for kingship, but he and his brother, he maintains, are not yet prepared for the rigors of rule. Since everyone unanimously agrees with him, it may be assumed that Bors's attitude is a common one, thereby revealing something about kingship in the romances.

Arthur, Galehaut, and Claudas are all great fighters, but they

48. Sommer, 5:337.

seldom fight in person, and, as has been seen, Galehaut is able to practice *cheualerie* only because he has not yet been crowned and after he has taken care that his kingdom will be well-governed in his absence. Obviously, Arthur's and Claudas's rule, however legitimate and beneficial, cannot be considered *cheualerie*. Bors's attitude reflects the distinction, implied elsewhere in the romances, between the two orders who participate in the life of *coutume, don,* and *aventure*—that of the knights who experience them and that of the king who must give them. The king is not to engage in *cheualerie,* but, on the other hand, he cannot therefore be criticized for not doing so. A knight is obliged to follow *cheualerie* till an unspecified time, *sil vit longement,* after which he may be suitable for kingship. While *cheualerie* is thus quite distinct from kingship, it does serve as a kind of preparation for it. Kings are to be judged as kings, not as knights, although Arthur's early kingship and his unique character seem to give him a place in both worlds. In the prose *Tristan,* for example, the point is made that Arthur is bound to the life of the court and is unable to adventure. Some, in fact, note that: "Ne portoit il mie armes si comme faisoient chevaliers errans, par quoy aucuns repputoient sa chevalerie estre perdue, et que domage estoit qu'il estoit roy, car s'il eust este chevalier errant, il eust este de grant renom."[49] Bors's reluctance reflects not a value judgment between knights and kings but a legitimate distinction which must be kept in mind when estimating Arthur in terms of Gawain, Lancelot, and the others.

Bors's distinction also serves another purpose. It indicates that the Vulgate *Lancelot* still belongs to the tradition of the early romances, or at best only anticipates from time to time later political ideas of the romances. The concern of the Vulgate *Lancelot* is for chivalry, not society or the *roiaume.* The spectrum of kingship is perforce broader here than in the earlier romances, and it often reflects the chronicle-world of the *chansons de geste,* particularly in the case of Claudas. The later parts, although they do not focus on kingship exclusively, deal at surprising length with technical questions of suzerainty, sovereignty, allegiance, fidelity, kingship,

49. Cited by Pickford, *L'Evolution du roman arthurien en prose,* p. 223.

knighthood, delegated authority, and the constitution of the court. The royal shortcomings most feared are the prolonged absence or death of the king, the king's failure to maintain *largesce* and *droiture,* and the instability of the king caused by momentary passions. The last of these, however, is usually treated in conjunction with political problems. The king's personal failures usually reappear in terms of political disorders.

If the *Lancelot* concentrates on the virtues of the *cheualerie terriene,* the *Queste del Saint Graal* consists of a powerful indictment of that institution.[50] Although structurally it is simply another *aventure* in the story of Lancelot and Arthur, it is expanded into a critique of earthly chivalry. Its ecclesiastical orientation, its repeated emphasis on the failure of the knights, and its replacing of Lancelot with Galahad, the perfect knight, amount almost to a wholesale condemnation of the values praised by Bors when he refused the crown of Gannes. The *Queste* does not emphasize the figure of Arthur, although in one striking scene the king realizes that this quest will diminish the honor of his court and perhaps ultimately destroy it. He is further faced with the dilemma that *aventure,* hitherto the raison d'être of his court, suddenly looms up as the element that will cause its downfall. The highest *aventure* of all, the grail-quest, will contribute most strongly to the destruction of the fellowship of the Round Table, by holding up to the *cheualerie terriene* the glass of the *cheualerie celestiele* and by turning *aventure,* the essence of *cheualerie,* against those who had lived by it for so long.

The *Queste* centers on other rulers than Arthur. It gives a new account of the *Roi-Mehaignié* and describes his ultimate cure by Galahad. The Maimed King becomes, in fact, the mirror image of Arthur. In the earlier parts of the Vulgate, Arthur's court had provided the knights with opportunities to win *honor* and *largesce.* The court at Corbenic, the grail-castle, however, demands that the knights prove themselves according to a different stan-

50. Sommer, 6:1–199. A more recent edition is that of A. Pauphilet (Paris, 1923). See Frappier in *ALMA,* pp. 302–07; A. Micha, "Etudes sur le *Lancelot* en prose, II: L'Esprit du Lancelot-Graal," *Romania* 82 1961): 357–78.

dard, against which all but Galahad fail. The *Roi-Mehaignié* thus occupies a place in the world of the *Queste* in which the healing of the king and the saving of the kingdom, not the individual honor of each knight, are the main objects of *aventure*.

The *Queste* had been prepared for as early as the *Charette* section of the *Lancelot,* in which Gawain encounters the knight with two swords, Eliezer, son of the Fisher King, Pelles. Gawain himself journeys to the grail-castle, but does not see the Maimed King or accomplish any of the *aventures* there. In the *Agravain* section Lancelot himself comes to Corbenic, accomplishes some, but not all, of the *aventures,* and is deceived into sleeping with Pelles's daughter, Helayne, in order that Galahad might be conceived. Bors is the next to visit the castle, but it is only at his second visit there that the question of the Maimed King comes up. Pelles asks casually if Bors has seen his father:

> Sire, fet il [Pelles] cest li roys mehaignies que on apele le roy pescheour le plus hardi cheualier et le plus preudomme qui fust a son tamps . . . Par le forfait quil fist quant il traist lespee du fuerre qui ne deuoit estre traite devant que cils le trairont qui les aventures del saint graal doit achever et pour chou fu il ferus parmi les .ii. cuisses de lespee et naura ia garison devant chou que li boins cheualiers vendra qui des goutes del sanc li oindra ses plaies.[51]

Only in the *Queste* proper do we learn more of these two kings. In the quest of Galahad, Bors, and Perceval there appear three kings, all of whom are linked with the coming of the best knight in the world and all of whom grew out of the two kings in Chrétien's *Perceval.* The first two are Pelles the Fisher King and his father, Pellinor the Maimed King. The third is Mordrain, originally a contemporary of Joseph of Arimathea who has been stricken blind because he presumed to look into the grail, but who has been allowed to wait on earth for the coming of the perfect knight in order to be healed by him. Mordrain has been

51. Sommer, 5:294–303. Bors's first visit is in Sommer, 5:128–47; his second, in Sommer, 5:294–303.

kept alive by a host for four hundred years and is thus identified with the mysterious old king sustained by the host in Chrétien. The other two kings belong to the generations of Utherpendragon and Arthur. Pelles is far too active and plays too complex a role to be maimed or enchanted. His father, however, is the *Roi-Mehaignié,* the Vulgate counterpart of Chrétien's Fisher King and of Amfortas. The version in the *Queste,* however, differs from all earlier versions. Pellinor's father, Lambor, had been killed by Urlain, a rival ruler, with a sword that Urlain had discovered on a ship to which he had fled. Urlain himself had been stricken dead, but the death of Lambor had caused pestilence, famine, and drought, and it had turned *la terre foraine* into *la terre gaste,* the wasteland.[52] The weapon which Urlain had used was the sword of David, and the ship into which he had fled was the ship of Solomon.[53] The sword had been broken once before, but Mordrain had rejoined the pieces. After the deaths of Lambor and Urlain, Lambor's son Pellinor found the ship and attempted to draw the sword himself. For his presumption he was stricken between the thighs and had to await the coming of the best knight in the world to be cured. Thus, the Vulgate version of the Dolorous Stroke.

The importance of these changes in the history of the Maimed King-Fisher King lies in their results. The king becomes the figure through whom the story of the grail's coming to Britain and the conversion of the Britons is connected to that of Arthur's reign. Moreover, the roles now given to David's sword and Solomon's ship and the story of the Dolorous Stroke draw the reader's attention to the sacrilegious character of Urlain's and Pellinor's actions, not to fertility symbolism, as the cause of the wasting of the land.

The final work in the Vulgate is the *Mort Artu.*[54] The romance

52. Sommer, 5:303. On the new name of the Fisher King, see J. D. Bruce, "Pelles, Pellinor, and Pellean in the Old French Arthurian Romances," *Modern Philology* 16 (1918/19): 113–28, 337–50.

53. See Schlauch, "The Allegory of Church and Synagogue."

54. Sommer, 6:201–391. See also J. Frappier, *Etude sur la Morte le Roi Artu* (rep. Paris, 1961); J. D. Bruce, "The Development of the Mort Arthur Theme in Medieval Romance." *Romanic Review* 4 (1913): 403–71.

begins with another view of the adventures recounted in the *Queste,* one which sees them in terms of their consequences to Arthur and his court. Gawain's unworthiness to participate in the adventure of the grail (although, ironically, he had been the first to vow to seek it) is reflected in the news that he alone had killed eighteen of the questing knights. Lancelot slips back into his illicit love of the queen, and the events begin which lead eventually to Arthur's war with Lancelot, Mordred's treachery, the battle on Salisbury Plain, and the deaths of Arthur, Guinevere, Lancelot, and Gawain.

The romance falls into two nearly equal parts. The first centers on Arthur's court and traces the origin of the intrigues that finally cause its destruction. In a sense the internal defects of *cheualerie,* which are revealed in the court scenes, break out in the second part onto the field of open warfare. The forest, the medium of *aventure,* plays no part at all in the *Mort Artu.* The first part of the *Lancelot* had opened with the siege of Benoyc; the *Mort Artu* has the siege of Benoyc as one of its climaxes. All the splendor, justice, and honor of Arthur's kingdom are destroyed from within. The despair of King Ban at the beginning of the *Lancelot* parallels the despair of Arthur at the end of the *Mort.* Micha has pointed out the effect which the whole *Lancelot-Queste-Mort* sequence gives of both "the highest awareness of the complexity of life and of human beings" and the daily mediocrities and failures that exist side by side with them.[55] Both aspects of courtly life exist side by side in the *Mort.* The early virtues of Arthur have become his vices. In order to maintain *droiture* he must wreak vengeance upon Lancelot. He must condemn the queen to death. He must attack Lancelot at *La Joyeuse Garde,* even though he knows that he cannot take the castle, in order to uphold his *honor.* He is driven by the unreasonable demands for vengeance on the part of Gawain, formerly the chief representative of *sens* and stability at the court.[56] In ensuring the welfare of his realm

55. Micha, "Etudes," p. 364.

56. A. Micha, "La Suite-Vulgate de Merlin," *ZfRPh* 71 (1955): 47, in which Micha notes that Arthur's kingship is diminished for literary purposes by the amount of political wisdom attributed to Merlin and the political courage given to Gawain.

when he leaves for the siege of Benoyc (as Galehaut had done when leaving Sorelois), Arthur makes the wrong choice: Mordred.[57] In turn, Mordred's *largesce,* formerly a king's chief virtue, ultimately turns Arthur's subjects against him. *Coutume, don, largesce, aventure,* which had governed the ethical and political world of the earlier romances, all operate to the destruction of that world in the *Mort.* Arthur's final dream of the Wheel of Fortune translates the causes of his disaster to extrapersonal forces but at the same time diminishes his own greatness as an individual. At the end Arthur says, echoing Charlemagne and foreshadowing Lear: "or ai iou trop vescu."[58]

The disasters which accumulate throughout the course of the later parts of the Vulgate are partly the results of human weakness operated upon by the corrosive effects of time. Arthur's claim to have lived too long is prefaced in the attack on Benoyc, when the author pauses in describing the duel between Lancelot and Gawain to remark that all present wondered at Gawain's endurance, since he was twenty-one years older than Lancelot, and that Lancelot himself was fifty-five! Arthur, who is older than Gawain, is close to ninety. The war on Benoyc is a battle of old men who, having lived in the timeless world of *aventure,* ultimately become subject to the ravages of time. Their devotion to personal honor, dignity, reputation, and love have become rigid categories which inhibit their recognizing their own human weakness. The forces who ally themselves with Mordred on Salisbury Plain are the same external enemies who had threatened Arthur's kingdom at the outset of his reign—the Scots, Irish, Welsh, and Saxons. The individual failings of the heroes become in the end the causes for the downfall of the kingdom.

The two later romances which depict the early history of the grail and that of Arthur, the *Estoire del Saint Graal* and the *Estoire de Merlin,* do not substantially change the picture of king-

57. For Mordred and the destruction of Logres, see J. D. Bruce, "Mordred's Incestuous Birth," in *Medieval Studies in Memory of Gertrude Schoepperle Loomis* (New York, 1927), pp. 197–208.

58. Sommer, 6:344.

ship given in the later works.[59] Their chief function, in fact, is to provide extrastructural changes in the whole Vulgate by expanding themes and incidents found in the *Lancelot-Queste-Mort* sequence backward in time. The *Estoire de Merlin,* however, gives other details concerning kingship in the *roiaume aventureus.* The account of Arthur's forebears with which the work begins reproduces the account given by Geoffrey of Monmouth of the machinations of Vortigern and the Saxons's defeat of the Britons. Arthur's uncle Maines, the first of King Constans's sons to succeed him, proves to be inept. The barons appeal to Vortigern himself to be their ruler, but he refuses until Maines is assassinated. In this version Vortigern is the complete tyrant who allies himself with invaders in order to destroy his own people, rather a prefiguration of Mordred. Ultimately, Constans's other two sons, Pandragon and Uter, defeat Vortigern and the Saxons. When Pandragon is murdered, Uter succeeds to the throne, changing his name to Uterpendragon. When Uterpendragon becomes too old to defend his people, Arthur succeeds him, but not without much baronial opposition. Merlin, however, guides Arthur's movements and arranges his confirmation as king. When he gives Arthur the sword at his coronation, he explains: "car quant nostres sires mist iustice en terre il le mist en glaive et en espee. Et la justice que sour la gent laie estoit et doit estre fu baillie au commenchement de .iii. ordres pour desfendre sainte eglize et droit justice a tenir."[60] When the barons ask Arthur to postpone his coronation, he agrees, but casts an interesting sidelight upon his view of kingship by remarking that he will not be king at all until he is crowned and anointed: "Et de ce que vous me dites que ie soie sires dou regne et ce ne puet estre devant ce que iaie eu le sacre et la coroune et lonor del empire. Mais . . . ie ne voeil avoir sacre ne honor se par la volente de dieu non et de vous."[61] The re-

59. *Estoire del Saint Graal,* ed. Sommer, vol. 1; *Estoire de Merlin,* ed. Sommer, vol. 2. See A. Micha, "The Vulgate Merlin," in *ALMA,* pp. 325–35; Bogdanow, *The Romance of the Grail,* p. 6, n. 2. For Arthur's forebears, see Sommer, 2:24–79.

60. Sommer, 2:82.

61. Sommer, 2:86–87.

mainder of the work deals with Arthur's wars against the rebels, among whom, surprisingly, are to be found Pelles of Listenois and Pellinor of the *Terre Gaste,* the Fisher King and the Maimed King of the *Queste.* Here, in a work written later than the *Lancelot,* they have become simply two more rebels, devoid of the mystery that had surrounded them in the earlier work. Indeed, the proliferation of wounded kings, evangelists, and knights in the two *Estoires* tends to detract from any mystery that had surrounded these rulers in other works. Whatever hint of the unorthodox supernatural had originally been attached to these figures, they had become, by the middle of the thirteenth century, purely human kings.

Vulgate romances ultimately fail to deal with kingship as an institution to the extent that they deal with *cheualerie.* Royal senility, sexual passion, self-defeating concerns for personal *honor,* all appear as individual personality traits. The *inutilitas* of the ruler is still considered in terms of *felonie* or personal shortcomings, not in terms of the welfare of the whole realm. The idea of Fortune seems to underlie Arthur's eventual failure, but it does so by universalizing the King, identifying Arthur with all kings and, in fact, all prominent men. From time to time Arthur's role as king briefly manages to transcend these conventional representations of royal inadequacy, an occurrence more frequent in the post-Vulgate works. The fragmentary interest in kingship as an institution in the Vulgate does not suffice to make the *rex inutilis* a consistent political category.

In the post-Vulgate *Roman du Graal,* however, and in Malory, Arthur and the *Roi-Mehaignié* both undergo a metamorphosis. These works, which center directly on the figure of Arthur and his reign, link the maiming of the Fisher King to Arthur's kingdom by further revising the tale of the Dolorous Stroke. At the same time, Arthur himself transcends the momentary weaknesses he had in the Vulgate and becomes a tragic figure whose fall bears little resemblance even to that of the Arthur who had protested against the whimsy of Fortune in the Vulgate *Mort Artu.*

The "New Arthuriad" of the post-Vulgate Arthurian romances subordinates the major figures of the earlier works to the history of the "*roi aventureux,* the king of chance and mischance, whose kingdom is the *roiaume aventureux.*"[62] The kingdom itself becomes the subject of *aventure,* a literary entity. Its ruler, Arthur, becomes "a just, unselfish, strong ruler, and father of his people, his virtues far outweighing his one weakness of undue partiality to his nephew Gawain."[63] With these works the figures of Arthur and the *Roi-Mehaignié* are so transformed that they no longer serve to illustrate the literary history of the *rex inutilis.* Their failure comes to be bound up with *mischeance* and *aventure,* not with technical details of political theory. The *regnum* finally assumes the center of interest and the romances become comprehensive accounts of human experience at many levels. Individual *aventure* becomes the *aventure* of the kingdom, its epic history. In terms of such history no one before Shakespeare would again discuss the implications of royal inadequacy from the double perspective of the individual human ruler and the complex abstract embodiment of suprapersonal public authority.

62. Bogdanow, *The Romance of the Grail,* pp. 152–53.

63. R. H. Wilson, *Characterization in Malory: A Comparison with His Sources* (Chicago, 1934), pp. 105–19.

6

Princeps Inutilis: Pope, Emperor, and King, 1294–1327

The sacerdotal—later papal—authority to coerce negligent or ineffective rulers had come to constitute, by the late thirteenth century, a suitable framework for political theory and political action on the part of laymen as well as clerics, for the public law touching monarchical power as well as the strictly papal authority to act on behalf of the common good of Christendom. Drawing upon increasingly articulate interpretations of Roman and canon law and upon the diplomatic experience of the papacy between the late eleventh and the late thirteenth centuries, the decretists and decretalists as well as the jurists and publicists habituated men to the discussion of royal power along juridical lines and to the conception of monarchical institutions as operating within a structure of public law. In the case of the *rex inutilis* this practice restricted the dynamic range of sources in which ideas of kingship might be developed and set off one against another. The earlier contributions made by Carolingian and later papal publicists between the ninth and the twelfth centuries, by literary representations of kingship within the context of an aristocracy-oriented and -controlled culture, and by the tentative analogies between royal and episcopal office drawn by the early canonists had been absorbed, transformed, or rejected in the process of shaping a style of governance and a conception of kingship which was genreally similar throughout the West and whose juridical outlines owed much to ecclesiastical legal thought.

The thirteenth century was as rich in the exchange of legal characteristics among the offices of pope, emperor, and king as earlier centuries had been in borrowing from the suggestive range of patristic thought and the traditions of Germanic culture. Kings and their publicists began to apply to monarchies such maxims as "rex est imperator in regno suo," the king claiming the same kind of authority in his kingdom as he believed the emperor to have in the Empire.[1] Some of the more ambitious *podestàs* of the Italian city-republics began to refer to themselves as holding office *"Dei gratia,"* borrowing terminology in turn from that which enhanced the office of king. An increasing homogeneity of the conceptual terminology of political discussions occurred at precisely the moment when rulers, publicists, lawyers, and even popes began also to provide a vigorous definition of the autonomy of *regna* against the universal claims of both church and Empire. This double movement of thirteenth- and fourteenth-century political theory greatly enhanced both the administration of public law within territorial monarchies and the ease with which lawyers could apply the same labels to all institutions of public authority, whether papacy, empire, or individual kingdoms such as England and France. Guillelmus Durantis could easily refer to the abstract "princeps, scilicet imperator vel papa," and his successors could extend the term to kings and even, by the time of Machiavelli, to any ruler.[2] Ecclesiastical theorists might give a new social meaning to the application of such terms as *civitas, regnum,* and *polis* to the church, and Dante could posit a rationale for the universal empire in terms very similar to those used by Remigio de' Girolami to describe a rationale for civic autonomy. As Wilks has remarked, "political society is not one; there are now many political societies."[3]

1. A comprehensive recent study, encompassing much of the bibliography on the topic, is that of Gaines Post, *Studies in Medieval Legal Thought,* pp. 453–82; R. Feenstra, "Jean de Blanot et la formule *Rex Franciae in regno suo princeps est,"* in *Etudes . . . LeBras,* 2:885–95.

2. See the remarks of M. Boulet-Sautel, "Le Princeps de Guillaume Durand," *Etudes . . . LeBras,* 2:803–13.

3. M. J. Wilks, *The Problem of Sovereignty in the Later Middle Ages: The Papal Monarchy with Augustinus Triumphus and the Publicists* (Cambridge, 1963), p. 432. For Dante and Remigio, see L. Minio-Paluello, "Remigio Girolami's *De Bono Communi,"* *Italian Studies* 11 (1956):

The common "political" character of these diverse societies afforded political theorists and publicists the opportunity to discuss them by using a set of abstract political concepts which could be applied with equal accuracy to both ecclesiastical and temporal societies and which may be considered as a contribution to the often discussed "secularization" or "laicization" of later medieval society.[4] The writings of John of Paris, Marsiglio of Padua, and William of Ockham thus drew not only upon the revival of Aristotelian political thought in the late thirteenth century but from the long process of formation of a juridical vocabulary in the work of ecclesiastical and secular lawyers as well. To be sure, such ideas as that of the public welfare, the limited powers of temporal rulers, and the impelling necessity of establishing justice in civil society had long been a part of Christian political literature. If the earliest uses of such ideas could only by extreme ingenuousness be made directly applicable to the political institutions of the ninth and tenth centuries, they could be and were made applicable to the complex ecclesiastical and temporal political structures of the fourteenth and fifteenth centuries. If the private character of royal power in the early Middle Ages had constituted the only effective guarantee of even rudimentary public stability, the public character of later medieval governance lessened the relevance of earlier moral judgments upon individual rulers and raised new questions concerning the nature of kingship.

Older theories of the just king and the tyrant, which had represented essentially an ecclesiastical attempt to regulate private individual power in terms of public morality, if not public law, no longer served to categorize the new public emphasis upon the ruler's task. The discussions by fourteenth-century lawyers upon

---

56–71, and Charles T. Davis, "Remigio de' Girolami and Dante; A Comparison of their Conceptions of Peace," *Studi Danteschi* 36 (1959): 105–36.

4. Relevant studies are those of J. R. Strayer, "The Laicization of French and English Society in the Thirteenth and Fourteenth Centuries," *Speculum* 15 (1940): 76–86; G. de Lagarde, *La Naissance de l'esprit laïque au déclin du moyen âge,* vol. 1 (3d ed., Paris, 1956); vol. 2 (2d ed., Paris, 1958).

the differences between the good man and the good citizen reflect the new criteria for political life: the moral criteria for early Christian kingship no longer completely sufficed to evaluate the good or evil fourteenth-century prince.

The formation of a homogeneous, abstract political terminology affected even the church. Although students of political thought have long concentrated their attention upon the absorption by temporal societies of characteristics and powers hitherto reserved to the pope, the *ecclesia,* or to Christendom as a whole, few have traced the reverse influence within the church itself. If such writers as John of Paris, Ockham, and Marsiglio could claim that the church was no political society at all, that did not prevent them from discussing the inner workings of that respiritualized institution in terms strikingly similar to those they used to describe temporal institutions. Even the nonpolitical church had a common good, the pope had a *status,* and the rulers of the church had to act for the common welfare of Christendom, just as temporal rulers had to act for the common welfare of their kingdoms. Thus the concepts of *utilitas ecclesiae* and *utilitas publica* might sound very much alike insofar as they were instruments invoked by strong popes and kings to enhance and rationalize the public powers they claimed for themselves. At the same time, the same concepts might be invoked by subordinates or opponents of weak or incompetent rulers to diminish individual powers, either in the name of the *Sedes Petri* or the *corona regni* under ostensible pressure of evident necessity for the common welfare of the church or realm.[5]

The history of the *rex inutilis* in the early fourteenth century should be traced with these changes in mind. In the church, the Empire, and the territorial monarchies, kings, popes, and subjects alike found at hand a vocabulary of public law which described the nature and needs of political society and placed all public actions within recognizable forms of law. In fact, the period

5. See Post, *Studies in Medieval Legal Theory,* for general considerations. Wilks, *The Problem of Sovereignty,* also discusses the application of these new "political" attitudes to the church.

1300–1450 witnessed a crisis of rulership during which the question of who would profit most from the new theories, the king or the commonwealth, seems to have been in considerable doubt. Although kings, emperors, and popes fell, and those who had caused their falls claimed that they did so according to law, that "law" was for several centuries yet to work more to the benefit of individual monarchs than to the benefit of those who would check or limit their power.[6] The transformation of the late medieval ruler from a private to a public man was accompanied, as Kantorowicz and others have shown, by the progressive enlargement of his human character. The ruler, hedged about by "mysteries of state," sustained by elaborate legal fictions which magnified his human nature, and transformed into the personal embodiment of sovereignty, law, and justice, was to weather the crisis of constitutionalism until the early modern period. When James I of England, for example, expressed his great displeasure with those who pried too deeply into his "mysteries of state," he was wisely, if not discreetly, invoking one of the chief principles of the individual ruler's retention of powers which would only later devolve to the invisible "constitution," to the State, the law, or the "people."[7]

The period 1294–1327 may thus be regarded as an early stage in that crisis. Besides the conflict between Philip the Fair and Boniface VIII, Robert of Naples and Henry VII, and John XXII and the imperial publicists, there grew up also a "political public" which was fed by the pulpit and the publicistic tract, the chronicle and the *consilium.* The use of the new political ideas for propaganda purposes, the growth of representative assemblies, and the increasingly frequent appearance of political topics in the

6. See the still valuable study of J. N. Figgis, *Political Thought from Gerson to Grotius: 1414–1625* (rep. New York, 1960), and the numerous more recent contributions of Francis P. Oakley, particularly his "From Constance to 1688 Revisited," *Journal of the History of Ideas* 27 (1966): 429–32, and the works cited there, as well as in his article, "Figgis, Constance, and the Divines of Paris," *American Historical Review* 75 (1969): 368–86.

7. Discussion in Kantorowicz, "Mysteries of State."

quodlibetical literature of the period should be considered in terms of the magnitude of the isues which that public faced. The broader categories of political typology as well as the new political ideas appealed to and influenced such a public, unprepared and unable as it was to consider political affairs with the subtlety and precision of an Innocent IV or a John of Paris. The older traditions surrounding the figure of the *rex inutilis,* for example, became equally common currency with the newer talk about the welfare of kingdoms, the relations between the papacy and the realm, and the king as the embodiment of the public safety. Popular invective, literary satire, and a genuine concern for political stability is reflected, for example, in Dante's portraits of the negligent princes in *Purgatorio,* vii.[8] The adaptation of legal and political theories to a wider public thus helped to perpetuate both the older and the more recent theories of royal inadequacy.

Medieval political thought had rarely concentrated upon the means by which rulers might be removed.[9] By 1300, to be sure, certain powers of deposition had been long attributed to the pope, but these could not always be appropriated safely by others. There did exist, however, in the large body of legal and political commentary produced in the twelfth and thirteenth centuries many precepts about what kings should and should not do, so that in one sense there existed a rationale for deposition before there existed a deposition process. The actual means available to those wishing to depose an unsuitable ruler were more frequently those based upon momentary aggregations of actual power and their expedient disposition. The nature of royal power was not so precisely definable that men could easily distinguish between the power of individual rulers and the public authority they embodied. The thrust of power necessary to remove an unsuitable ruler could never be so precisely regulated as to divide neatly

8. For Dante's negligent princes, see my study "I Principi negligenti di Dante e le concezioni medioevali del *Rex Inutilis,*" *Rivista Storica Italiana* 80 (1968): 741–58.

9. Substantial studies in Carlyle; Ullmann, *Principles of Government and Politics;* E. Lewis, *Medieval Political Ideas* (New York, 1954), 1:241–331.

the *administratio,* for example, from the royal *dignitas,* without arousing destructive resistance or even threatening the stability of the kingdom. Even in the twentieth century, when the sight of exiled and deposed kings is rather more common than it was in the fourteenth, those kings do not customarily reside in their own countries, and they serve the historian as pale and frivolous reminders of those more somber political ghosts of the late thirteenth and fourteenth centuries, Pietro Morone, Edward of Carnarvon, and Richard of Bordeaux—once Pope Celestine V, Edward II, and Richard II of England.

Thus the future of the *rex inutilis* was to lie within the legal framework perfected by Innocent IV and soon to be taken over by laymen and clerics seeking a legal framework for theories of rightful resistance to royal authority. In these political structures, in which the distribution of real power was habitually more massive and abrupt than subtle and legally precise, the character of royal uselessness, like the character of tyranny, took on the shape of a criminal violation of law. It became part of that legal formalism which began to surround deposition proceedings and thus contributed to and helped to shape the increasing awareness that the forms of law, if not always its substance, were the safest assurance for the success of revolutions and that these forms could be found more easily by adapting principles from the two laws than by relying exclusively upon the scriptural invocations of tyranny, the feudal *diffidatio,* or alleged violations of the coronation oath.

In describing the English revolution of 1399 Gaillard Lapsley has observed:

> In a society in which the forms of law have been prized so highly as they have in England, revolutions may assume an important constitutional significance not because of the material alterations which they make, but on account of the discoveries about the law and its forms to which they lead.[10]

Lapsley's remarks pertain not only to England nor only to the

10. G. Lapsley, "Richard II's Last Parliament," *EHR* 53 (1937): 78.

events of 1399. In the first quarter of the fourteenth century men experimented with many forms of public law. Between 1294 and 1327 there occurred three political crises that may illustrate the applicability of these remarks to the problem of the *rex inutilis* in the political crisis which began in the late thirteenth century. The abdication of Pope Celestine V in 1294 and the depositions of the Emperor Adolf of Nassau in 1298 and Edward II of England in 1327 all illustrate the early fourteenth-century conception of the *princeps inutilis.* Pope, emperor, and king, the three greatest powers in medieval Christendom, were all accused (or accused themselves) of "uselessness" in proceedings which stressed the legal character of that category. Celestine's abdication shook the world of Boniface VIII (and perhaps those of Urban VI and John XXIII). The deposition of Adolf, lacking any official indication of papal authority, reflected the increasing power of the electors and the extent to which the title of emperor had become a political appointment at the disposal of local powers. The removal of Edward II was "to haunt the dreams of his great-grandson, Richard II; it smoothed the path of the revolutionaries of 1399 and it opened the way for dynastic conflict and the decline of the medieval [English] monarchy."[11] All three crises raised the question of the *princeps inutilis.* All three reflect the history of the type in the new political world of the early fourteenth century.

Dante's ambiguous condemnation of Celestine V hardly indicates the impact of that pope's renunciation of the papacy upon the ecclesiological and political thought of the fourteenth century.[12] Among canonists and theologians Celestine's action and

11. May McKisack, *The Fourteenth Century, 1307–1399,* Oxford History of England, vol. 5 (Oxford, 1959), p. 96.

12. That Dante intended that the spirit "che fece per viltà il gran rifiuto" in *Inferno,* iii, 59–60, be recognized as Celestine has been a matter of some dispute. The following works, however, make a convincing case and shed much light on Celestine's reputation in the early fourteenth century: F. Schneider, "Der grosse Verzicht Colestins V," *Deutsche Dante-Jahrbuch* 33, n.F. 24 (1954): 212–14 (refuting the Pilate-thesis earlier put forward by Yvonne Batard in her *Dante, Minerve et Apollon—Les*

the justification he cited had to be reconciled to several distinct legal problems, themselves related to the unique nature of the papacy and to the canonists' long tradition of refusing to consider any grounds save notorious heresy as sufficient to serve as the basis for the removal of a pope. The supremacy of the pope within the ecclesiastical hierarchy of juristic authority and the carefully detailed separation of the person of the pope from the papal office raised serious legal questions which Celestine's defenders had to answer. Moreover, the political crises of the 1920s gave Celestine's renunciation and the election of Boniface VIII an importance extending even beyond the juristic world of the canonists. Public reaction to Celestine's renunciation resulted in extensive speculation on the nature of the papacy both by those who supported and those who opposed Celestine's decision.

Elected pope in July of 1294, Celestine V renounced the papacy in December of the same year. Confronting the assembled cardinals, acording to Ferretti's version he announced:

> I, Celestine V, moved by valid reasons, that is, by reason of humility, by reason of [the desire for] a better life, by reason of a troubled conscience, of corporal defects, of a lack of knowledge, of personal shortcomings, and in order that I may be able to proceed to a more humble life, freely and voluntarily give up the papacy and renounce expressly the place and the dignity, the burdens and honors with full and free ability to do so and [it now remains for] the holy college of cardinals to elect and provide canonically a shepherd for the universal Church.[13]

Celestine then divested himself ritually of the papal regalia and

---

Images dans la Divine Comédie [Paris, 1952], pp. 480–81); B. Nardi, "Dante e Celestino V," in his *Dal Convivio alla Commedia,* Istituto Storico Italiano—Studi Storici, fasc. 35–39 (Rome, 1960), pp. 315–30. More recent and thorough is the work of G. Padoan, "Colui che fece per viltà il gran rifiuto," *Studi Danteschi* 38 (1961): 75–128, with copious citations from contemporary commentaries on Dante's work and on Celestine.

13. Baronius-Theiner, *Annales Ecclesiastici, ad. an.* 1294, no. 20.

resumed his customary monkish dress. Eleven days later the conclave of cardinals elected Benedetto Gaetani to the throne of St. Peter. The new pope, whom tradition had already begun to name the engineer of Celestine's renunciation, took the name Boniface VIII and set about, in his first official acts, to vindicate the right by which his predecessor had vacated that throne.[14]

Although Celestine did not base his renunciation exclusively—or even primarily—upon his alleged incapacity to govern the church, he did give that topic a prominent place among his other reasons and thus raised anew the vexing question of papal incompetence. A close examination of his statement, moreover, reveals another striking aspect of his grounds: the text cites strictly those canonical reasons which allowed all prelates, with papal permission, to renounce high ecclesiastical office. By neglecting carefully those aspects of the papacy which did not apply to all higher prelates generally, Celestine avoided—and thus left for others to consider—a number of knotty theological and legal questions. Thus Celestine's action could not help but invite review of some of the most difficult questions with which canonists had ever dealt. The creators of a science which had as one of its chief objects the juristic demonstration of the doctrine that the pope was supreme in the church were now faced with the reverse of that doctrine, the problem of papal unsuitability. Not only the canonists and the new pope but the new pope's enemies as well were drawn to open the nature of the papal office to legal analysis at a time when such investigations could not but be seriously influenced by contemporary political, legal, and philosophical arguments.

However inept Celestine's government of the church may in fact have been, the legal reasoning contained in his statement of renunciation indicates that he had received sound advice from scholars who knew their canon law. The one lawyer whom tradition quickly named the chief architect of the renunciation, Benedetto Gaetani, may not have needed to resort to the legen-

14. On Boniface and Celestine, see G. Digard, *Philippe le Bel et le Saint-Siege* (Paris, 1936), 1:166–207; L. Tosti, *Pope Boniface VIII and His Times,* trans. E. Donnelly (New York, 1933), pp. 60–98, 463–70; T. S. R. Boase, *Boniface VIII* (London, 1933), pp. 22–88.

dary means by which he is supposed to have persuaded Celestine to resign.[15] The first three reasons which Celestine advanced—*humilitas, melior vita,* and *conscientia illaesa*—all pertain to his well-publicized fear for the salvation of his own soul under the burden of the *onera et honores* of the papal office, a concern which canonists had long recognized as sufficient grounds for a prelate's renunciation (with, of course, papal approval) and which even Dante was maliciously to take note of in the *Purgatorio.*[16] The fourth, fifth, and seventh reasons—*debilitas corporis, defectum scientiae,* and *infirmitas personae*—are familiar terms from canonists' earlier discussions of general prelatal inadequacy. It is in his citation of these last terms that Celestine is of relevance to the history of the *princeps inutilis.*

As Tierney has pointed out, the dialectical structure of Gratian's *Decretum* necessarily brought the canonists to discussions not only of papal supremacy within Christendom but also of the possible limitations of that supremacy.[17] For the most part, to be sure, canonist commentators were understandably reluctant to outline a systematic theory justifying the removal of a canonically elected pope for any reason. The character of the texts pertaining to papal unsuitability which Gratian had included in his collection, the aims of the glossators of the canon law, and the powerful traditional separation of the person of the pope from the dignity of the papal office all contributed to that reluctance and should be borne in mind during the following discussion.

Certainly several popes in the history of the church through

15. See below, n. 25. Also L. Moehler, *Die Kardinäle Jakob und Petrus Colonna* (Paderborn, 1914), pp. 251–77, for anti-Bonifatian propaganda.

16. *Purgatorio* XIX, 97–145. The speaker is Pope Adrian V.

17. B. Tierney, "Pope and Council: Some New Decretist Texts," *Medieval Studies* 19 (1957): p. 198; see pp. 197–218. Other studies by Tierney trace the twelfth- and thirteenth-century beginnings of attempts at discussions of the limitation of papal power: "Grosseteste and the Theory of Papal Sovereignty," *Journal of Ecclesiastical History* 6 (1955): 1–17; *Foundations of the Conciliar Theory* (Cambridge, 1955); "A Conciliar Theory of the Thirteenth Century," *CHR* 36 (1950/51): 415–40.

the tenth century had been subjected to trial and deposition, to the institution of powerful antipopes, and to sustained personal invective. In the eleventh century Gregory VII, and in the twelfth, Alexander III, to name only two of the most prominent examples, both faced severe tests of their right to hold office. Of the earlier group, perhaps the cases of Formosus and Marcellinus were best known to later canonists, the latter in fact having received more than usual attention since a reference to his case appeared in the *Decretum.*[18] Another pope, parts of whose correspondence also appeared in the *Decretum,* Leo IV, had written to Charles the Bald concerning his own *inutilitas* and the danger of Charles's interpreting the pope's personal shortcomings in prejudice to the *dignitas* of the whole church.[19] In most of these cases, however, as Ullmann and others have shown, both the institution of the papacy and the personal failings of individual popes were protected by the careful distinction between person and office, which had constituted so large a part of medieval theories of papalism from the fifth century on.[20]

The juristic rationale for that distinction was embodied in a number of canonical texts, none of which was to prove more useful than that of Cardinal Humbert, attributed by Gratian to St. Boniface and included in the *Decretum* as D.40 c.6 *Si papa:*

18. D.21 c.7 *Nunc autem.* The glosses to this passage always refer to D.40 c.6 *Si papa,* discussed below.

19. C.2 q.7 c.41 *Nos si aliquid incompetenter.* See Ullmann, "*Nos si aliquid incompetenter.*" The other sections of Leo IV's correspondence are in MGH *Epp. V. Epp. kar. aev.* III, 585–612; see also nos. 24, 39, and 40; P. Ewald, "Die Papstbriefe der Britischen Sammlung," *Neues Archiv* 5 (1880): 277–414, esp. 291f.

20. Ullmann's numerous studies are summarized in his *Principles of Government and Politics* and *The Growth of Papal Government.* On the heretical pope, see also L. Buisson, *Potestas und Caritas* (Graz, 1958), pp. 166–216; V. Martin, "Comment S'est formée la doctrine de la supériorité du concile sur le pape," *Revue des Sciences Religieuses* 17 (1937): 121–43, 261–89, 405–27. Besides the studies of Tierney cited above, see also J. A. Watt, "The Early Medieval Canonists and the Foundation of the Conciliar Theory," *Irish Theological Quarterly* 24 (1957): 13–31; M. J. Wilks, *The Problem of Sovereignty,* pp. 455–523.

> Si Papa suae et fraternae salutis neglegens reprehenditur inutilis et remissus in operibus suis et insuper a bono taciturnus . . . Huius culpas istic redarguere presumit mortalium nullus, quia cunctos ipse iudicaturus a nemine est iudicandus, nisi deprehendatur a fide devius.[21]

The reservation "nisi deprehendatur a fide devius," standing in juristic as well as syntactic opposition to *inutilis et remissus,* became the canonists' guide for regulating the discussion of papal unsuitability.[22] Following Humbert, they consistently restricted their concern to the question of papal heresy rather than to other aspects of possible papal unsuitability, as other texts might have led them to do. In view of the increasingly juristic concepts of the papal office, moreover, the phrase "Papa a nemine iudicatur" expressed in legal terms the supremacy of the pope within the hierarchy of Christendom: the pope could not be judged because there was, literally, no one to judge him.[23] In view of earlier canonist lines of thought, then, Celestine could not very well have availed himself of the one type of papal unsuitability to which the canonists had devoted most attention, that of heresy. Nor could he have appealed to other canonical exemptions which might conceivably be applied to a pope of unsound mind, since his renunciation had to be at once theologically and legally valid. Finally, he did not choose, or was not permitted, to be deposed, and papal deposition had received far more attention than had papal abdication.

21. Accurate text in P. E. Schramm, *Kaiser, Rom und Renovatio* (rep. 1957), 2:120–36, at 128–29. On the significance of the text, see W. Ullmann, "Cardinal Humbert and the *Ecclesia Romana," Studi Gregoriani* 4 (1952): 111–27, and J. T. Gilchrist, "Humbert of Silva Candida and the Political Concept of *Ecclesia* in the Eleventh-Century Reform Movement," *Journal of Religious History* 2 (1962): 13–28.

22. The implications of these views for later approaches to the problems raised by papal abdication are discussed in W. Ullmann, "Medieval Views Concerning Papal Abdication," *Irish Ecclesiastical Record* 71 (1949): 125–33, and J. Leclerq, "La Renonciation de Célestin V et l'opinion théologique en France du vivant de Boniface VIII," *Revue de l'Histoire de l'Eglise de France* 25 (1939): 183–92.

23. See Wilks, *The Problem of Sovereignty,* pp. 455–78.

In his first letter Boniface painted a dramatic picture of the turmoil to which the church had been subjected since 1292, stressing particularly the legitimacy of Celestine's renunciation and that of his own election.[24] That he should be so concerned to establish the legality of those events is easily understandable. Never had a pope resigned the papacy. Only rarely had earlier canonists even discussed the possibility of such an event. Celestine was obviously not a heretic, and Boniface had many enemies. At the most opportune of times the candidacy of Boniface would have attracted much opposition. Coupled with the resignation of a canonically elected pope who was, in the opinion of many, a saint, Boniface's pontificate added complications to an already complex period. Celestine's action may well have seemed to the assembled cardinals, as Ferretti remarks, a "res nova . . . plena periculi"; and indeed it was.

Boniface, then, had other than strictly legal reasons for his apprehension. Not only problems of theology and canon law but specific political conflicts threatened to turn the case into a political crisis in the relations between the papacy and all of Christendom. In 1297 the Colonna cardinals attempted to precipitate just such a crisis when, taking advantage of other opposition to Boniface, they issued their famous manifesto impugning Boniface's right to the papacy, chiefly on the grounds that his predecessor had had no right to resign at all.[25] Boniface replied with the bull *Quoniam aliqui,* which he incorporated into his official collection of canons, the *Liber sextus,* published in 1298.[26] *Quoniam aliqui*

24. *Les Régistres de Boniface VIII,* ed. G. Digard (Paris, 1907), vol. 1, cols. 1–4. The legal background to theories of renunciation is discussed by Riesenberg in *The Inalienability of Sovereignty,* pp. 63–80.

25. For these manifestoes, see, besides the works cited above, H. Denifle, "Die Denkschriften der Colonna gegen Bonifaz VIII. und die Cardinäle gegen die Colonna," *Archiv fur Literatur– und Kirchengeschichte des Mittelalters* 5 (Freiburg i.B., 1889): 493–529; Leclercq, "La Renonciation de Célestin V." A general survey is provided by R. Mols, art. "Célestin V," in the *Dictionnaire d'histoire et de géographie ecclésiastique,* fasc. LXVII (Paris, 1950), cols. 79–101.

26. *Liber sextus* 1.7.1 *Quoniam aliqui.*

thus opened the range of inquiry into the legitimacy of Celestine's case to the glossators of the canon law, a group of men who had been called upon frequently in the past to justify and expand similar papal pronouncements of great import.

When Innocent IV had been faced with a case of royal incompetence, it may be recalled, he borrowed certain approaches to the problem from the canonists' work on the problem of prelatal incompetence. By "equiparating" Sancho II of Portugal to any incompetent higher prelate, Innocent could justify the assigning of that political monstrosity the *curator* to Portugal, depriving the king of the *administratio* of the kingdom while leaving to him the royal *dignitas*. Such a solution could not, however, be applied in reverse. Although Celestine had availed himself of some of the grounds often used to qualify prelates as incompetent, the *sedes Petri* was to prove ultimately less vulnerable to such a division of powers than were the territorial monarchies. The idea of papal *coadiutores* had been worked out, moreover, in terms of the cardinals.[27] In the fourteenth and fifteenth centuries the division of powers between pope and cardinals or pope and general council representing the whole body of the faithful was indeed to become the object of much legal and theological discussion.[28] The complexity of the cardinalate possessing the *administratio* of the church while an incompetent pope retained the papal *dignitas* was an idea which only the most extreme and ingenuous of the early conciliarists attempted to consider.[29] In any case, the assigning of a *curator* or *coadiutor* would still have left Celestine possessed of the papal dignity, a burden which he declared himself incapable of sustaining. When such a solution was in fact suggested, it was not the pope but one of the cardinals, possibly Gaetani, who maintained that Innocent IV's solution to the prob-

27. See Wilks, *The Problem of Sovereignty,* pp. 455–63, with bibliography cited.

28. See Tierney, *Foundations of the Conciliar Theory;* H. Jedin, *A History of the Council of Trent,* trans. E. Graf (St. Louis, 1957), 1:5–61, as well as the Studies of Martin, Watt, and Ullmann cited above.

29. See the instance cited by W. Ullmann, *The Origins of the Great Schism* (London, 1948), p. 167.

lems of Portugal in 1245 would be inapplicable to the papacy in 1294.

Just as earlier canonists had agreed, however, that a heretic and perhaps a tyrant ought not be pope, Celestine had now come forward with the powerful assertion that in spite of the protection afforded the person of the pope by generations of skilled canonists, an incompetent pope was equally unfit to rule the church. Within fifty years of the first juristic occurrence of the *rex inutilis,* a reigning pontiff had raised the question, although he did not use the term, of the *papa inutilis.* By neglecting many of the canonists' theories which had prevented the problem of papal incompetence from becoming a much-discussed topic during the preceding century and a half, Celestine approached the papal office from another direction and applied to it all of the canonists' observations on incompetent prelates. That approach led to an act unique in papal history, to a disputed pontificate, the events of which forever weakened the papacy as an institution, and to the entrance into discussions of the church of ideas concerning the public welfare of Christendom, the restriction of the powers of the ruler, and the topic of the relation between the person of the pope and the papal office. Celestine's act, if it was indeed a *res nova,* was also a turning point in fourteenth-century ecclesiastical approaches to the powers of the *princeps.*

The jurists, theologians, and publicists who commented upon Celestine's case soon erected an elaborate structure of legal reasoning to justify his action. If Celestine himself was not imbued with neo-Aristotelian theories of the common good of Christendom, his advisors certainly were. His application to the papacy of standards hitherto restricted to other prelates, moreover, certainly suggested to others not only that an inept pope could endanger the common good but also that theories hitherto reserved to other powers might be applicable in such a case. An examination of some of the responses to Celestine's abdication may reflect some of that pope's contributions to the idea of the *princeps inutilis.*

Peter Olivi, one of the earliest defenders of Celestine, answered in 1295 and again in 1297 a number of objections to the legality of Celestine's renunciation, including some of those brought forward by the Colonna cardinals.[30] After having shown, not for the first time certainly, that papal power could be lost through notorious heresy, Olivi concentrated upon the theological distinction between the sacramental capacity of the pope, his *potestas ordinis,* which resembled that of all other bishops and could not be lost, and the pope's juridical capacity, his *potestas iurisdictionis,* which was *mobilis et transitoria* and could be lost.[31] By arguing that the pope has the same authority over himself as he has over other bishops, Olivi even went further and claimed for him not only the right to resign, "ex maxima et evidentissima necessitate et sub tali circumstantiarum moderamine, quod nullum notabile scandalum immineat,"[32] but to nominate his own successor as well.[33] In drawing a sharp distinction between the person of the pope and the *sedes Petri,* Olivi may be said to anticipate the English barons and their advisors of 1308, who also drew painfully sharp distinctions, and then between the individual person of the English king and the *corona regni.*[34]

The theologians Godefroid des Fontaines and Pierre d'Auvergne continued Olivi's defense of Celestine and developed it into a consideration of the whole task of the papacy, the assurance of the *utilitas ecclesiae,* finally reaching the argument that any pope who

30. For Olivi, see Decima L. Douie, *The Nature and the Effect of the Heresy of the Fraticelli* (Manchester, 1932), pp. 81–119; F. Ehrle, "Petrus Johannis Olivi, sein Leben und seine Schriften," *Archiv für Literatur- und Kirchengeschichte des Mittelalters* 3 (Berlin, 1887): 409–552; L. Hodl, "Die Lehre des Petrus Johannis Olivi O.F.M. von der Universalgewalt des Papstes," *Mitteilungen des Grabmann-Institut der Universitat Munchen* (Munich, 1958), 1:19–25.

31. Brief discussion in Wilks, *The Problem of Sovereignty,* p. 379.

32. Ehrle, "Petrus Iohannis Olivi," pp. 527–28. Olivi's material on Celestine V is printed in P. L. Oliger, "Petrus Iohannis Olivi de renunciatione papae Coelestini V quaestiones et epistola," *Archivium Fransciscanum Hist.* 11 (1918): 309–73.

33. Wilks, *The Problem of Sovereignty,* p. 467, n. 3, discusses other references to the papal nomination of a successor, but does not note Olivi's view. See also Ehrle, p. 526.

34. The text of the declaration is in H. G. Richardson and G. O. Sayles, *The Governance of Medieval England from the Conquest to Magna Carta* (Edinburgh, 1963), pp. 466–69.

felt unable to accomplish that task ought to resign.[35] The influence of other political ideas, however, is evident in Pierre d'Auvergne's work. Since, he states, every being is ordered toward a specific operation, the pope's "specific operation" being the maintaining of the *ecclesia,* any pontiff who proves unable to fulfill that task ought to step down and leave it to another. Pierre d'Auvergne, like other contemporary philosophers, here adds an Aristotelian dimension to the older ecclesiological arguments cited by his contemporaries. Thus it may be seen that Boniface VIII's decretal *Quoniam aliqui* encountered substantial agreement among theologians and philosophers. Publicists and jurists also provided a certain measure of agreement.

John of Paris's treatise *De potestate regia et papale* was written in 1302 as a partisan tract on behalf of Philip the Fair in his quarrel with Boniface VIII. The last chapters of this tract are devoted to the general question of the papal right to renounce the papacy, doubtless inspired by Celestine's action eight years before.[36] Although he was favorable to Philip throughout his tract, John strongly maintained the legitimacy of the papal renunciation. Since the pope is only elected, John says,

> for the common good of the church and the flock of the Lord . . . If, after his election to the papacy a pope should find himself or should be discovered to be totally inept or useless or if an impediment should arise, such as insanity or anything similar, he should request to be relieved by the people or by

35. Texts discussed by Leclerq, "La Renonciation de Célestin V," pp. 186–89; Riesenberg, *The Inalienability of Sovereignty,* pp. 64–65. See also P. G. Caron, *La Rinuncia all' ufficio ecclesiastico nella storia del diritto canonico dalla età apostolica alla riforma cattolica* (Milan, 1946), pp. 167–272. See also G. de Lagarde, "La Philosohie sociale d'Henri de Gand et Godefroid de Fontaines," *Archives de l'histoire doctrinale et littéraire au moyen-âge,* 18 (1943/45): 73–142.

36. For John of Paris, see J. Leclerq, *Jean de Paris et l'ecclésiologie du XIIIe siècle* (Paris, 1942). The text of the *De potestate regia et papali* is edited on pp. 173–260. See also Tierney, *Foundations of the Conciliar Theory,* pp. 158–78; Ullmann, *Principles of Government and Politics,* pp. 263–67; Wilks, *The Problem of Sovereignty,* index, s.v. John of Paris.

> the cardinals who in such a case represent the whole clergy and people, and he should, permission received or not, cede his high place. Otherwise, indeed, that which had been instituted out of charity would militate against charity, if uselessly and to the evil and confusion of the church and to the damnation of his own soul a presiding pontiff were not able to renounce [the papacy].[37]

Not only, then, may the pope freely resign the papacy, but he may be forced to do so:

> Hence, if there should arise any sort of spiritual degeneracy or ineptitude or a scandal within the church or anything which disturbs the church or divides the flock of God, setting one group at another and creating scandal, and if the pope, having been warned of this, does not desist, he may be even compelled to resign . . . since even the pope, just like any other prelate, rules not for his own benefit but for that of the people, the agreement of the people would be better in this case that he be deposed, even if he is unwilling, if he should seem completely useless, and another should be elected.[38]

In John of Paris's work the chief emphasis is strictly upon the welfare of the whole church, the *bonum commune ecclesiae,* or the *bonum gregis Domini,* which the divine vicariate of the pope appears no longer able to sustain by itself. Not only the papal office but the person of each individual pope must be sufficient to assure the good of the whole church.

John of Paris may be considered an extreme but very articulate example of the trend in political thought which prevented Celestine's case from becoming a duplicate of that of Sancho of Portugal. That a division of authority and power did not occur in 1294 and was not again to be considered until 1378 reflects the reluctance of later medieval thinkers to separate juridically the dignity and governance pertaining to any public office, in spite of the increased sophistication of legal thought which allowed such a division to

37. Leclerq, *Jean de Paris,* p. 254.
38. Ibid.

become a possibility. Even the most propapalist of political writers, as Wilks's study has shown, men like Augustinus Triumphus, could not remain unaffected by the forceful theses of a John of Paris.[39] A brief glance at some of Augustinus's remarks concerning the nature of the papacy may illustrate dramatically the intellectual milieu into which Celestine's resignation threw a timely, if extremely difficult, problem.

The pope must be, Augustinus observes, a man of sufficient ability to ensure the well-being of the church: "It should be noted that the college of cardinals ought to elect as pope a man of sufficient knowledge . . . because the greatest of sciences is the rule of souls [*ars artium est regimen animarum*]."[40] The last phrase is a favorite of Augustinus and should call to mind the increasing emphasis which political writers placed upon *scientia, certa scientia,* and *sapientia* in governmental affairs during the late thirteenth and fourteenth centuries. Further, Augustinus claims that a law forbidding the pope to renounce the papacy would be "contra veritatem et contra reipublicae utilitatem . . . contra bonum totius ecclesie . . . ecclesia langueret."[41] When he comes to the case of Celestine, Augustinus continues his theme of knowledge and skill: "But Celestine renounced [the papacy] because of his imperfect knowledge. Seeing himself powerless and insufficient for the governance of the church, he renounced the papacy, led by the advice of the Holy Spirit."[42] In spite of the arguments of the Colonna cardinals and other opponents of Boniface, then, substantial theological and philosophical agreement concurred in the case of Celestine. To be sure, some agreement was to be expected after the facts of a resignation and a new election, but the philosophers' response to Celestine's renunciation does not sound much like a *post facto* rationale con-

39. For Augustinus, see Wilks, *The Problem of Sovereignty.* See also J. Rivière, "Une Première 'Somme' du pouvoir pontifical. Le pape chez Augustin d'Ancône," *Revue des Sciences Religieuses* 18 (1938): 149–83.

40. Augustinus Triumphus de Ancona, *Summa de potestate ecclesiastica* (Lyons, a. 1484), *Q.*3 *ad* 3.

41. Ibid. *Q.*4 *ad* 5. The whole of *Quaestio* 4 deals with the renunciation of the papacy.

42. *Q.*4 *ad* 8. Cf. *Q.*46.

structed to please Benedetto Gaetani. The themes of political theory brought to bear upon Celestine's case were too varied and, in some cases, too dangerous to any theory of papal untouchability for them to be wholly orthodox replies to clerical and lay opposition charges.

Even the canon lawyers, long the most intelligent and tough-minded supporters of papal supremacy, often sound very much like John of Paris when they comment on *Quoniam aliqui,* bringing to bear upon the question of papal unsuitability much of the political considerations earlier applied to the case by others. In his ordinary gloss to the *Liber sextus* and in his *Novella* Johannes Andreae was to rely on both theologians and publicists. Johannes's work may be in fact considered as threading a difficult middle road between two extreme views of papal authority. The pope may resign, Johannes says,

> But he may not be deposed: because the pope may be deposed only for heresy. 40 dist. *si papa* [D.40 c.6]. But other prelates may be deposed by the pope for insufficiency, both ecclesiastical and secular 18 q.2 [C.18 q.2 c.15] *quis abbas.* 15 quaestio 6 *alius* [C.15 q.6 c.3] and on account of negligence, 81 distinctio dictum [d.g.a. D.81].[43]

In his gloss to *Quoniam aliqui,* however, Johannes strongly supports the pope's right to resign for any reason, whether he is insufficient or not (glo. *ad.* VI 1.7.1 *ad. v. maxime):* "Comparativum: unde etiam sufficiens sit, renunciare poterit." The pope, whether *sufficiens* or *insufficiens,* may resign the papacy voluntarily. Concerning insufficiency, Johannes goes on to note (ibid. *ad. v. insufficientiam):* "Et posset ex multis insurgere insufficientia haec, ut ex defectu litteraturae, ex senectute, ex infirmitate, vel similibus." Perhaps one of the reasons for the ease with which canonists adopted the views

43. Johannes Andreae, *glo. ord. ad VI* 1.7.1 *ad v. insufficientem.* The linking of such concepts as *negligentia, insufficientia,* and *dilapidatio* may be seen by glancing at Hostiensis's definition of negligentia *(Summa Aurea* [rep. Turin, 1963], col. 168): "Quid sit negligentia. Eius, quod fieri debet, et potest, omisio." A century later Antonio a Butrio remarks *(In sextum Decretalium volumen commentaria,* [rep. Turin, 1967], vol. 5) *ad* VI 1.8.2, no. 8: "Sed negligentia et dilapidatio est insufficientia."

of later political thinkers and publicists may have been the fact that these views were not wholly new to canonist scholarship. They had all been expressed before in terms of lesser prelates and their relation to the pope. From the injunctions of Gregory the Great to the deposition of Rothad by Hincmar of Rheims to the disputes concerning the sacramental powers of simoniacs in the eleventh century, the ability of bishops had been a reiterated theme in ecclesiastical pronouncements, both by popes and councils. The case of Celestine and the responses to it by other political thinkers did not face the canonists with completely unheard-of theses. Johannes Andreae and others simply applied to the pope some of the traditional canonist observations concerning the suitability of prelates. They added to the body of discussions of papal unsuitability a number of views concerning renunciation, an area which had not received much attention before 1294. To be sure, they still reserved deposition for a notoriously heretical pope, but they made the further step of admitting that the *bonum commune ecclesiae* might indeed be threatened or destroyed by an incompetent pope, and they admitted the freedom of the pope to resign his office. As Wilks notes, "The very suggestion that a pope may be incapable of carrying out his function means that a crack had appeared in the apparently solid edifice of papal supremacy."[44] One may remark that the edifice was not as solid as the more thoroughgoing papalists might have liked to think. Yet the canonists' and theologians' acceptance of Celestine's rationale and the consequent view of the papacy which it entailed did indeed represent a crack. It underlined the shift in emphasis in political thought from the dignity of the individual incumbent, who was legally untouchable and "perfect" by virtue of his identification with the powers of his office, to the purpose of the office itself.

The papacy, as the events subsequent to the Councils of Constance and Basle were to show, was to survive analysis of John of Paris and other political theorists of the fourteenth century. In the years following 1294, however, men had been given the opportu-

44. Wilks, *The Problem of Sovereignty,* p. 497. See generally, pp. 488–523.

nity to discuss that institution in a language and according to political views which threatened any sort of absolute lordship. If Celestine's case did not set a precedent for the future of the *papa inutilis,* it at least provided an occasion for discussions of uselessness sharpened by current ideas about the nature of political society and generating theories which, if they could not always be applied to the papacy, could be applied by astute men to less protected political figures, whether emperors or kings, with much greater impact and with less easily predictable results.

The depositions of Adolf of Nassau in 1298 and Edward II of England in 1327 may illustrate the assimilation of the figure of the *princeps inutilis* into fourteenth-century deposition theory.[45] Adolf of Nassau had been elected emperor of the Romans largely by the power of the western ecclesiastical electors in an attempt to prevent the continuation of Habsburg control of the imperial title.[46] His election had cost him the support of the eastern magnates, led by Albert of Austria, and his attempts to increase his own family's holdings and power and to accommodate French foreign policy cost him eventually the support of the western electors. In 1298 Archbishop Gerhard of Mainz declared him deposed, the electors of Saxony and Brandenburg concurring.[47] From 800 to 1298 the office of emperor had been the subject of countless analyses, restrictions, and pretensions on the part of theorists, popes, electors, and emperors. If the reigns of Charlemagne, Otto I, Henry

45. For perceptive remarks on both cases, see Caspary, "The Deposition of Richard II."

46. See Geoffrey Barraclough, *The Origins of Modern Germany* (rep. New York, 1963), pp. 303–05; idem, "Edward I and Adolf of Nassau: A Chapter in Medieval Diplomatic History," *The Cambridge Historical Journal* 6 (1940): 225–62; W. Stubbs, *Germany in the Later Middle Ages,* ed. A. Hassall (London, 1908), pp. 80–87; F. W. E. Roth, *Geschichte des romischen Königs Adolf I von Nassau* (Wiesbaden, 1879); H. Otto, "Die Absetzung Adolfs von Nassau und die romische Kurie," *Historische Vierteljahrschrift* 2 (1899): 1–17; V. Samanek, "Studien zur Geschichte König Adolfs," Akad. Wien., Phil.-hist. Kl., S.B. 207, Bd. 3 (1930), esp. pp. 234–49.

47. MGH *Const.* III, nos. 588–90, pp. 548–63.

IV, Frederick I, and Frederick II had represented the periods of greatest temporal preponderance over the imperial idea, other reigns had equally weakened it. From the pontificates of Alexander III and Innocent III, in fact, popes and canonists consistently viewed the emperor as a subordinate of the pope, in an official as well as a theological sense. The emperor came to be considered the "vicar of the pope."[48] Standards for imperial suitability were spelled out far more explicitly than papal standards for royal suitability. Between 1198 and 1220 Innocent III and Honorius III found numerous occasions to intervene in imperial affairs, and the numerous studies of Innocent's views on the relations between *sacerdotium* and *imperium,* if they do not always agree on all aspects, nevertheless concur in Innocent's creation of firm juridical bonds between emperor and pope. The political crises which the papacy faced in the late twelfth and thirteenth centuries may well have contributed to forcing Innocent's hand on strong pronouncements, and certainly the relations between Frederick II and Innocent IV did not afford the pope any occasions to relax the strong claims on the imperial office made by his predecessors.

More than those of pope or king, the duties of the emperor had been reiterated again and again by canonists and publicists. As the idea of the imperial office as a papal vicariate was worked out by popes and canonists, the personal character of the emperor, as well as his duties and the papal authority to punish his offenses, became frequent themes of political speculation. Upon the emperor fell the papal requirements of *idoneitas,* of "usefulness" on a broad scale. Against the emperor charges of criminal negligence could be

48. See Stickler, "Imperator vicarius papae"; Wilks, *The Problem of Sovereignty,* pp. 103–08, 199, 223–315. The deposition of Adolf provided a precedent for the deposition of the Emperor Wenceslaus IV in 1400. See T. Lindner, *Geschichte des deutschen Reiches unter König Wenzel* (Leipzig, 1880), 2:427–43, 515–24. Documents are in *Deutsche Reichtagsakten,* vol. 3, ed. J. Weizacker (Munich, 1877), pp. 254–78 Wenceslaus had been deposed: "Propter multas pregnantes causas nos urgentes et intolerabiles exorbitationes amovemus ac deponimus had nostra sententia dominum Wenceslaum ceu inutilem ignavum et penitus ineptum ad Romanum imperium ab ipso Romano imperio atque ab omni sibi debita gloria honore et majestate."

brought most explicitly. For the very reason that the imperial office came most frequently under papal scrutiny, the figure of the *imperator inutilis* fails to develop parallel to the type *rex inutilis.* The remarks of Ullmann concerning general "uselessness" on the part of medieval rulers apply most consistently to the imperial office as that office was considered by Gregory VII, Innocent III, and Innocent IV.[49] Few canonists found it profitable to speak of separating the imperial dignity from the institutions of imperial governance: the emperor could lay claim to few of the dynastic rights that strengthened the claims of kings. If the imperial office was thus weakened by generations of canonist reservations, the simultaneous imperial claims for temporal sovereignty were muted by the far more articulate papal claims for supremacy within Christendom.

The charges against Adolf of Nassau resemble both the earlier papal pronouncements against criminal emperors and the more recent views that incompetent temporal rulers ought to be deposed outright. The Archbishop of Mainz called the electors together, he said, because:

> When evident utility urges and imminent necessity demands, we may, and indeed we ought out of the care which our office imposes upon us, to call not only those princes to whom pertains the right of electing a king of the Romans who afterward is raised to emperor, but also that ruler himself . . . at a certain place and time . . . and those princes ought to recognize this, and they do in fact recognize it.[50]

The archbishop, rhetorically arrogating to himself and to the other electors rights hitherto reserved to the pope, goes on to list the charges against Adolf, the reasons for the *evidens utilitas* and the *imminens necessitas* of the Empire. Adolf had violated the liberties of the church; he had permitted the mistreatment of laymen and clerics alike; he failed to protect the rights of widows and orphans;

49. See the citations above, p. 25, n. 51.
50. MGH *Const.* III, p. 549.

he was guilty of perjury and sacrilege.[51] So far, the charges parallel those against Frederick II, the decree of whose deposition was certainly used as a model for Archbishop Gerhard's own pronouncement. Adolf, however, was guilty of other shortcomings. His failure to keep the peace, for example, had rendered him *inutilis*—incompetent— as well as criminal:

> The Lord Adolf, king of the Romans, by these and other immense, notorious, and manifold excesses is manifestly convicted and otherwise found to be insufficient for such a dignity [*insufficiens inventus ad tantae regimen dignitatis*] . . . During his reign the breaking of peace could not be contained, but evils multiplied upon the earth.[52]

Further, the "said king is found to be insufficient and useless in such a high dignity." Adolf, guilty of both *iniquitates* and *inutilitas*, reaped the harvest planted by Innocent III and Innocent IV.

It may seem at first uncommon that accusations of both wickedness and incapacity were simultaneously leveled at the emperor. That both kinds of offense were intended to apply to him, however, cannot be doubted. The vernacular *Osterreichische Reimchronik* links both his incapacity and the criminal character of his actions:

> Count Adolf of Nassau,
> Out of sin and out of foolishness,
> I place you in God's own ban
>
> . . .
>
> he is an unworthy king.[53]

If the accusations of insufficiency, uselessness, and indignity here derive from the Innocentian tradition of standards for imperial suitability, they nevertheless also reflect the more popular aspects

51. See the perceptive remarks of Caspary in "The Deposition of Richard II and the Canon Law."

52. MGH *Const.* III, p. 552.

53. *Ottakars österreichische Reimchronik*, ed. J. Seemüuller, MGH *SS vern. lingua* V, pars. II, p. 948, vv. 71696–704.

of the type of ineffective ruler whom "frevel" and "sunde" have rendered incompetent. The deposition of Adolf, stemming as it does from the form of that of Frederick II in 1245, also borrows some of its aspects from that of Sancho II. The protection which *Grandi* afforded to incompetent kings, however, was not intended to apply to the emperor. Adolf's uselessness simply added grounds of unsuitability to more severe criminal charges, which alone would have been juridically sufficient to depose him. In the course of the fourteenth century political philosophers were consistently to maintain the thesis that an emperor might be deposed for criminal actions or for simple incompetence. The imperial office, at the end of a long tradition of considering it specifically as an *office,* was the one which was to suffer the greatest damage from the linking of theories of office and incapacity that grew up in the late thirteenth and fourteenth centuries.

The process of deposition against Adolf, cloaked in rhetorical terms borrowed from earlier papal decretals, imitative of the statements of canon lawyers, and profiting from the considerable attention to the *imperium* as an office in earlier political writings nevertheless presented the appearance of a legitimate act of public law performed by those who were justly empowered to execute it. In 1327 the barons and higher clergy of England acted against Edward II, ostensibly in similar fashion and for similar reasons.[54] The differences between the two depositions, however, particularly in their consideration of the ruler's alleged "uselessness," may reflect some of the remaining distinctions between the imperial and regal offices, in spite of the similarity in political literature of *regnum* and *imperium* as political abstractions. The political position of the barons in 1327 was far more constitutionally ambiguous than was that of the electors in 1298. The electors might well have profited from the claims put forward by the cardinals and their publicists in 1297 and 1298 concerning the juridical relations between that group

54. T. F. Tout, *The Place of the Reign of Edward II in English History* (2d ed., Manchester, 1936); J. Taylor, "The French Brut and the Reign of Edward II," *EHR* 72 (1957): 423–37. Relevant documents in S. B. Chrimes and A. L. Brown, *Select Documents of English Constitutional History, 1307–1485* (New York, 1961), esp. pp. 33–38.

and the pope. The English barons, on the other hand, had no such theoretical grounds of approach, save the older and juridically less easily supportable claims of deceived vassals. To be sure, the magnates of the realm had been traditionally associated with the royal council, and they had on occasion attempted to coerce temporarily weak or otherwise incapacitated rulers—for example, Stephen, John, and Henry III. Previous efforts at justifying baronial control of the king, however, had themselves been influenced by the views of popes and canonists. In 1327 the magnates borrowed a complete deposition theory, one which owed as much to the depositions of Frederick II, Sancho II, and Adolf (and perhaps to that of Celestine V) as to any previous tradition of feudal resistance.

The renunciation of Celestine and the deposition of Adolf may well have been on the minds of some of the ecclesiastical magnates who participated in the rebellion against and deposition of Edward II. Both these events had raised questions about the relationship between the inadequacy or criminality of a ruler and the good of the community at whose head he stood. The series of restrictions placed upon Henry III in the preceding century and the barons' declaration of 1308 that they owed allegiance only to the "crown" of England, not to the "person" of the king, represented a substantial degree of restraint placed upon the monarch by men who borrowed theories of constitutionalism and public law in order to preserve their own private interests. Such restraints, on the one hand, and the king's anointed character and personal preponderance, on the other, resulted in some degree of tension among the members of the community of the realm of England. Those juridical tensions, however, could not overcome consistently the political superiority of the ruler. Kingship was never to become simply a juristically defined office. The king was to remain the firmly attached head of the *corpus politicum* for several centuries to come.

The magnates of 1327 were not all skilled canonists, however. The overriding desire of the assembly at London to rid itself and the kingdom of Edward II was far greater than its concern for exact legal proprieties. Thus the steps in the process of deposition, as Maitland remarked, constitute a precedent for revolution to a far greater extent than the institution of anything resembling "due process" for the removal of a king.[55] "Revolution," however, is perhaps too broad a term to apply to the actions of men who would not have known what it meant and who certainly had no intention of changing the "form" of government under which they lived. If the barons of 1327 were less skillful than their successors of 1399, it may have been because:

> they had to find an answer to a question which had not been asked seriously in England since the Norman Conquest. By what means might an undoubted king lawfully be removed? The constitution, as Stubbs observed, had no rule or real precedent for deposing a worthless king; and, although it is unlikely that any of the revolutionaries fully appreciated the momentous significance of the task on which they were engaged, the act was fraught with sufficient danger to make them go warily and do all in their power to give the proceedings an air of legality.[56]

Their dilemma lies in the words "lawfully" and "an air of legality." What law applied to the removal of a king?

The actions of the assembly of 1327 may thus be regarded as an experiment in public law. Like many experiments, it may have been undertaken rashly, without sufficient controls, in an ill-equipped laboratory. It was undertaken nevertheless, and one of its less noted aspects was that it raised the question of the *rex inutilis* within the framework of a purely national assembly without prior appeal to Rome. Thus papal participation in the removal of a legitimate ruler, a fact of political theory from the eleventh century on, is no longer a requisite. The assembly of 1327 picked up the problem of a people's deposition of its own ruler almost where it had been left in the tenth and early eleventh centuries. By 1327, however, the universalism of canon and Roman law and the concentration by political thinkers upon the kingdom as the elementary political unit had given to the deposition process several new dimensions. These dimensions might be adapted to the needs of local powers, as they

55. Maitland, *The Constitutional History of England,* pp. 190–93.
56. McKisack, *The Fourteenth Century,* p. 91.

were in fact adapted in 1298 and 1327 in the matter of depositions and in 1264 and 1308 in the matter of exerting control on a legitimate ruler. The deposition of Edward II may therefore be regarded as a political crisis in which the principles of the two laws and the new philosophy of politics were applied to the more particularistic principles of *diffidatio* and the consequent abandonment of the ruler. A survey of the events of January 1327 may reveal this interaction.

The first step in the process of removing Edward II from the throne was the acclamation of Edward III as king before any action whatever had been taken in law to stop the reign of Edward II. Later, Edward II made a forced resignation of the royal dignity, and still later, a representative of the assembly formally renounced allegiance to Edward, and the steward of the royal household broke his staff of office. The outward form of the deposition thus resembles elements of political conduct which originated many centuries earlier and in which the kingdom's renunciation of allegiance to its king echoes the single vassal's renunciation of allegiance to his lord. Only by extending the limits of political analogy beyond logic might the kingdom be considered legally identical in all respects with the deceived vassal. Within the framework of *diffidatio* and *gravamina* there were other legal ideas at work. The feudal bond between lord and man might account for the vassal's justified renunciation of allegiance to a lord who had failed to prove trustworthy, as historical experience and its reflection in the literature of the *chansons de geste* made clear. The lord could never renounce homage from a true vassal; that is, the breaking of the feudal contract by the lord could not legitimately be seen as "abdication." For abdication, however, there existed other models, most of them discussed in the canon law and its glosses. The prelate might resign, with papal permission. The pope himself might resign. An incorrigibly wicked or inept ruler might conceivably resign, although this last instance was overshadowed by the development of deposition theory. Finally, the division of power between king-with-*dignitas* and *curator*-with-*administratio* might be considered a partial abdication, although no king so far had ever agreed to such a division of power, and for good reason. In this instance, as in others of the thirteenth and fourteenth centuries, the development of theories of public law had proceeded farther and faster than the development of political institutions that could effectively use them.

One political institution which threatened several English kings in the thirteenth and fourteenth centuries does in some respects resemble the office of *curator* as Innocent IV and other glossators of the canon law had envisaged it. The role of Simon de Montfort in the governmental revolt against Henry III is well-known. In the reign of Edward II, moreover, claims were put forth by Thomas of Lancaster in his capacity as High Steward of England which strongly resembled the duties of the temporal *curator* in canon law. In October 1326 Edward, Prince of Wales, was named *custos,* or keeper, of the realm. Given the political circumstances of the time, one may perhaps suggest that one of the greatest dangers to the crown constituted by the existence of "over-mighty subjects" was the possibility of those subjects' assuming legitimate office under the king and exercising governmental control, even if in the king's name, often against the king himself. The chronicle of Geoffrey le Baker, in fact, contains a passage supposedly delivered by the commission to Edward at Kenilworth in which the king, if he resigns the crown to his son, is promised that he will be maintained in honor, "post honeris deposicionem quam antea solebat ab omnibus habere regia celsitudo."[57] It may not be excessive to see in this offer something of the intention of Innocent IV when he separated the royal *dignitas* and *administratio* of Portugal, the difference being, of course, that Edward III would be king instead of *curator.* The fourteenth century, unlike the twentieth, never really thought out the position of such political phenomena as *Dominus Edwardus de Karnarvon nuper regi.*

The charges against Edward II are on much more solid ground, particularly insofar as they form part of the history of the legal theory of the *princeps inutilis.*[58] Like that of Celestine, "la persone ly Roy n'est past suffisaunt de governer." He has been "led and

57. Chrimes and Brown, *Documents,* p. 34.
58. Ibid., pp. 37–38, from *Foedera,* II, i, 650.

ruled" by others, who have counseled him evilly. He refused to follow good counsel, spending his time in unseemly occupations, neglecting the needs of his kingdom. Like Sancho, he has lost territory: "par défaute de bon gouvernement, ad il perdu le roialme d'Escoce, et autres terres et seigneuries en Gascoygne et Hyrland." He has caused the misery of ecclesiastics and has murdered, imprisoned, and disherited his own nobles. He ignored his own promises made at his coronation. He has been guilty of criminal negligence and has caused the loss of his realm and people. By the criminal character of these actions *and by the defects of his own person (défaute de sa personne),* he is found to be incorrigible and without any hope of reform, like Frederick II. Lastly, his acts have been so notorious that they cannot be controverted. The short French text which contains these charges is not an official document, although it strongly resembles those other official documents relative to the depositions of Frederick II, Sancho II, and Adolf of Nassau and the statement attributed to Celestine V concerning his own insufficiency. Moreover, the charges are carefully drawn up so as to include as much of thirteenth-century deposition theory as they possibly can. The models of Frederick, Sancho, Celestine, and Adolf are finally capped by the necessary charges of hopeless incorrigibility and notoriety which justify the public character of the deposition. If Bishop Stratford's memorandum was not as all-encompassing as the list of *gravamina* compiled by the Lancastrians in 1399, it was at least sufficient for its purposes. Every quality attributable to the *rex inutilis* by 1300 finds a place in the charges against Edward. But Edward's deficiencies are not conceived in the abstract: every charge carefully notes the consequences of the king's *inutilitas:* damage and destruction of *eglise, poeple,* and *roialme.*

It should not be altogether surprising that the magnates of 1327 should resemble so strongly their ninth- and tenth-century predecessors in considering *dilapidatio* and other related offenses as crimes justifying the abandonment or deposition of the legitimate ruler. In the earlier period social and economic necessity often drove men to abandon those kings who were incapable of fighting, ruling, or affording protection to those who legitimately looked for it, not because they saw these shortcomings as abstractly conceived crimes against the "realm," "people," or "State," but because their own immediate lives, welfare, or personal interests demanded such a course of action. The development of theories of public law and the State, of a common good, community of the realm, and public welfare between the eleventh and fourteenth centuries, however, broadened the scope of possible royal offenses not only against individuals in the face of immediate physical danger but against the abstract entities *eglise, poeple, roialme,* which possessed abstract *utilitas, necessitas,* and *bosoignes.* The concepts of community of the realm and public welfare had sufficiently broadened in scope so as to impose upon the *princeps* a new series of obligations which were less strictly private and moral than early theories of Christian kingship, yet also less specific and abstract than later ideas of "constitutional monarchy." In the later Arthurian romances the kingdom becomes possessed of an "epic history." In fourteenth-century deposition theory it becomes possessed of an abstract welfare and a claim to the legal authority to defend it. In the romances the fate of the kingdom transcends the fate and character of individual rulers. In law the welfare of the kingdom has come to be different from the welfare of the individual king. To the fourteenth-century *princeps* applies John of Paris's description of the purpose of papal rule: the *princeps* rules, "not for himself, but for the good of all." The distinction between "crimes" and "uselessness" has become less important than the consequences of these offenses upon the realm.

In 751 Childeric III was deprived of the *nomen* of king, having already lost the *potestas.* The pope had only to absolve the king's subjects from the oaths of fidelity which they had made to him. In 1399 Richard II absolved his subjects not only from their oaths of fealty but from all bonds of "homage . . . allegiance, regality, and lordship by which they were bound to him, and absolved them also from every obligation or oath *quantum ad suam personam attinet,* and from every effect of law ensuing therefrom." He renounced not only the *nomen* and *potestas* of king "but likewise the royal dignity, majesty, and crown . . . lordship, rule, governance, administration, empire, jurisdiction . . . honor, regality, and highness of king."[59] Even after such renunciations, the Lancastrians still felt the necessity to note that Richard was deprived of any other trace of the royal dignity, "quantum in eo remanserit." "To such extent as any remained in him" is a clear milestone in the history of Western kingship. In spite of the Lancastrians' precise terminology and legal expertise, the exact amount of "kingship" was not to be determined for several centuries to come: for England, not until 1649 and 1688; for France, not until 1789. The idea of the remnants of royalty in a deposed king were still to fascinate Shakespeare and Marlowe in the early seventeenth century. Sixteenth-century jurists were to discuss the metaphysical relation between the king's two bodies. The royal funeral ceremony in sixteenth-century France perpetuated in ritual and ceremony the fiction that the king never dies.[60] Later, Parliament claimed to act on behalf of the King when it consented to the execution of Charles Stuart. All these fictions, as the work of Kantorowicz, Giesey, Dunham, and others has shown, reflect the birth pangs of the abstract State, which is itself, as Cassirer and Auden remind us, also a myth.

The history of the *rex inutilis* constitutes a chapter in the intellectual history of kingship in the political world of Christendom. The "private" king of the early Middle Ages and his "public" counterpart in the thirteenth and fourteenth centuries were the focus of much of the thought and action of politics in early Europe. If men drew from many different sources for their theories of kingship, that is perhaps because the institution of kingship itself touched upon aspects of social organization and imagination which were not clearly differentiated until a later period. The reluctance or inability of later medieval men substantially to alter the nature of kingship accounts for both the continuing strength of the institution in later centuries and the difficulty men experienced in articulating meaningful definitions of royal crime and inadequacy. Government was to remain royal government, and the king, as well as his op-

59. S. B. Chrimes, *English Constitutional Ideas in the Fifteenth Century* (Cambridge, 1936), pp. 5–6. See also Richard H. Jones, *The Royal Policy of Richard II: Absolutism in the Later Middle Ages* (Oxford, 1968).

60. See R. E. Giesey, *The Royal Funeral Ceremony in Renaissance France* (Geneva, 1960).

ponents or rivals, could manipulate the new resources provided by changing ideas and institutions of public law. The persistence of the sacral prestige of kingship reflects the royal retention of power in theory as well as practice.[61]

Just as the increasingly complex character of royal power between the eighth and the fourteenth centuries required the proliferation of terms with the listing of which this section opened to describe all of its aspects, so did the experience of real or literary rulers from Childeric III to Edward II reflect the changing ways in which men described and conceived royal power and those who wielded it or failed to. The kingdoms of the later fourteenth and fifteenth centuries were to have their own experience of ineffective rulers: Richard II of England, Charles VI of France, Henry VI of England, and Juana of Castile. They were also to experience the rule of kings whose governance was so out of keeping with their individual early "character" that historical accounts of their rules seem inevitably to fall into two parts, one describing a careless young manhood, the other an effective and successful reign—for example, Henry V and Charles VII. Finally, there also appeared rulers who successfully (too successfully, some men thought) realized the effective use of public power: Louis XI, Edward IV, Henry VII, Ferdinand of Aragon. The political experience of the later fourteenth and fifteenth centuries proved that if the king himself was incapable of governing, there were men who could and would govern in his name. The struggle for positions of advantage and theorists' concern for the place and power of the king within what Lewis calls "the interplay of forces of this political society" were to determine the later history of the idea of royal ineffectiveness and influence the later terms *roi fainéant* and *Schattenkönig,* the "perfect shadow" of Marlowe's epithet with which this study opened.

The preceding pages have certainly not exhausted the early medieval history of the *rex inutilis.* In suggesting that the formation of political typology between the eighth and the fourteenth cen-

61. See the discussion in P. S. Lewis, *Later Medieval France: The Polity* (New York, 1968).

turies constitutes a more complex process than historians of political theory are often willing to allow, and that "political" thought during this period ought not to be considered apart from related notions of human character and the representation of political problems in purely "literary" works, it has simply drawn the outlines of a model for one aspect of the social and intellectual history of kingship. If I have not treated the fourteenth and fifteenth centuries in the detail they deserve, it is because they represent the extension of a process which was complete in its outlines by 1327 and hence require a separate study of their own, one which would draw upon the rich source materials of chronicles, sermons, treatises on political theory and law, as well as the changing institutions of royal governance, public ceremonies, and the experience of individual rulers. Between 751 and 1327 the figure of the *rex* itself, like that of the *rex inutilis,* was flexible, dynamic, and responsive to changes in social and intellectual movement. Political structures, like ecclesiastical ones, were created and sustained by rulers and the men who supported or rationalized their actions. In the interplay of experience and theorizing, of governance and resistance to being governed, and of legitimacy and expedience is to be found the historical nature of medieval kingship.

Bibliographical Note

Manuscripts cited

Admont Stiftsbibliothek MS 7: Huguccio of Pisa, *Summa.*
University of Pennsylvania MS Lat. 114: Bernardus Raymundus, *Summa* to the *Liber sextus.*
Vatican Borghese 287: Stephen of Tournai, *Summa.*
Vatican Pal. Lat. 629: Bernardus Compostellanus Jr., *Casus.*
Vatican Pal. Lat. 8071: anon. glosses on *Liber sextus.*
Yale Law Library MS no. 1: Henricus Merseburgensis, *Summa.*

Sources of Medieval Canon Law

During the past several decades scholars have come to realize increasingly the importance of medieval canon law and its commentaries for the study of political thought and policy between the twelfth and the fourteenth centuries. The importance of this realization has been described by Brian Tierney in "Medieval Canon Law and Western Constitutionalism," *CHR* 52 (1966): 1–17. A survey of recent work and further needs in this field may be found in Robert L. Benson, *The Bishop-Elect* (Princeton, 1968), pp. 387–90. To the recent work there cited, should be added the *Collectanea Stephan Kuttner,* vols. 11–14 of *Studia Gratiana,* and G. Le Bras, C. Lefebvre, and J. Rambaud, *L'Age classique, 1140–1378, Sources et théorie du droit,* vol. 3 of *Histoire du droit et des institutions de l'église en occident,* ed. G. Le Bras (Paris, 1965).

Index

With the exception of the names of minor characters in the literary works discussed and of peripheral historical figures, the index of names is reasonably complete. Key single terms in Latin and Old French have been cited in their most important locations, but there is no concordance of these. In the matter of names, I have tried to index the most common forms of medieval names (e.g. Johannes Faventinus, but John of Paris). Standard abbreviations for title and office have been used (e.g. emp. = emperor; k. = king; abp. = archbishop).